Supreme Court DRAMA

Cases That Changed America

Supreme Court DRAMA

Cases That Changed America

Daniel E. Brannen, &
Dr. Richard Clay Hanes
Elizabeth Shaw, Editor

VOLUME 1

FREEDOM OF ASSEMBLY AND ASSOCIATION

FREEDOM OF THE PRESS

FREEDOM OF RELIGION AND THE ESTABLISHMENT CLAUSE

FREEDOM OF SPEECH

RIGHT TO PRIVACY

U·X·L®

AN IMPRINT OF THE GALE GROUP

DETROIT · NEW YORK · SAN FRANCISCO
LONDON · BOSTON · WOODBRIDGE, CT

Supreme Court Drama: Cases That Changed America

DANIEL E. BRANNEN
RICHARD CLAY HANES

Staff

Elizabeth M. Shaw, U•X•L Editor
Carol DeKane Nagel, U•X•L Managing Editor
Thomas L. Romig, U•X•L Publisher

Shalice Shah-Caldwell, Permissions Associate (Pictures)
Maria Franklin, Permissions Manager
Robyn Young, Imaging and Multimedia Content Editor

Rita Wimberley, Senior Buyer
Evi Seoud, Assistant Manager, Composition Purchasing and Electronic Prepress
Dorothy Maki, Manufacturing Manager
Mary Beth Trimper, Production Director
Michelle DiMercurio, Senior Art Director

Pamela A. Reed, Imaging Coordinator
Randy Basset, Image Database Supervisor
Barbara Yarrow, Imaging and Multimedia Content Manager

Linda Mahoney, LM Design, Typesetting

Cover photographs: Reproduced by permission of the Library of Congress and the Supreme Court of the United States.

Library of Congress Cataloging-in-Publication Data

Brannen, Daniel E., 1968-
Supreme Court drama: cases that changed the nation / Daniel E. Brannen, Jr. and Richard Clay Hanes ; Elizabeth M. Shaw, editor.
p. cm.
Includes bibliographical references and index.
ISBN 0-7876-4877-9 (set) – ISBN 0-7876-4878-7 (v.1) – ISBN 0-7876-4879-5 (v.2) –ISBN 0-7876-4880-9 (v.3) – ISBN 0-7876-4881-7 (v.4)
1.Constitutional law–United States–Cases–Juvenile literature. 2. United States. Supreme Court–Juvenile Literature. [1. Constitutional law–United States–Cases. 2. United States. Supreme Court.] I. Hanes, Richard Clay, 1946- II. Shaw, Elizabeth M., 1973- III. Title.

KF4550.Z9 B73 2001
347.73'26'0264–dc21

00-056380

Printed in Canada

10 9 8 7 6 5 4 3 2

Contents

Contents

Contents

VOLUME 2: CRIMINAL JUSTICE AND FAMILY LAW

Contents

Contents

Contents

Trials Alphabetically

A

B

C

D

E

F

G

H

I

J

K

L

M

N

O

P

R

S

Trials Alphabetically

T

U

V

W

Y

Trials Chronologically

Trials Chronologically

1936

1937

1938

1940

1941

1942

1943

1944

1945

1947

1948

1951

1954

1955

1957

1958

1967

1968

1969

1970

1971

1972

1973

1974

1975

1976

1977

1978

Trials Chronologically

1979

1980

1981

1982

1984

1985

1986

1987

1988

1989

1990

Trials Chronologically

1998

1999

2000

Reader's Guide

U.S. citizens take comfort and pride in living under the rule of law. Our elected representatives write and enforce the laws that cover everything from family relationships to the dealings of multi-billion-dollar corporations, from the quality of the air to the content of the programs broadcast through it. But it is the judicial system that interprets the meaning of the law and makes it real for the average citizen through the drama of trials and the force of court orders and judicial opinions.

The four volumes of *Supreme Court Drama: Cases that Changed America* profile approximately 150 cases that influenced the development of key aspects of law in the United States. The case profiles are grouped according to the legal principle on which they are based, with each volume covering one or two broad areas of the law as follows:

- **Volume : Individual Liberties** includes cases that have influenced such First Amendment issues as freedom of the press, religion, speech, and assembly. It also covers the right to privacy.
- **Volume 2: Criminal Justice and Family Law** covers many different areas of criminal law, such as capital punishment, crimnal procedure, family law, and juvenile law.
- **Volume 3: Equal Protection and Civil Rights** includes cases in the areas of affirmative action, reproductive rights segregation, and voting rights, as well as areas of special concern such as immigrants, the disabled, and gay and lesbian citizens. Sexual harassment and the right to die are also represented in this volume.

- **Volume 4: Business and Government Law** also encompasses two major spheres of the law. Monopolies, antitrust, and labor-related cases supplement the business fundamentals of corporate law. The government cases document the legal evolution of the branches of the federal government as well as the federal government's relation to state power. Separate topics address military issues, taxation, and legal history behind some Native American issues.
- **Appendixes** to all volumes also present the full text of the U.S. Constitution and its amendments and a chronological table of Supreme Court justices.

Coverage

Issue overviews, averaging 2,000 words in length provide the context for the case profiles that follow. Case discussions range from 750 to 2,000 words according, to their complexity and importance. Each provides the background of the case and issues involved, the main arguments presented by each side, and an explanation of the Supreme Court's decision, as well as the legal, political, and social impact of the decision. Excerpts from the Court's opinions are often included. Within each issue section, the cases are arranged from earliest to most recent.

When a single case could be covered under several different areas—the landmark reproductive rights decision in *Roe v. Wade,* for example, is also based upon an assertion of privacy rights—the case is placed with the issue with which it is most often associated. Users should consult the cumulative index that appears in each volume to find cases throughout the set that apply to a particular topic.

Additional Features

- The issues and proceedings featured in *Supreme Court Drama* are presented in language accessible to middle school users. Legal terms must sometimes be used for precision, however, so a Words to Know section of more than 300 words and phrases appears in each volume.
- A general essay providing a broad overview of the Supreme Court of the United States and the structure of the American legal system.
- **Bolded** cross-references within overview and case entries that point to cases that appear elsewhere in the set.

- Tables of contents to locate a particular case by name or in chronological order.
- A cumulative index at the end of each volume that includes the cases, people, events and subjects that appear throughout *Supreme Court Drama.*

Suggestions Are Welcome

We welcome your comments on *Supreme Court Drama: Cases That Changed America.* Please write, Editors, *Supreme Court Drama,* U•X•L, 27500 Drake Road, Farmington Hills, MI 48331-3535; call toll-free: 1-800-877-4253; fax to 248-414-5043; or send e-mail via http://www.galegroup.com.

Advisors

The editor is grateful for all the assistance and insight offered by the advisors to this product.

- Mary Alice Anderson, Media Specialist, Winona Middle School, Winona, Minnesota
- Sara Brooke, Librarian, Ellis School, Pittsburgh, Pennsylvania
- Marolynn Griffin, Librarian, Desert Ridge Middle School, Albuquerque, New Mexico
- Dr. E. Shane McKee, Instructor, The Putney School at Elm Lea Farm, Putney, Vermont

The editor and writers would also like to acknowledge the tireless review and copy editing work done by:

- Aaron Ford, The Ohio State University, Columbus, Ohio
- Kathleen Knisely, Franklin County Courts, Columbus, Ohio
- Courtney Mroch, Freelance Writer, Jacksonville, Florida
- Melynda Neal, Franklin County Courts, Columbus, Ohio
- Berna Rhodes-Ford, Franklin County Courts, Columbus, Ohio
- Gertrude Ring, Freelance Writer, Los Angeles, California
- Lauren Zupnic, Franklin County Courts, Columbus, Ohio

Guide to the Supreme Court of the United States

The United States Supreme Court is the highest court in the judicial branch of the federal government. That means the Supreme Court is equal in importance to the president, who heads the executive branch, and Congress, which heads the legislative branch. Congress makes laws, the president enforces them, and the Supreme Court interprets them to make sure they are properly enforced.

The Supreme Court's main job is to review federal (national) and state cases that involve rights or duties under the U.S. Constitution, the document outlining the laws and guidelines for lawmaking and enforcement in the United States. The Court does this to make sure that all federal and state governments are obeying the Constitution.

For example, if Congress passes a law that violates the First Amendment freedom of speech, the Supreme Court can strike the law down as unconstitutional. If the president violates the Fourth Amendment by having the Federal Bureau of Investigation search a person's home without a warrant, the Supreme Court can fix the violation. If a state court violates the Constitution by convicting someone of a crime in an unfair trial, the Supreme Court can reverse the conviction.

As the highest court in the United States government, the Supreme Court also has the job of interpreting federal law. Congress creates law to regulate crimes, drugs, taxes, and other important issues across the nation. When someone is accused of violating a federal law, a federal court must interpret the law to decide whether the accused has broken the law. In this role, the Supreme Court makes the final decision about what a federal law means.

The Federal Court System

The Supreme Court was born in 1789, when the United States adopted the Constitution. Article III of the Constitution says, "The judicial Power of the United States, shall be vested in one supreme Court, and in such inferior Courts as the Congress may from time to time ordain and establish." With this sentence, the Constitution made the Supreme Court the highest Court in the judicial branch of the federal government. It also gave Congress the power to create lower courts.

Congress used that power to create a large judicial (court) system. The system has three levels. Trial courts, called federal district courts, are at the lowest level. There are ninety-four federal district courts covering different areas of the country. Each federal district court handles trials for cases in its area.

Federal district courts hold trials in both criminal and civil cases. Criminal trials involve cases by the government against a person who is accused of a crime, like murder. Civil trials involve cases between private parties, such as when one person accuses another of breaking a contract or agreement.

When a party loses a case in federal district court, she usually may appeal the decision to a U.S. court of appeals. Federal courts of appeals are the second level in the federal judicial system. There are twelve courts of appeals covering twelve areas, or circuits, of the country. For example, the district courts in Connecticut, New York, and Vermont are part of the Second Circuit. Appeals from district courts in those states go to the U.S. Court of Appeals for the Second Circuit.

During an appeal, the losing party asks the court of appeals to reverse or modify the trial court's decision. In essence, she argues that the trial court made an error when it ruled against her.

The party who loses before the court of appeals must decide whether to take her case to the U.S. Supreme Court. The Supreme Court is the third and highest level of the federal judicial system. The process of taking a case to the U.S. Supreme Court is described below.

State Court Systems

Most states have a judicial system that resembles the federal system. Trial courts hold trials in both criminal and civil cases. Most states also have special courts that hear only certain kinds of cases. Family, juvenile, and traffic courts are typical examples. There also are state courts, such as justices of the peace and small claims courts, that handle minor matters.

Appeals from all lower courts usually go to a court of appeals. The losing party there may take her case to the state's highest court, often called the state supreme court. When a case involves the U.S. Constitution or federal law, the losing party sometimes may take the case from the state supreme court to the U.S. Supreme Court.

Bringing a Case to the U.S. Supreme Court

There are three main ways that cases get to the U.S. Supreme Court. The most widely used method is to ask the Supreme Court to hear the case. This is called filing a petition for a writ of *certiorari.* The person who files the petition, usually the person who lost the case in the court of appeals, is called the petitioner. The person on the other side of the case is called the respondent. The Court only grants a small percentage of the writ petitions it receives each year. It usually tries to accept the cases that involve the most important legal issues.

The second main way to bring a case to the Supreme Court is by appeal. An appeal is possible only when the law that the case involves says the parties may appeal to the Supreme Court. The losing party who files the appeal is called the appellant, while the person on the other side of the case is a called the appellee.

The third main way to bring a case to the Supreme Court is by filing a petition for a writ of habeas corpus. This petition is mainly for people who have been imprisoned in violation of the U.S. Constitution. For example, if an accused criminal is convicted and jailed after the police beat him to get a confession (a police act that is illegal), the prisoner may ask the Supreme Court to release him by filing a petition for a writ of habeas corpus. The person who files the petition is called the petitioner, while the person holding the petitioner in jail is called the respondent.

The process of arguing and deciding a case in the Supreme Court is similar no matter how the case gets there. The parties file briefs that explain why they think the lower court's decision in their case is either right or wrong. The Supreme Court reviews the briefs along with a record of the evidence presented during trial in the federal district court or state trial court. The Supreme Court also may allow the parties to engage in oral argument, which is a chance for the lawyers to explain their clients' cases. During oral argument, the Supreme Court justices can ask questions to help them make the right decision.

After the justices read the briefs, review the record, and hear oral argument, they meet privately in chambers to discuss the case. Eventually, the nine justices vote for the party they think should win the case. A party must receive votes from five of the nine justices to win the case. The justices who cast the votes for the winning party are called the majority, while the justices who vote for the losing party are called the minority.

After the justices vote, one justice in thc majority writes an opinion to explain the Court's decision. Other justices in the majority may write concurring opinions that explain why they agree with the Court's decision. Justices in the minority may write dissenting opinions to explain why they think the Court's decision is wrong.

The Supreme Court's decision is the final word in a case. Parties who are unhappy with the result have no place to go to get a different ruling. The only way to change the effect of a Supreme Court decision is to have Congress change the law, have the entire nation change, or amend, the Constitution, or have the president appoint a different justice to the Court when one retires or dies. This is part of the federal government's system of checks and balances, which prevents one branch from becoming too strong.

Supreme Court Justices

Supreme Court justices are among the greatest legal minds in the country. Appointment to the job is usually the high point of a career that involved some combination of trial work as a lawyer, teaching as a professor, or service as a judge on a lower court.

Under the Constitution, the president appoints Supreme Court justices with the advice and consent of the Senate when one of the nine justices retires, dies, or is removed from office. Supreme Court justices cannot be removed from office except by impeachment and conviction by Congress for serious crimes. That means the process of appointing a new justice usually begins when one of the justices retires or dies.

The president begins the process by nominating someone to fill the empty seat on the Court. The president usually names someone who he thinks will interpret the Constitution favorably to his political party's wishes. In other words, democratic presidents typically nominate liberal justices, while republican presidents nominate conservative justices.

The next step in the process is for the Senate Judiciary Committee to review the president's recommendation. If the Senate is controlled by the president's political party, the review process usually results in Senate approval of the president's selection.

If the president's political opposition controls the Senate, the review process can be fierce and lengthy. The Judiciary Committee calls the nominee before it to answer questions. The Committee's goal is to determine whether the nominee is qualified to be a Supreme Court justice. The Committee also uses the investigation to try to figure out how the nominee will decide controversial cases, such as cases involving abortion. After its investigation, the Committee recommends whether the Senate should confirm or reject the president's nomination. Two-thirds of the senators must vote for the nominee to confirm him as a new Supreme Court justice.

The Supreme Court has changed greatly over the years. One of the Court's greatest liberal periods was when Chief Justice Earl Warren headed the Court from 1953 to 1969. In 1954, the Warren Court decided one of its most famous cases, *Brown v. Board of Education,* in which it forced public schools to end the practice of separating black and white students in different schools.

The Warren Court was followed by one of the Court's greatest conservative periods, under Chief Justice Warren E. Burger from 1969 to 1986, followed by Chief Justice William H. Rehnquist from 1986 onward. In one of the Rehnquist Court's most important decisions, *Clinton v. Jones* (1997), the Court said the president may be sued while in office for conduct unrelated to his official duties. The decision allowed Paula Jones to sue President William J. Clinton for sexual harassment.

Unfortunately, the justices on the highest court in a nation of diversity have not been very diverse themselves. Until 1916, all Supreme Court justices were white, Christian men. That year, Louis D. Brandeis became the first Jewish member of the Supreme Court. In 1967, Thurgood Marshall became the first African American justice. Clarence Thomas became just the second in 1991. In 1981, President Ronald Reagan nominated Sandra Day O'Connor to be the first woman on the Supreme Court. Ruth Bader Ginsburg joined her there in 1993.

Research and Activity Ideas

Activity 1: New School Rule

Assignment: Imagine that your school principal has just announced a new school rule for detention. Students who get detention are not allowed to explain themselves, even if they did nothing wrong. Instead, they must sit in the principal's office during lunch. They are not allowed to eat lunch, not allowed to talk at all, and must listen to Frank Sinatra music during the entire period. Your teacher has asked you to prepare a written report on whether this new rule violates the U.S. Constitution.

Preparation: Begin your research by reading the Bill of Rights, which contains the first ten amendments to the U.S. Constitution, along with the Fourteenth Amendment. These amendments contain many rights that might apply to the principal's new rule. Do you see any that might help? Continue your research by looking in *Supreme Court Drama: Cases That Changed America* for essays and cases on the freedom of speech, cruel and unusual punishment, and students' rights in school. Consult the library and Internet web sites for additional research material. Does it seem to matter whether you are in a public or private school?

Presentation: After you have gathered your information, prepare a report that explains what you found. Does the principal's new rule violate the Constitution? Why or why not? Explain your conclusions by referring to specific amendments from the Constitution and specific cases from *Supreme Court Drama.*

Activity 2: Taking a Case to Court

Assignment: Pretend you were in a bookstore that was being robbed. When the police arrived to arrest the criminal, they accidentally arrested you. During the arrest they treated you roughly and broke your arm. Your lawyer has informed you that you may sue the police to recover damages in either state or federal court. Before deciding which court system to use, you must do some research about both systems.

Preparation: Begin by reading the Introduction to *Supreme Court Drama: Cases That Changed America* so you can learn about the federal and state court systems in general. Continue with library and Internet research for more information about these systems. Then figure out which courts you need to use for your case. For the state system, use the library and Internet to find your local trial court for civil cases. Then find your state court of appeals and supreme courts in case you lose in the trial court. For the federal system, find the federal district court and U.S. court of appeals for your area. Write to the state supreme court and the U.S. court of appeals to find out what percentage of cases make it from those courts to the U.S. Supreme Court each year.

Presentation: Write a letter to your attorney explaining what you found. Tell her where you need to file your case if you choose the state system, and where you need to take appeals in that system. Do the same for the federal system. Tell her what your chances are of getting to the U.S. Supreme Court with your case.

Activity 3: Oral Argument

Activity: Imagine that a new religious group called Planterism has moved into your community. Planters are a group of men who worship trees, flowers, and other plant life. Once every week they hold an all-night ceremony during which they burn a tree as a sacrifice for all living plants. The ceremony disturbs neighbors who are trying to sleep and threatens to eliminate rare trees in your town.

Your mayor or other local leader decides he does not like Planters, so he enacts the following law:

> **Everyone in this town must follow Christianity, Judaism, or some other popular religion. Anyone who follows a false religion, including Planterism, is guilty of a felony. Anyone who burns a tree as a**

sacrifice during a religious ceremony is guilty of a felony. Anyone who disturbs the peace with a religious ceremony at night is guilty of a felony.

Violation of this law by men is punishable by life in prison without a trial. If the local police suspect a man is violating this law, they shall enter his house immediately without a warrant, arrest him, and take him to jail for imprisonment. Violation of this law by women is punishable by thirty days in jail only after a jury finds the woman guilty in a fair trial.

Your teacher has instructed the class to convene a Supreme Court to determine whether this law violates the U.S. Constitution.

Preparation: Select nine members of your class to be justices on the Court. The rest of your class should divide into three teams. One team will represent the mayor, who will argue in favor of the law. The second team will represent a group of Planters who want to challenge the law. The third team will represent a group of Christians, who want to burn palms on Palm Sunday, a religious holiday that happens once a year.

The justices and all three teams should begin by reading the Bill of Rights and the Fourteenth Amendment of the U.S. Constitution. Continue by reading *Supreme Court Drama: Cases That Changed America* for essays and cases on the freedom of religion, the establishment clause, search and seizure, cruel and unusual punishment, governmental power, due process of law, and gender discrimination. Supplement this with research from library materials and Internet web sites. You may want to assign small groups from each team to handle specific issues.

Presentation: When everyone has completed the research, all three teams should prepare to argue before the Supreme Court. The team representing the mayor should explain why the law should be upheld. The teams representing the Planters and the Christians should explain why the law should be struck down as unconstitutional. During the argument, the justices are allowed to ask questions of each team. After every team has made its argument, the justices should meet to discuss the case and to make a ruling. Is the law unconstitutional? Which parts are valid and which are not?

Words to Know

A

Accessory Aiding or contributing in a secondary way to a crime or assisting in or contributing to a crime.

Accomplice One who knowingly and voluntarily helps commit a crime.

Acquittal When a person who has been charged with committing a crime is found not guilty by the courts.

Admissible A term used to describe information that is allowed to be used as evidence or information in a court case.

Adultery Voluntary sexual relations between an individual who is married and someone who is not the individual's spouse.

Affidavit A written statement of facts voluntarily made by someone in front of an official or witness.

Affirmative action Employment programs required by the federal government designed to eliminate existing and continuing discrimination, to remedy lingering effects of past discrimination, and to create systems and procedures to prevent future discrimination; commonly based on population percentages of minority groups in a particular area. Factors considered are race, color, sex, creed (religious beliefs), and age.

Age of consent The age at which a person may marry without parental approval.

Words to Know

Age of majority The age at which a person, formerly a minor or an infant, is recognized by law to be an adult, capable of managing his or her own affairs and responsible for any legal obligations created by his or her actions.

Aggravated assault A person is guilty of aggravated assault if he or she tries to cause serious bodily injury to another or causes such injury purposely, knowingly, or recklessly without any concern for that person or without remorse.

Alien Foreign-born person who has not been naturalized to become a U.S. citizen under federal law and the Constitution.

Alimony Payment a family court may order one person in a couple to make to the other when the couple separates or divorces.

Amendment An addition, deletion, or change to an original item, such as the additions to the Constitution.

Amicus curiae Latin for "friend of the court"; a person with strong interest in, views on, or knowledge of the subject matter of a case, but is not a party to the case. A friend of the court may petition the court for permission to file a statement about the situation.

Amnesty The action of a government by which all persons or certain groups of persons who have committed a criminal offense—usually of a political nature that threatens the government (such as treason)—are granted immunity from prosecution.

Appeal Timely plea by an unsuccessful party in a lawsuit to an appropriate superior court that has the power to review a final decision on the grounds that the decision was made in error.

Appellate court A court having jurisdiction to review decisions of a lower court.

Apportionment The process by which legislative seats are distributed among those who are entitled to representation; determination of the number of representatives that each state, county, or other subdivision may send to a legislative body.

Arbitration Taking a dispute to an unbiased third person and agreeing in advance to comply with the decision made by that third person, after both parties have had a chance to argue their side of the issue.

Arraignment The formal proceeding where the defendant is brought before the trial court to hear the charges against him or her and to enter a plea of guilty, not guilty, or no contest.

Arrest The taking into custody of an individual for the purpose of answering the charges against him or her.

Arrest warrant A written order issued by an authority of the state and commanding that the person named be taken into custody.

Arson The malicious burning or exploding of a house, building, or property.

Assault Intentionally harming another person.

Attempt Unsuccessfully preparing and trying to carry out a deed.

B

Bail An amount of money the defendant needs to pay the court to be released while waiting for a trial.

Bankruptcy A federally authorized procedure by which an individual, corporation, or municipality is relieved of total liability for its debts by making arrangements for the partial repayment of those debts.

Battery An intentional, unpermitted act causing harmful or offensive contact with another person.

Beneficiary One who inherits something through the last will and testament (will) of another; also, a person who is entitled to profits, benefits, or advantage from a contract.

Bigamy The offense of willfully and knowingly entering into a second marriage while married to another person.

Bill A written declaration that one hopes to have made into a law.

Bill of rights The first ten amendments to the U.S. Constitution, ratified (adopted by the states) in 1791, which set forth and guaranteed certain fundamental rights and privileges of individuals, including freedom of religion, speech, press, and assembly; guarantee of a speedy jury trial in criminal cases; and protection against excessive bail and cruel and unusual punishment.

Black codes Laws, statutes, or rules that governed slavery and segregation of public places in the South prior to 1865.

Bona fide occupational qualification An essential requirement for performing a given job. The requirement may even be a physical condition beyond an individual's control, such as perfect vision, if it is absolutely necessary for performing a job.

Brief A summary of the important points of a longer document.

Burden of proof The duty of a party to convince a judge or jury of their position, and to prove wrong any evidence that damages the position of the party. In criminal cases the party must prove their case beyond a reasonable doubt.

Burglary The criminal offense of breaking and entering a building illegally for the purpose of committing a crime.

Bylaws The rules and regulations of an association or a corporation to provide a framework for its operation and management.

C

Capacity The ability, capability, or fitness to do something; a legal right, power, or competency to perform some act. An ability to comprehend both the nature and consequences of one's acts.

Capital punishment The lawful infliction of death as a punishment; the death penalty.

Cause A reason for an action or condition. A ground of a legal action.

Censorship The suppression of speech or writing that is deemed obscene, indecent, or controversial.

Certiorari Latin for "to be informed of"; an order commanding officers of inferior courts to allow a case pending before them to move up to a higher court to determine whether any irregularities or errors occurred that justify review of the case. A device by which the Supreme Court of the United States exercises its discretion in selecting the cases it will review.

Change of venue The removal of a lawsuit from one county or district to another for trial, often permitted in criminal cases in which the court finds that the defendant would not receive a fair trial in the first location because of negative publicity.

Charter A grant from the government of ownership rights of land to a person, a group of people, or an organization, such as a corporation.

Circumstantial evidence Information and testimony presented by a party in a civil or criminal case that allows conclusions to be drawn about certain facts without the party presenting concrete evidence to support their facts.

Citation A paper commonly used in various courts that is served upon an individual to notify him or her that he or she is required to appear at a specific time and place.

Citizens Those who, under the Constitution and laws of the United States, owe allegiance to the United States and are entitled to the enjoyment of all civil rights awarded to those living in the United States.

Civil law A body of rules that spell out the private rights of citizens and the remedies for governing disputes between individuals in such areas as contracts, property, and family law.

Civil liberties Freedom of speech, freedom of press, freedom from discrimination, and other rights guaranteed and protected by the Constitution, which were intended to place limits on government.

Civil rights Personal liberties that belong to an individual.

Class action A lawsuit that allows a large number of people with a common interest in a matter to sue or be sued as a group.

Clause A section, phrase, paragraph, or segment of a legal document, such as a contract, deed, will, or constitution, that relates to a particular point.

Closing argument The final factual and legal argument made by each attorney on all sides of a case in a trial prior to the verdict or judgment.

Code A collection of laws, rules, or regulations that are consolidated and classified according to subject matter.

Collective bargaining agreement The contractual agreement between an employer and a labor union that controls pay, hours, and working conditions for employees which can be enforced against both the employer and the union for failure to comply with its terms.

Commerce Clause The provision of the U.S. Constitution that gives Congress exclusive power over trade activities between the states and with foreign countries and Native American tribes.

Words to Know

Commercial speech The words used in advertisments by commercial companies and service providers. Commercial speech is protected under the First Amendment as long as it is not false or misleading.

Common law The principles and rules of action, embodied in case law rather than legislative enactments, applicable to the government and protection of persons and property, Common laws derive their authority from the community customs and traditions that evolved over the centuries as interpreted by judicial tribunals (types of courts).

Common-law marriage A union of two people not formalized in the customary manner but created by an agreement by the two people to consider themselves married followed by their living together.

Community property The materials and resources owned in common by a husband and wife.

Complaint The possible evidence that initiates a civil action; in criminal law, the document that sets in motion a person's being charged with an offense.

Concurring opinion An opinion by one or more judges that provides separate reasoning for reaching the same decision as the majority of the court.

Conditional Subject to change; dependent upon the occurrence of a future, uncertain event.

Confession A statement made by an individual that acknowledges his or her guilt of a crime.

Conflict of interest A term used to describe the situation in which a public official exploits his or her position for personal benefit.

Consent Voluntary agreement to the proposal of another; the act or result of reaching an agreement.

Conspiracy An agreement between two or more persons to engage in an unlawful or criminal act, or an act that is innocent in itself but becomes unlawful when done by those participating.

Constituent A person who gives another person permission to act on his or her behalf, such as an agent, an attorney in a court of law, or an elected official in government.

Constitution of the United States A document written by the founding fathers of the United States that has been added to by Congress over the centuries that is held as the absolute rule of action and decision for all branches and offices of the government, and which all subsequent laws and ordinances must be in accordance. It is enforced by representatives of the people of the United States, and can be changed only by a constitutional amendment by the authority that created it.

Contempt An act of deliberate disobedience or disregard for the laws or regulations of a public authority, such as a court or legislative body.

Continuance The postponement of an action pending (waiting to be tried) in a court to a later date, granted by a court in response to a request made by one of the parties to a lawsuit.

Corporations Business entities that are treated much like human individuals under the law, having legally enforceable rights, the ability to acquire debt and pay out profits, the ability to hold and transfer property, the ability to enter into contracts, the requirement to pay taxes, and the ability to sue and be sued.

Counsel An attorney or lawyer.

Court of appeal An intermediate court of review that is found in thirteen judicial districts, called circuits, in the United States. A state court of appeal reviews a decision handed down by a lower court to determine whether that court made errors that warrant the reversal of its final decision.

Covenant An agreement, contract, or written promise between two individuals that frequently includes a pledge to do or refrain from doing something.

Criminal law A body of rules and statutes that defines behavior prohibited by the government because it threatens and/or harms public safety, and establishes the punishments to be given to those who commit such acts.

Cross-examination The questioning of a witness or party during a trial, hearing, or deposition by the opposing lawyer.

Cruel and unusual punishment Such punishment as would amount to torture or barbarity, any cruel and degrading punishment, or any fine, penalty, confinement, or treatment so disproportionate to the offense as to shock the moral sense of the community.

Custodial parent The parent to whom the court grants guardianship of the children after a divorce.

D

Death penalty See Capital punishment.

De facto Latin for "in fact"; in deed; actually.

Defamation Any intentional false communication, either written or spoken, that harms a person's reputation; decreases the respect, regard, or confidence in which a person is held; or causes hostile or disagreeable opinions or feelings against a person.

Defendant The person defending or denying; the party against whom recovery is sought in an action or suit, or the accused in a criminal case.

Defense The forcible reaction against an unlawful and violent attack, such as the defense of one's person, property, or country in time of war.

De jure Latin for "in law"; legitimate; lawful, as a matter of law. Having complied with all the requirements imposed by law.

Deliberate Willful; purposeful; determined after thoughtful evaluation of all relevant factors. To act with a particular intent, which is derived from a careful consideration of factors that influence the choice to be made.

Delinquent An individual who fails to fulfill an obligation or otherwise is guilty of a crime or offense.

Domestic partnership laws Legislation and regulations related to the legal recognition of nonmarital relationships between persons who are romantically involved with each other, have set up a joint residence, and have registered with cities recognizing said relationships.

Denaturalization To take away an individual's rights as a citizen.

Deportation Banishment to a foreign country, attended with confiscation of property and deprivation of civil rights.

Deposition The testimony of a party or witness in a civil or criminal proceeding taken before trial, usually in an attorney's office.

Desegregation Judicial mandate making illegal the practice of segregation.

Disclaimer The denial, refusal, or rejection of a right, power, or responsibility.

Discrimination The grant of particular privileges to a group randomly chosen from a large number of people in which no reasonable difference exists between the favored and disfavored groups. Federal laws prohibit discrimination in such areas as employment, housing, voting rights, education, access to public facilities, and on the bases of race, age, sex, nationality, disability, or religion.

Dismissal A discharge of an individual or corporation from employment.

Dissent A disagreement by one or more judges with the decision of the majority on a case before them.

Divorce A court decree that terminates a marriage; also known as marital dissolution.

Double jeopardy A second prosecution for the same offense after acquittal or conviction or multiple punishments for the same offense. The evil sought to be avoided by prohibiting double jeopardy is double trial and double conviction, not necessarily double punishment.

Draft A mandatory call of persons to serve in the military.

Due process of law A fundamental, constitutional guarantee that all legal proceedings will be fair and that one will be given notice of the proceedings and an opportunity to be heard before the government acts to take away one's life, liberty, or property. Also, a constitutional guarantee that a law shall not be unreasonable, random, or without consideration for general well-being.

Duress Unlawful pressure exerted upon a person to force that person to perform an act that he or she ordinarily would not perform.

E

Emancipation The act or process by which a person is liberated from the authority and control of another person.

Entrapment The act of government agents or officials that causes a person to commit a crime he or she would not have committed otherwise.

Equal Pay Act Federal law that commands the same pay for all persons who do the same work without regard to sex, age, race, or ability.

Equal protection The constitutional guarantee that no person or class of persons shall be denied the same protection of the laws that is enjoyed by other persons or other classes in like circumstances in their lives, liberty, property, and pursuit of happiness.

Words to Know

Establishment Clause The provision in the First Amendment that provides that there will be no laws created respecting the establishment of a religion, inhibiting the practice of a religion, or giving preference to any or all religions. It has been interpreted to also denounce the discouragement of any or all religions.

Euthanasia The merciful act or practice of terminating the life of an individual or individuals inflicted with incurable and distressing diseases in a relatively painless manner.

Exclusionary rule The principle based on federal constitutional law that evidence illegally seized by law enforcement officers in violation of a suspect's right to be free from unreasonable searches and seizures cannot be used against the suspect in a criminal prosecution.

Executive agreement An agreement made between the head of a foreign country and the president of the United States. This agreement does not have to be submitted to the Senate for consent, and it supersedes any contradicting state law.

Executive orders When the president uses some part of a law or the Constitution to enforce some action.

Executor The individual legally named by a deceased person to administer the provisions of his or her will.

Ex parte Latin for "on one side only"; done by, for, or on the application of one party alone.

Expert witness A witness, such as a psychological statistician or ballisticsexpert, who possesses special or superior knowledge concerning the subject of his or her testimony.

Ex post facto laws Latin for "after-the-fact laws"; laws that provide for the infliction of punishment upon a person for some prior act that, at the time it was committed, was not illegal.

Extradition The transfer of a person accused of a crime from one state or country to another state or country that seeks to place the accused on trial.

F

Family court A court that presides over cases involving: (1) child abuse and neglect; (2) support; (3) paternity; (4) termination of custody due to constant neglect; (5) juvenile delinquency; and (6) family offenses.

Federal Relating to a national government, as opposed to state or local governments.

Federal circuit courts The twelve circuit courts making up the U.S. Federal Circuit Court System. Decisions made by the federal district courts can be reviewed by the court of appeals in each circuit.

Federal district courts The first of three levels of the federal court system, which includes the U.S. Court of Appeals and the U.S. Supreme Court. If a participating party disagrees with the ruling of a federal district court in its case, it may petition for the case to be moved to the next level in the federal court system.

Felon An individual who commits a felony, a crime of a serious nature, such as burglary or murder.

Felony A serious crime, characterized under federal law and many state statutes as any offense punishable by death or imprisonment in excess of one year.

First degree murder Murder committed with deliberately premeditated thought and malice, or with extreme atrocity or cruelty. The difference between first and second degree murder is the presence of the specific intention to kill.

Fraud A false representation of a matter of fact—whether by words or by conduct, by false or misleading allegations, or by concealment of what should have been disclosed—that deceives and is intended to deceive another so that the individual will act upon it to her or his legal injury.

Freedom of assembly See Freedom of association.

Freedom of association The right to associate with others for the purpose of engaging in constitutionally protected activities, such as to peacefully assemble.

Freedom of religion The First Amendment right to individually believe and to practice or exercise one's religious belief.

Freedom of speech The right, guaranteed by the First Amendment to the U.S. Constitution, to express beliefs and ideas without unwarranted government restriction.

Freedom of the press The right, guaranteed by the First Amendment to the U.S. Constitution, to gather, publish, and distribute information and ideas without government restriction; this right encompasses freedom from prior restraints on publication and freedom from censorship.

Fundamental rights Rights that derive, or are implied, from the terms of the U.S. Constitution, such as the Bill of Rights, the first ten amendments to the Constitution.

G

Gag rule A rule, regulation, or law that prohibits debate or discussion of a particular issue.

Grandfather clause A portion of a statute that provides that the law is not applicable in certain circumstances due to preexisting facts.

Grand jury A panel of citizens that is convened by a court to decide whether it is appropriate for the government to indict (proceed with a prosecution against) someone suspected of a crime.

Grand larceny A category of larceny—the offense of illegally taking the property of another—in which the value of the property taken is greater than that set for petit larceny.

Grounds The basis or foundation; reasons sufficient in law to justify relief.

Guardian A person lawfully invested with the power, and charged with the obligation, of taking care of and managing the property and rights of a person who, because of age, understanding, or lack of self-control, is considered incapable of administering his or her own affairs.

Guardian ad litem A guardian appointed by the court to represent the interests of infants, the unborn, or incompetent persons in legal actions.

H

Habeas corpus Latin for "you have the body"; a writ (court order) that commands an individual or a government official who has restrained another to produce the prisoner at a designated time and place so that the court can determine the legality of custody and decide whether to order the prisoner's release.

Hate crime A crime motivated by race, religion, gender, sexual orientation, or other prejudice.

Hearing A legal proceeding in which issues of law or fact are tried and evidence is presented to help determine the issue.

Hearsay A statement made out of court that is offered in court as evidence to prove the truth of the matter asserted.

Heir An individual who receives an interest in, or ownership of, land or tenements from an ancestor who died through the laws of descent and distribution. At common law, an heir was the individual appointed by law to succeed to the estate of an ancestor who died without a will. It is commonly used today in reference to any individual who succeeds to property, either by will or law.

Homicide The killing of one human being by another human being.

Hung jury A trial jury selected to make a decision in a criminal case regarding a defendant's guilt or innocence that is unable to reach a verdict due to a complete division in opinion.

I

Immunity Exemption from performing duties that the law generally requires other citizens to perform, or from a penalty or burden that the law generally places on other citizens.

Impeachment A process used to charge, try, and remove public officials for misconduct while in office.

Inalienable Not subject to sale or transfer; inseparable.

Incapacity The absence of legal ability, competence, or qualifications.

Income tax A charge imposed by government on the annual gains of a person, corporation, or other taxable unit derived through work, business pursuits, investments, property dealings, and other sources determined in accordance with the Internal Revenue Code or state law.

Indictment A written accusation charging that an individual named therein has committed an act or admitted to doing something that is punishable by law.

Indirect tax A tax upon some right, privilege, or corporation.

Words to Know

Individual rights Rights and privileges constitutionally guaranteed to the people as set forth by the Bill of Rights; the ability of a person to pursue life, liberty, and property.

Infant Persons who are under the age of the legal majority—at common law, twenty-one years, now generally eighteen years. According to the sense in which this term is used, it may denote the age of the person, the contractual disabilities that nonage entails, or his or her status with regard to other powers or relations.

Inherent rights Rights held within a person because he or she exists.

Inheritance Property received from a person who has died, either by will or through state laws if the deceased has failed to execute a valid will.

Injunction A court order by which an individual is required to perform or is restrained from performing a particular act. A writ framed according to the circumstances of the individual case.

In loco parentis Latin for "in the placeof a parent"; the legal doctrine under which an individual assumes parental rights, duties, and obligations without going through the formalities of legal adoption.

Insanity defense A defense asserted by an accused in a criminal prosecution to avoid responsibility for a crime because, at the time of the crime, the person did not comprehend the nature or wrongfulness of the act.

Insider Relating to the federal regulation of the purchase and sale of stocks and bonds, anyone who has knowledge of facts not available to the general public.

Insider trading The trading of stocks and bonds based on information gained from special private, privileged information affecting the value of the stocks and bonds.

Intent A determination to perform a particular act or to act in a particular manner for a specific reason; an aim or design; a resolution to use a certain means to reach an end.

Intermediate courts Courts with general ability or authority to hear a case (trial, appellate, or both) but are not the court of last resort within the jurisdiction.

Intestate The description of a person who dies without making a valid will.

Involuntary manslaughter The act of unlawfully killing another human being unintentionally.

Irrevocable Unable to cancel or recall; that which is unalterable or irreversible.

J

Judicial Relating to courts and the legal system.

Judicial discretion Sound judgment exercised by a judge in determining what is right and fair under the law.

Judicial review A court's authority to examine an executive or legislative act and to invalidate (cancel) that act if it opposes constitutional principles.

Jurisdiction The geographic area over which authority (such as a cout) extends; legal authority.

Jury In trials, a group of people selected and sworn to inquire into matters of fact and to reach a verdict on the basis of evidence presented to it.

Jury nullification The ability of a jury to acquit the defendant despite the amount of evidence against him or her in a criminal case.

Just cause A reasonable and lawful ground for action.

Justifiable homicide The killing of another in self-defense or in the lawful defense of one's property; killing of another when the law demands it, such as in execution for a capital crime.

Juvenile A young individual who has not reached the age whereby he or she would be treated as an adult in the area of criminal law. The age at which the young person attains the status of being a legal majority varies from state to state—as low as fourteen years old, as high as eighteen years old; however, the Juvenile Delinquency Act determines that a youthful person under the age of eighteen is a juvenile in cases involving federal jurisdiction.

Juvenile court The court presiding over cases in which young persons under a certain age, depending on the area of jurisdiction, are accused of criminal acts.

Juvenile delinquency The participation of a youthful individual, one who falls under the age at which he or she could be tried as an adult, in illegal behavior.

L

Larceny The unauthorized taking and removal of the personal property of another by a person who intends to permanently deprive the owner of it; a crime against the right of possession.

Legal defense A complete and acceptable response as to why the claims of the plaintiff should not be granted in a point of law.

Legal tender All U.S. coins and currencies—regardless of when coined or issued—including (in terms of the Federal Reserve System) Federal Reserve notes and circulating notes of Federal Reserve banks and national banking associations that are used for all public and private debts, public charges, taxes, duties, and dues.

Legislation Lawmaking; the preparation and enactment of laws by a legislative body.

Liability A comprehensive legal term that describes the condition of being actually or potentially subject to (responsible for) a legal obligation.

Libel and slander The communication of false information about a person, a group, or an entity, such as a corporation. Libel is any defamation that can be seen, such as in print or on a film or in a representation such as a statued. Slander is any defamation that is spoken and heard.

Litigation An action brought in court to enforce a particular right; the act or process of bringing a lawsuit in and of itself; a judicial contest; any dispute.

Living will A written document that allows a patient to give explicit instructions about medical treatment to be administered when the patient is terminally ill or permanently unconscious; also called an advance directive.

Lobbying The process of influencing public and government policy at all levels: federal, state, and local.

M

Magistrate Any individual who has the power of a public civil officer or inferior judicial officer, such as a justice of the peace.

Majority Full age; legal age; age at which a person is no longer a minor. The age at which, by law, a person is capable of being legally responsible for all of his or her acts (i.e., contractual obligations) and is entitled to manage his or her own affairs and to the enjoy civic rights (i.e., right to vote). Also the status of a person who is a major in age.

Malice The intentional commission of a wrongful act, without justification, with the intent to cause harm to others; conscious violation of the law that injures another individual; a mental state indicating a disregard of social responsibility.

Malpractice When a professional, such as a doctor or lawyer, fails to carry out their job correctly and there are bad results.

Mandate A judicial command or order from a court.

Manslaughter The unjustifiable, inexcusable, and intentional killing of a human being without deliberation, premeditation, or malice.

Material Important; significant; substantial. A description of the quality of evidence that possesses such value as to establish the truth or falsity of a point in issue in a lawsuit.

Mediation Settling a dispute or controversy by setting up an independent person between the two parties to help them settle their disagreement.

Minor An infant or person who is under the age of legal competence. In most states, a person is no longer a minor after reaching the age of eighteen (though state laws might still prohibit certain acts until reaching a greater age; i.e., purchase of liquor).

Misdemeanor Offenses lower than felonies and generally those punishable by fine, penalty, or imprisonment other than in a penitentiary.

Mistrial A courtroom trial that has been ended prior to its normal conclusion. A mistrial has no legal effect and is considered an invalid trial. It differs from a new trial, which recognizes that a trial was completed but was set aside so that the issues could be tried again.

Mitigating circumstances Circumstances that may be considered by a court in determining responsibility of a defendant or the extent of damages to be awarded to a plaintiff. Mitigating circumstances do not justify or excuse an offense but may reduce the charge.

Monopoly An economic advantage held by one or more persons or companies because they hold the exclusive power to carry out a particular business or trade or to manufacture and sell a particular task or produce a particular product.

Moratorium A suspension (ending) of activity or an authorized period of delay or waiting. A moratorium is sometimes agreed upon by the interested parties, or it may be authorized or imposed by operation of law.

Motion A written or oral application made to a court or judge to obtain a ruling or order directing that some act be done in favor of the applicant.

Motive An idea, belief, or emotion that causes a person to act in a certain way, either good or bad.

Murder The unlawful killing of another human being without justification or excuse.

N

National origin The country in which a person was born or from which his or her ancestors came. One's national origin is typically calculated by employers to provide equal employment opportunity statistics in accordance with the provisions of the Civil Rights Act.

Naturalization A process by which a person gains nationality and becomes entitled to the privileges of citizenship. While groups of individuals have been naturalized in history by treaties or laws of Congress, such as in the case of Hawaii, typically naturalization occurs on the individual level upon the completion of a list of requirements.

Necessary and Proper Clause The statement contained in Article I, Section 8, Clause 18 of the U.S. Constitution that gives Congress the power to pass any laws that are necessary and proper to carrying out its specifically granted powers.

Negligence Conduct that falls below the standards of behavior established by law for the protection of others against unreasonable risk of harm.

Nonprofit A corporation or an association that conducts business for the benefit of the general public rather than to gain profits for itself.

Notary public A public official whose main powers include administering oaths and witnessing signatures, both important and effective ways to minimize fraud in legal documents.

O

Obscenity An act, spoken word, or item tending to offend public morals by its indecency or lewdness.

Ordinance A law, statute, or regulation enacted by a municipality.

P

Palimony The settlement awarded at the end of a non-marital relationship, where the couple lived together for a long period of time and where there was an agreement that one partner would support the other in return for the second making a home and performing domestic duties.

Pardon When a person in power, such as a president or governor, offers a formal statement of forgivenss for a crime and takes away the given punishment.

Parental liability A statute (law), enacted in some states, that makes parents responsible for damages caused by their children if it is found that the damages resulted from the parents' lack of control over the acts of the child.

Parole The release of a person convicted of a crime prior to the end of that person's term of imprisonment on the condition that they will follow certain strict rules for their conduct, and if they break any of those rules they will return to prison.

Patents Rights granted to inventors by the federal government that permit them to keep others from making, using, or selling their invention for a definite, or restricted, period of time.

Peremptory challenge The right to challenge the use of a juror in a trial without being required to give a reason for the challenge.

Perjury A crime that occurs when an individual willfully makes a false statement during a judicial proceeding, after he or she has taken an oath to speak the truth.

Petition A formal application made to a court in writing that requests action on a certain matter.

Petit larceny A form of larceny—the stealing of another's personal property—in which the value of the property that is taken is generally less than $50.

Words to Know

Plaintiff The party who sues in a civil action.

Plain view doctrine In the context of searches and seizures, the principle that provides that objects that an officer can easily see can be seized without a search warrant and are fair to use as evidence.

Plea The phase in a court case where the defendant has to declare whether they are guilty or not guilty.

Police power The authority that states to employ a police force and give them the power to enforce the laws and protect the community.

Poll tax A specified sum of money to be paid by each person who votes.

Polygamy The offense of having more than one wife or husband at the same time.

Precedent A court decision that is cited as an example to resolve similar questions of law in later cases.

Preponderance of evidence A rule that states that it is up to the plaintiff to convince the judge or the jury of their side of the case in or to win the case.

Prima facie [*Latin,* On the first appearance.]A fact presumed to be true unless it is disproved.

Prior restraint Government violating freedom of speech by not allowing something to be published.

Privacy In constitutional law, the right of people to make personal decisions regarding intimate matters; under the common law, the right of people to lead their lives in a manner that is reasonably secluded from public scrutiny, whether such scrutiny comes from a neighbor's prying eyes, an investigator's eavesdropping ears, or a news photographer's intrusive camera; and in statutory law, the right of people to be free from unwarranted drug testing and electronic surveillance.

Privilege An advantage or benefit possessed by an individual, company, or class beyond those held by others.

Privileges and immunities Concepts contained in the U.S. Constitution that place the citizens of each state on an equal basis with citizens of other states with respect to advantages resulting from citizenship in those states and citizenship in the United States.

Probable cause Apparent facts discovered through logical inquiry that would lead a reasonably intelligent person to believe that an accused person has committed a crime.

Probate court Called Surrogate or Orphan's Court in some states, the probate court presides over wills, the administration of estates, and, in some states, the appointment of guardians or approval of the adoption of minors.

Probation A sentence whereby a convict is released from confinement but is still under court supervision; a testing or a trial period. It can be given in lieu of a prison term or can suspend a prison sentence if the convict has consistently demonstrated good behavior.

Procedural due process The constitutional guarantee that one's liberty and property rights may not be affected unless reasonable notice and an opportunity to be heard in order to present a claim or defense are provided.

Property A thing or things owned either by government—public property—or owned by private individuals, groups, or companies—private property.

Prosecute To follow through; to commence and continue an action or judicial proceeding to its conclusion. To proceed against a defendant by charging that person with a crime and bringing him or her to trial.

Prosecution The proceedings carried out before a court to determine the guilt or innocence of a defendant. The term also refers to the government attorney charging and trying a criminal case.

Punitive damages Money awarded to an injured party that goes beyond that which is necessary to pay for the individual for losses and that is intended to punish the wrongdoer.

Q

Quorum A majority of an entire body; i.e., a quorum of a legislative assembly.

Quota The number of persons or things that must be used, or admitted, or hired in order to be following a rule or law.

R

Rape A criminal offense defined in most states as forcible sexual relations with a person against that person's will.

Ratification The confirmation or adoption of an act that has already been performed.

Words to Know

Reapportionment The realignment of voting districts done to fulfill the constitutional requirement of one person, one vote.

Referendum The right reserved to the people to approve or reject an act of the legislature, or the right of the people to approve or reject legislation that has been referred to them by the legislature.

Refugees Individuals who leave their native country for social, political, or religious reasons, or who are forced to leave as a result of any type of disaster, including war, political upheaval, and famine.

Rehabilitation Work to restore former rights, authority, or abilities.

Remand To send back.

Replevin A legal action to recover the possession of items of personal property.

Reprieve The temporary hold put on a death penalty for further review of the case.

Rescind To declare a contract void—of no legal force or binding effect—from its beginning and thereby restore the parties to the positions they would have been in had no contract ever been made.

Reservation A tract of land under the control of the Bureau of Indian Affairs to which a Native American tribe retains its original title of ownership, or that has been set aside from the public domain for use by a tribe.

Reserve Funds set aside to cover future expenses, losses, or claims. To retain; to keep in store for future or special use; to postpone to a future time.

Resolution The official expression of the opinion or will of a legislative body.

Retainer A contract between attorney and client specifying the nature of the services and the cost of the services.

Retribution Punishment or reward for an act. In criminal law, punishment is based upon the theory that every crime demands payment.

Reverse discrimination Discrimination against a group of people that is generally considered to be the majority, usually stemming from the enforcement of some affirmative action guidlelines.

Revocation The recall of some power or authority that has been granted.

Robbery The taking of money or goods in the possession of another, from his or her person or immediate presence, by force or intimidation.

S

Sabotage The willful destruction or impairment of war material or national defense material, or harm to war premises or war utilities. During a labor dispute, the willful and malicious destruction of an employer's property or interference with his or her normal operations.

Search warrant A court order authorizing the examination of a place for the purpose of discovering evidence of guilt to be used in the prosecution of a criminal action.

Second degree murder The unlawful taking of human life with malice, but without premeditated thought.

Sedition A revolt or an incitement to revolt against established authority, usually in the form of treason or defamation against government.

Seditious libel A written communication intended to incite the overthrow of the government by force or violence.

Segregation The act or process of separating a race, class, or ethnic group from a society's general population.

Self-defense The protection of one's person or property against some injury attempted by another.

Self-incrimination Giving testimony in a trial or other legal proceeding that could subject one to criminal prosecution.

Sentencing The post-conviction stage of a criminal justice process, in which the defendant is brought before the court for penalty.

Separate but equal The doctrine first accepted by the U.S. Supreme Court in *Plessy v. Ferguson* establishing that different facilities for blacks and whites was valid under the Equal Protection Clause of the Fourteenth Amendment as long as they were equal.

Separation of church and state The separation of religious and government interest to ensure that religion does not become corrupt by government and that government does not become corrupt by religious conflict. The principle prevents the government from supporting the practices of one religion over another. It also enables the government to do what is necessary to prevent one religious group from violating the rights of others.

Separation of powers The division of state and federal government into three independent branches.

Settlement The act of adjusting or determining the dealings or disputes between persons without pursuing the matter through a trial.

Sexual harassment Unwelcome sexual advances, requests for sexual favors, and other verbal or physical conduct of a sexual nature that tends to create a hostile or offensive work environment.

Share A portion or part of something that may be divided into components, such as a sum of money. A unit of stock that represents ownership in a corporation.

Shield laws Statutes that allow journalists not to disclose in legal proceedings confidential information or sources of information obtained in their professional capacities.

Statutes that restrict or prohibit the use of certain evidence in sexual offense cases, such as evidence regarding the lack of chastity of the victim.

Shoplifting Theft of merchandise from a store or business establishment.

Small claims court A special court that provides fast, informal, and inexpensive solutions for small claims.

Solicitation The criminal offense of urging someone to commit an unlawful act.

Statute An act of a legislature that declares, or commands something; a specific law, expressed in writing.

Statute of limitations A type of federal or state law that restricts the time within which legal proceedings may be brought.

Statutory law A law which is created by an act of the legislature.

Statutory rape Sexual intercourse by an adult with a person below a designated age.

Subpoena Latin for "under penalty"; a formal document that orders a named individual to appear before an officer of the court at a fixed time to give testimony.

Suffrage The right to vote at public elections.

Summons The paper that tells a defendant that he or she is being sued and asserts the power of the court to hear and determine the case. A form of legal process that commands the defendant to appear before the court on a specific day and to answer the complaint made by the plaintiff.

Supreme court The highest court in the U.S. judicial system.

Surrogate mother A woman who agrees under contract to bear a child for an infertile couple. The woman is paid to have a donated fertilized egg or the fertilized egg of the female partner in the couple (usually fertilized by the male partner of the couple) artificially placed into her uterus.

Suspended sentence A sentence that states that a criminal, in waiting for their trial, has already served enough time in prison.

Symbolic speech Nonverbal gestures and actions that are meant to communicate a message.

T

Testify To provide evidence as a witness in order to establish a particular fact or set of facts.

Testimony Oral evidence offered by a competent witness under oath, which is used to establish some fact or set of facts.

Trade secret Any valuable commercial information that provides a business with an advantage over competitors who do not have that information.

Trade union An organization of workers in the same skilled occupation or related skilled occupations who act together to secure for all members favorable wages, hours, and other working conditions.

Treason The betrayal of one's own country by waging war against it or by consciously or purposely acting to aid its enemies.

Treaty A compact made between two or more independent nations with a view to the public welfare.

Trespass An unlawful intrusion that interferes with one's person or property.

Trial A judicial examination and determination of facts and legal issues arising between parties to a civil or criminal action.

Trial court The court where civil actions or criminal proceedings are first heard.

Truancy The willful and unjustified failure to attend school by one required to do so.

Words to Know

U

Unenumerated rights Rights that are not expressly mentioned in the written text of a constitution but instead are inferred from the language, history, and structure of the constitution, or cases interpreting it.

Unconstitutional That which is not in agreement with the ideas and regulations of the Constitution.

Uniform commercial code A general and inclusive group of laws adopted, at least partially, by all of the states to further fair dealing in business.

V

Valid Binding; possessing legal force or strength; legally sufficient.

Vandalism The intentional and malicious destruction of or damage to the property of another.

Venue A place, such as a city or county, from which residents are selected to serve as jurors.

Verdict The formal decision or finding made by a jury concerning the questions submitted to it during a trial. The jury reports the verdict to the court, which generally accepts it.

Veto The refusal of an executive officer to approve a bill that has been created and approved by the legislature, thereby keeping the bill from becoming a law.

Voir dire Old French for "to speak the truth"; the preliminary examination of possible jurors to determine their qualifications and suitability to serve on a jury, in order to ensure the selection of a fair and impartial jury.

Voluntary manslaughter The unlawful killing of a person where there is no malice, premeditation or deliberate intent but too near to these standards to be classified as justifiable homicide.

W

Waive To intentionally or voluntarily give up a known right or engage in conduct that caused your rights to be taken away.

Ward A person, especially an infant or someone judged to be incompetent, placed by the court in the care of a guardian.

Warrant A written order issued by a judicial officer commanding a law enforcement officer to perform a duty. This usually includes searches, seizures and arrests.

White collar crime Term for nonviolent crimes that were committed in the course of the offender's occupation.

Will A document in which a person explains the management and distribution of his or her estate after his or her death.

Workers' compensation A system whereby an employer must pay, or provide insurance to pay, the lost wages and medical expenses of an employee who is injured on the job.

Writ An order issued by a court requiring that something be done.

Z

Zoning Assigning different areas within a city or county different uses, whereby one area cannot be used for any other purpose other than what it is designated. For example, if an area is assigned as residential, an office building could not be built there.

When people hold a town meeting to complain about a local problem, such as poor road conditions, they exercise the right to freedom of assembly. So do people who gather to protest unfair treatment of racial minorities, such as African Americans. As long as a group is not breaking the law, freedom of assembly protects its right to have such meetings. It prevents the government from stopping the meeting, even if the government or its citizens do not like the group or its reason for gathering.

The freedom of association is a separate right that is related to the freedom of assembly. An assembly can be an informal meeting, such as citizens who gather at a state capitol to protest a law. An association, however, is usually a formal organization devoted to a particular cause or group of people. The National Rifle Association, for example, supports the right to own and use firearms. The freedom of association protects our right to form and join such organizations.

The freedom of assembly comes from the U.S. Constitution's First Amendment, which says "Congress shall make no law . . . abridging . . . the right of the people peaceably to assemble." The First Amendment is part of the Bill of Rights, which contains the first ten amendments to the

Constitution. The United States adopted the Bill of Rights in 1791 to prevent the federal government from interfering with important individual rights, including the freedom of assembly. Although the First Amendment does not mention the freedom of association, the U.S. Supreme Court decided it also is a First Amendment right.

The Bill of Rights applies only to the federal government, so state governments did not have to obey the First Amendment for a long time. Then in 1868, after the Civil War (1861-1865) ended, the United States adopted the Fourteenth Amendment. Part of it says that states may not "deprive any person of life, liberty or property without due process of law." Over time, the Supreme Court decided that "liberty" in the Fourteenth Amendment refers to many of the rights in the Bill of Rights. Because of this, state governments today must honor the freedoms of assembly and association.

Expanding the right to assemble

At first, the freedom of assembly protected only the right to petition the government, which means to ask the government to take particular action. Before the United States declared independence from Britain in 1776, the British king often refused to hear the American colonists' wishes and demands. The Americans who adopted the First Amendment wanted to make sure the U.S. government would listen to its citizens.

Over time, however, the freedom of assembly has grown to protect groups that gather to express their ideas without petitioning the government. For example, ***De Jonge v. Oregon*** (1937) was about a Communist Party member named Dirk De Jonge. (The Communist Party is a political organization that favors ownership of property by communities or the government instead of by individual people.) De Jonge organized a meeting of the party in Portland, Oregon, to protest police brutality against workers who went on strike. (A strike is when employees stop work to protest poor working conditions, such as low pay or unsafe factories.) At the meeting De Jonge sold pamphlets about communism. Although the meeting was peaceful, an Oregon court convicted De Jonge of breaking a law prohibiting efforts to change business or government by violence. The U.S. Supreme Court reversed the conviction, saying there was no evidence De Jonge had advocated violence and that "peaceable assembly for lawful discussion cannot be made a crime."

The right to freedom of assembly also protects the least popular groups, even those that offend or outrage most citizens. For example, in

Smith v. Collin (1978), the courts ordered the Chicago suburb of Skokie, Illinois, to allow the American Nazi Party to march in neighborhoods where tens of thousands of Jewish persons lived. This angered many people because under Adolf Hitler, the German Nazi government killed millions of Jews during World War II (1939-1945); this mass killing is known as the Holocaust. Some Jews who survived the Holocaust lived in the Skokie neighborhoods where the American Nazi Party was allowed to march. For the freedom of assembly to survive, however, it must protect not only people and ideas that most of us consider good but also those we despise.

The freedom of assembly is not unlimited. The government may limit the freedom if the instance under consideration satisfies three conditions. First, the limitation must serve an important governmental interest. For example, a law preventing people from gathering to start a violent revolution is valid.

Second, the limitation must be content neutral. This means it must not control assemblies based on the kinds of people who gather, their reason for gathering, or their beliefs. A law preventing people from gathering to support flag burning, for example, would violate the freedom of assembly.

Third, the limitation must restrict the freedom of assembly as little as possible to serve the important governmental interest. In *Cox v. New Hampshire* (1941), for instance, the Supreme Court decided that the government may require permits for parading on public streets. As long as it issues the permits without discrimination (treating different groups unequally), the government may control the time, place, and manner of assemblies for the sake of public safety and convenience.

Freedom of association

The First Amendment does not mention the freedom of association. The Supreme Court, however, decided it is a First Amendment right because it is closely related to the First Amendment freedoms of speech and assembly. It did so in ***NAACP v. Alabama ex rel. Patterson*** (1958), a case that grew out of the African American struggle for civil rights in the 1950s. (Civil rights are those protected by the U.S. Constitution, especially the Bill of Rights.) The National Association for the Advancement of Colored People (NAACP) was a leader in that struggle. The government of Alabama opposed the civil rights movement and tried to stop the NAACP from operating in the state.

To accomplish this, Alabama attorney general John Patterson determined that the NAACP had not registered to operate in Alabama. To shut it down, Patterson got a court order requiring the NAACP to provide a list of its members. When the NAACP refused in order to protect its members' privacy, the court held the NAACP in contempt (in violation of a court order) and told it to stop operating in Alabama until it produced the list.

The U.S. Supreme Court reversed this ruling. It announced "that the freedom to engage in association for the advancement of beliefs and ideas" cannot be separated from the freedom of speech. That freedom also includes membership privacy, especially for associations with unpopular beliefs. Requiring unpopular groups to share membership lists may result in harm to some members. That would discourage people from exercising their freedom of association.

Like the freedom of assembly, the freedom of association is not unlimited. Governments may restrict it under the same three conditions explained above. For example, in *Communist Party of the United States v. Subversive Activities Control Board* (1961), the Supreme Court said the federal government may require the Communist Party of America to register with the U.S. attorney general and reveal the names of its officers. The Supreme Court said this does not violate the freedom of association because the Communist Party supported violent revolution against the federal government. Preventing a violent revolution is an important governmental interest.

The freedom of association also includes the freedom not to associate. This means people cannot be forced to join organizations that are contrary to their beliefs. In *Abood v. Detroit Board of Education* (1977), the Supreme Court ruled that school board employees in Detroit, Michigan, could not be forced to join a union and pay union dues. (A union is an organization that protects workers' rights.)

The right not to associate also is limited. The Supreme Court decided that governments may fight discrimination by forcing public associations to allow certain groups of people to become members. For example, in ***Roberts v. U.S. Jaycees*** (1984), the Supreme Court decided that a national association dedicated to developing young men's civic organizations could be forced to accept female members.

Even with some limitations, however, the freedoms of assembly and association are an important part of every Americans' right to say and believe what they want.

Suggestions for further reading

King, David C. *Freedom of Assembly.* Brookfield, CT: Millbrook Press, 1997.

Klinker, Philip A. *The First Amendment.* Englewood Cliffs, NJ: Silver Burdett Press, 1991.

Pascoe, Elaine. *Freedom of Expression: The Right to Speak Out in America.* Brookfield, CT: Millbrook Press, 1992.

DeJonge v. Oregon 1937

Petitioner: Dirk De Jonge

Respondent: State of Oregon

Petitioner's Claim: That his conviction for attending and speaking at a meeting organized by the Communist Party violated the Due Process Clause of the Fourteenth Amendment.

Chief Lawyer for Petitioner: Osmond K. Fraenkel

Chief Lawyer for Respondent: Maurice E. Tarshis

Justices for the Court: Louis D. Brandeis, Pierce Butler, Benjamin N. Cardozo, Charles Evans Hughes (writing for the Court), James Clark McReynolds, Owen Josephus Roberts, George Sutherland, Willis Van Devanter

Justices Dissenting: None (Harlan Fiske Stone did not participate)

Date of Decision: January 4, 1937

Decision: Conviction for attending a peaceable assembly violates the Due Process Clause of the Fourteenth Amendment.

Significance: Although the First Amendment prevents only the federal government from violating the right to freedom of assembly, the Court protected freedom of assembly from state action by using the Due Process Clause of the Fourteenth Amendment.

Chief Justice Charles Evans Hughes.
Courtesy of the Supreme Court of the United States.

Freedom to revolt

The U.S. Constitution protects freedom for all citizens, even those who want to overthrow the federal government. Communism, for example, competed with the U.S. system of capitalism for world domination during most of the twentieth century. Communism is a political and economic system that aims to achieve equality for all people through government ownership of property. Capitalism is based on property ownership by individuals. Communists believe that workers under capitalism suffer to make business and property owners wealthy.

In 1917 the Communist Party took control of the government in Russia. In 1922 Russia and neighboring communist countries formed the Union of Soviet Socialist Republics (USSR), known as the Soviet Union for short. The Soviet government's goal was to spread communism throughout the world, by force and violence if necessary.

In the United States at the time, workers and members of the Communist Party tried to fight against capitalism. In 1905, for example, workers formed a labor union called the Industrial Workers of the World (IWW). The union's goal was to replace capitalism with an economy run by the workers. Because the Soviet Union became a powerful country under communism, some people in the United States feared that groups like the IWW would succeed.

To fight against communism and the IWW, many states, including Oregon, passed laws called criminal syndicalism statutes (syndicalism is an economic system in which workers own and manage industry). Oregon's law made it a felony to support crime, violence, or destruction to make changes in government or industry. Because communism supported the violent overthrow of capitalist governments, Oregon used its syndicalism statute to put members of the Communist Party in jail.

Protesting police brutality

Dirk De Jonge was a member of the Communist Party. On July 27, 1934, De Jonge spoke at a meeting held by the Communist Party in Portland, Oregon. The purpose of the meeting was to protest police raids of workers' halls and homes, and police shootings of seamen who were on strike. At the meeting, De Jonge advertised communist literature and asked everyone to work harder to recruit members for the Communist Party. De Jonge did not, however, speak in favor of violence, destruction, or other criminal means of change or revolution.

Oregon charged De Jonge with violating its criminal syndicalism statute. At his trial, De Jonge made a motion to dismiss the case, which means to throw it out of court. De Jonge argued that there was no evidence that he had spoken in favor of unlawful conduct. The trial court denied De Jonge's motion, convicted him, and sentenced him to imprisonment for seven years. The Supreme Court of Oregon affirmed, that is, agreed with the decision. De Jonge appealed to the U.S. Supreme Court.

A victory for freedom of assembly

The Supreme Court reversed De Jonge's conviction. It saw no evidence that De Jonge had spoken in favor of violence against government or industry. Instead, the conviction violated De Jonge's right to freedom of assembly. The Communist Party held the meeting to protest peacefully against police brutality. The Court said, "The very idea of a government, republican in form, implies a right on the part of its citizens to meet peaceably."

The First Amendment, which is the source for the guarantee of freedom of assembly, applies only to the federal government. The Court wrote, however, that state governments, including Oregon's, must guarantee freedom of assembly because of the Due Process Clause of the Fourteenth Amendment. That clause says, "No State . . . shall deprive

INDUSTRIAL WORKERS OF THE WORLD

U.S. industry thrived at the beginning of the twentieth century thanks to inventions such as electricity and the internal combustion engine. The growth of factories, however, led to poor and unsafe working conditions for employees. Some people formed labor unions to fight for better working conditions.

The Industrial Workers of the World (IWW), formed in 1905, had more radical plans. IWW's goal was to replace capitalism with an economy run by the workers. IWW supported strikes and other forms of interference with factory production lines. Composers inspired IWW members with songs such as "Dump the Bosses off Your Back." Other unions, however, were more popular with workers who wished to preserve American capitalism, and the IWW faded away by the late 1920s.

any person of life, liberty, or property, without due process of law." The Court said this means that "peaceable assembly cannot be made a crime."

The freedom of assembly provided by the First Amendment is only one of many rights protected by the Bill of Rights, which contains the first ten amendments to the U.S. Constitution. The Bill of Rights requires only the federal government to recognize these freedoms. The *De Jonge* decision was part of an important trend to prevent state governments from interfering with rights contained in the Bill of Rights. Over time, the Supreme Court has used the Due Process Clause of the Fourteenth Amendment to hold state governments to almost everything in the Bill of Rights.

Suggestions for further reading

King, David C. *Freedom of Assembly.* Brookfield, CT: Millbrook Press, 1997.

Klinker, Philip A. *The First Amendment.* Englewood Cliffs, NJ: Silver Burdett Press, 1991.

Lucas, Eric. *Corky: Adventure Stories for Young People.* New York, NY: International Publishers, 1938.

Pascoe, Elaine. *Freedom of Expression: The Right to Speak Out in America.* Brookfield, CT: Millbrook Press, 1992.

World Book Encyclopedia, 1997 ed., entries on "Communism," "Industrial Workers of the World," "Labor movement," "Syndicalism." Chicago, IL: World Book, 1997.

National Association for the Advancement of Colored People v. Alabama 1958

Petitioner: National Association for the Advancement of Colored People (NAACP)

Respondent: State of Alabama

Petitioner's Claim: That forcing the NAACP to reveal the names of its Alabama members violated their freedom of association.

Chief Lawyer for Petitioner: Robert L. Carter

Chief Lawyer for Respondent: Edmond L. Rinehart, Assistant Attorney General of Alabama

Justices for the Court: Hugo Lafayette Black, William J. Brennan, Jr., Harold Burton, Tom C. Clark, William O. Douglas, John Marshall Harlan II (writing for the Court), Potter Stewart, Earl Warren, Charles Evans Whittaker

Justices Dissenting: None

Date of Decision: June 30, 1958

Decision: The NAACP did not have to reveal the names of its Alabama members.

Significance: The decision said privacy is an essential part of the freedom of association. Privacy was important for many African Americans during the civil rights movement, which was unpopular among many white Americans.

FREEDOM OF ASSEMBLY

Separate is not equal

In the landmark case of ***Brown v. Board of Education*** (1954), the U.S. Supreme Court said segregation in public schools is unconstitutional. Segregation was the practice of separating black and white people in different facilities. After *Brown,* however, segregation continued in public places such as restaurants, buses, restrooms, and water fountains.

The National Association for the Advancement of Colored People ("NAACP") is an organization that works to ensure equality for minorities in the United States. It has headquarters in New York and branch offices throughout the nation. In the 1950s, the NAACP fought to help African Americans end segregation. Many white Americans who did not want African Americans to be equal fought against the NAACP. This was especially true in southern states.

Way down south

In Alabama in the 1950s, the NAACP had a branch office plus affiliate organizations, which acted as local associations. The NAACP worked in

The arrest of NAACP worker Rosa Parks in 1955 spurred a great deal of civil rights activism in Alabama. Reproduced by permission of AP/Wide World Photos.

Alabama to recruit members, seek donations, and help African American students get into the state university. In 1955, an African American and NAACP worker named Rosa Parks was arrested for violating a bus segregation law in Montgomery, Alabama, by refusing to give her bus seat to a white person. In protest, African Americans boycotted the Montgomery buses for over one year, forcing Montgomery to close some bus lines. The NAACP supported the boycott.

At the time, Alabama had a law that required corporations with headquarters outside the state to register with the Alabama Secretary of State before operating in Alabama. The NAACP did not register because it did not think the law applied to its organization. In 1956, during the Montgomery bus boycott, Alabama attorney general John Patterson filed a lawsuit against the NAACP for breaking the law. Patterson asked the court to ban the NAACP from ever working in the state again.

To prove that the NAACP was operating in Alabama, Patterson asked it to turn over records and papers, including a list of all NAACP members in Alabama. Because the NAACP was unpopular in some areas, revealing its members was dangerous. In the past, members had been physically attacked and fired from their jobs for being part of the association. Because of these dangers, the NAACP refused to turn over its membership list.

Upon Patterson's request, the court ordered the NAACP to turn over its membership list plus other papers related to its business in Alabama. The NAACP refused, so the court held the NAACP in contempt and fined it $10,000. The court said the fine would increase to $100,000 if the NAACP failed to comply with its order within five days.

At the end of five days, the NAACP turned over all of the business papers Alabama sought except the membership list. As it had threatened to do, the court raised the fine to $100,000. The NAACP appealed this order twice to the Alabama Supreme Court, which refused to review the case. As its last resort, the NAACP took the case to the U.S. Supreme Court.

Before the Supreme Court, the NAACP argued that revealing its members would violate their freedom of association. The freedom of association comes from the First Amendment freedom of assembly. It protects the right to form an organization to fight for a cause. States, including Alabama, must obey the freedom of association under the Due Process Clause of the Fourteenth Amendment.

ROSA PARKS

One of the reasons Alabama went after the NAACP was an African American boycott of the public buses in Montgomery. That boycott was sparked by one woman, Rosa Parks, an African American who lived in Montgomery in 1955. Parks used the public buses to go to her job at the NAACP. In Montgomery at the time, the law required blacks and whites to sit in separate sections of the bus. If the white section filled up, blacks had to give up their seats for whites who were standing.

On December 1, 1955, Parks was riding home from work when the white section filled up. The bus driver told Parks to stand to allow a white person to sit. Tired of being treated unfairly, Parks refused to get up. She was arrested and eventually convicted of violating the bus segregation law. In protest, African Americans—led by Dr. Martin Luther King, Jr.—boycotted the public buses in Montgomery for over one year. In November 1956, the U.S. Supreme Court finally declared that bus segregation was illegal. In honor of Parks, Montgomery eventually renamed the street on which she rode home from work the Rosa Parks Boulevard.

Privacy prevails

With a unanimous decision, the Supreme Court ruled in favor of the NAACP and reversed the contempt order. Writing for the Court, Justice John Marshall Harlan II said privacy is an essential part of the freedom of association. Without privacy, members might be attacked, fired, or otherwise punished by persons who were hostile to the NAACP. With such fears, minorities might not join or remain with the NAACP, an organization that was fighting for their rights. In this way, lack of privacy would interfere with the freedom of association.

Justice Harlan said Alabama could interfere with the freedom of association only if had a very good reason for doing so. Alabama said it needed the membership list to prove that the NAACP was operating in the state without obeying the registration law. Alabama, however, could prove this with the other business records that the NAACP turned over. It did not need to know the names and addresses of ordinary members who were not even working for the NAACP. Because Alabama did not have a good reason for seeking the membership list, the trials court's order violated the freedom of association. Justice Harlan overturned that order and eliminated the $100,000 fine.

Suggestions for further reading

Farish, Leah. *The First Amendment: Freedom of Speech, Religion, and the Press.* Hillside, NJ: Enslow Publishers, Inc., 1998.

King, David C. *Freedom of Assembly.* Brookfield, CT: Millbrook Press, 1997.

Klinker, Philip A. *The First Amendment.* Englewood Cliffs, NJ: Silver Burdett Press, 1991.

Moss, Joyce, and George Wilson. *Profiles in American History: Significant Events and the People Who Shaped Them.* Vol. 7, *Great Depression to the Cuban Missile Crisis.* Detroit: Gale Research, 1995.

Pascoe, Elaine. *Freedom of Expression: The Right to Speak Out in America.* Brookfield, CT: Millbrook Press, 1992.

Cox v. Louisiana 1965

Appellant: Reverend B. Elton Cox

Appellee: State of Louisiana

Appellant's Claim: That convicting him for leading a peaceful demonstration against segregation violated the First Amendment.

Chief Lawyer for Appellant: Carl Rochlin

Chief Lawyer for Appellee: Ralph L. Roy

Justices for the Court: Hugo Lafayette Black (in *Cox* I), William J. Brennan, Jr., Tom C. Clark (in *Cox* I), William O. Douglas, Arthur Goldberg (writing for the Court), Potter Stewart, Earl Warren

Justices Dissenting: Hugo Lafayette Black (in *Cox* II), Tom C. Clark (in *Cox* II), John Marshall Harlan II, Byron R. White

Date of Decision: January 18, 1965

Decision: Cox's convictions violated the freedoms of speech and assembly.

Significance: The Court said states cannot use public welfare laws to punish unpopular speech or to discriminate against minority viewpoints.

Stop segregation

In the landmark case of ***Brown v. Board of Education*** (1954), the U.S. Supreme Court declared segregation in public schools to be unconstitutional. Segregation was the practice of separating black and white people

Associate Justice Arthur Goldberg.
Courtesy of the Supreme Court of the United States.

in different facilities. After *Brown,* however, segregation continued in public places such as restaurants, buses, restrooms, and water fountains.

In the 1960s, African Americans such as Martin Luther King, Jr. led a civil rights movement to end segregation and achieve equality for African Americans. Public protests were a popular and important part of this movement. By gathering in public to oppose segregation and other unfair practices, protestors exercised the First Amendment freedoms of speech and assembly.

The government did not always like the civil rights protests. White Americans, who did not want African Americans to achieve equality, sometimes controlled governments. Some government officials were concerned that protests would get out of control and lead to riots and other illegal behavior. Efforts to silence civil rights protestors often interfered with First Amendment rights. That is what happened in *Cox v. Louisiana.*

Protests in Baton Rouge

On December 14, 1961, the Congress of Racial Equality ("CORE") organized a protest in Baton Rouge, Louisiana. The protestors were twenty-three black students from Southern University. They picketed segregated lunch counters in Baton Rouge and urged people to boycott stores with such counters. The twenty-three students were arrested and jailed in the courthouse in Baton Rouge.

The following day, about 2,000 black students marched from Southern University to downtown Baton Rouge to protest against the arrests and segregation in general. Reverend B. Elton Cox, a member of CORE and a Congregational minister, led the students in their march. He instructed them to be orderly and peaceful.

When the group arrived downtown, two city officials approached Cox and asked him what his group was doing. Cox said they were protesting the arrests and segregation by marching to the courthouse to say prayers, sing hymns, and display signs. The officials asked Cox to disband the group and return to the university, but Cox refused.

When Cox's group arrived at the courthouse, Police Chief Wingate White asked Cox what he was doing. After Cox explained, White told him to confine the students to the sidewalk across the street from the courthouse, which Cox did. Approximately eighty police officers positioned themselves in the street between the protestors and the courthouse. A group of about 300 white people gathered in front of the courthouse to watch.

Cox's group held a peaceful protest. They said prayers and sang "God Bless America" and other songs. When the group sang, the twenty-three students jailed in the courthouse could be heard singing along with the others. Cox's group applauded loudly. Some cried. During the entire protest, many students displayed pickets urging people to boycott stores that supported segregation.

At the end of the protest, Cox announced that it was lunchtime. He urged the black students to go downtown to eat at the lunch counters reserved for white people. Cox said the students should sit there for one hour if the stores refused to serve them. Many of the white onlookers reacted by "muttering" and "grumbling."

Here comes the law

The Baton Rouge sheriff then decided that Cox was causing a breach of the peace. He used a loudspeaker to order Cox's group to break up and go home. Cox and the students refused to leave. Minutes later the police fired tear gas into the crowd, causing the people to break up and flee. After trying to calm the students, Cox was the last one to leave.

The next day Cox was arrested and charged with four offenses. At trial he was convicted of disturbing the peace, obstructing (blocking) a public passage, and picketing before a courthouse. Cox was sentenced to a total of one year and nine months in jail and fined $5,700. Cox appealed to the Louisiana Supreme Court, which affirmed (approved) his convictions. He then appealed to the U.S. Supreme Court. Cox argued that his convictions violated the First Amendment freedoms of speech and assembly.

No breach of the peace

The Supreme Court reversed all of Cox's convictions. Writing for the Court, Justice Arthur Goldberg explained the decision for each specific violation.

Louisiana's breach of the peace statute made it a crime to gather in public for the purpose of causing a public disturbance. The Supreme Court said that convicting Cox under that statute violated the First Amendment. The First Amendment says, "Congress shall make no law . . . abridging [limiting] the freedom of speech . . . or the right of the people peaceably to assemble." States, including Louisiana, must obey the First Amendment under the Due Process Clause of the Fourteenth Amendment. The Due Process Clause prevents state and local governments from violating a person's right to life, liberty (or freedom), and property.

The Court voted unanimously to reverse Cox's conviction for disturbing the peace. Justice Goldberg explained that the First Amendment was designed to allow people to do exactly what Cox did. It protects a person's right to gather in public to demonstrate peacefully against the government. Cox's students protested peacefully. Although they occasionally applauded or sang loudly, they did not cause violence or any other disturbance. Because punishing Cox for a peaceful protest violated the First Amendment, the Court struck down the entire breach of the peace statute as unconstitutional.

Public passages

Louisiana's public passages statute made it illegal to obstruct (block) a public sidewalk. After reviewing a video of the protest, Justice Goldberg said there was no doubt that Cox's group had blocked the entire sidewalk across the street from the courthouse. Justice Goldberg also said

Louisiana was allowed to make blocking the sidewalk a crime. Even if people are exercising their right to free speech, they may not endanger public safety by blocking public walkways. The Court, however, voted 7–2 to overturn Cox's conviction under the public passages statute. The statute outlawed all obstructions, but the Court saw evidence that local officials gave some groups permission to use streets and sidewalks for parades and demonstrations. The Court said the U.S. Constitution prevents local governments from favoring some groups over others. Louisiana could not give some people permission to demonstrate but convict Cox just because it did not like the message of his protest.

Picketing before a courthouse

The Court reported its decision on the picketing charge in a second opinion, called *Cox* II. Writing for the Court again, Justice Goldberg explained that the Louisiana statute made it illegal to picket before a courthouse to try to influence a judge or jury. Justice Goldberg said that Louisiana is allowed to have such a law so that judges and juries will decide cases based on the evidence in court, instead of on the protests outside.

Again, however, the Court decided to overturn Cox's conviction. With a 5–4 vote, the Court said that Cox had permission to protest across the street from the courthouse. Police Chief Wingate White specifically told Cox that his group should confine itself to that area. Justice Goldberg said that it would be unfair to give Cox permission to picket on the sidewalk and then to convict him for doing so.

Four justices dissented, meaning disagreed, with this part of the Court's decision. They thought Police Chief White was trying to control a potentially violent situation. They did not agree that White gave Cox's group permission to break the law against picketing in front of a courthouse. In his dissenting opinion Justice Tom C. Clark said, "I have always been taught that this Nation was dedicated to freedom under law not under mobs."

Impact

The *Cox* cases reminded America about some basic rights under the First Amendment, such as the right to gather in public to protest against the government. Although the government is allowed to regulate protests for public safety, it may not allow some groups to protest and deny the right to others. Most importantly, the government may not punish a group for protesting because it does not like the group's message.

MONTGOMERY BUS BOYCOTT

One of history's most famous protests against segregation happened in Montgomery, Alabama. On December 1, 1955, African American Rosa Parks was arrested for violating a segregation law by refusing to give up her bus seat to a white person. Outraged by the arrest, African Americans gathered in the basement of the Dexter Avenue Baptist Church, where Dr. Martin Luther King, Jr. was pastor. The group decided to boycott Montgomery's buses on Monday, December 5. That day, fewer than twelve of the city's 30,000 African Americans rode the public buses.

Led by Dr. King, African Americans formed the Montgomery Improvement Association to continue the boycott. For 381 days, African Americans refused to use Montgomery's public buses. People formed car-pools to provide transportation to work. Taxi cab drivers helped by charging the bus fare of ten cents per ride. That year was difficult for African Americans. Police arrested African Americans waiting at bus stops for taxis and charged them with violating public nuisance laws. Police also arrested car-poolers for minor traffic violations.

In the end, justice prevailed. In November 1956, the U.S. Supreme Court declared Alabama's bus segregation law unconstitutional. The next month, blacks and whites rode Montgomery's buses together, sitting where they desired. For Dr. King, it was a visible beginning of his long battle for civil rights.

Suggestions for further reading

Dubovoy, Sina. *Civil Rights Leaders.* New York: Facts on File, 1997.

Evans, J. Edward. *Freedom of Speech.* Minneapolis: Lerner Publications, Inc., 1990.

Farish, Leah. *The First Amendment: Freedom of Speech, Religion, and the Press.* Hillside, NJ: Enslow Publishers, Inc., 1998.

King, David C. *The Right to Speak Out.* Brookfield, CT: Millbrook Press, 1997.

Klinker, Philip A. *The First Amendment.* Englewood Cliffs, NJ: Silver Burdett Press, 1991.

Moss, Joyce, and George Wilson. *Profiles in American History: Significant Events and the People Who Shaped Them.* Vols. 7 and 8. Detroit: Gale Research, 1995.

Pascoe, Elaine. *Freedom of Expression: The Right to Speak Out in America.* Brookfield, CT: Millbrook Press, 1992.

Rediger, Pat. *Great African Americans in Civil Rights.* New York: Crabtree Publishing Co., 1996.

Steele, Philip, Philip Skele, and Penny Clarke. *Freedom of Speech?* New York: Franklin Watts, 1997.

Zeinert, Karen. *Free Speech: From Newspapers to Music Lyrics.* Enslow Publishers, Inc., 1995.

Roberts v. U.S. Jaycees 1984

Petitioner: Kathryn R. Roberts, Acting Commissioner, Minnesota Department of Human Rights, et al.

Respondent: U.S. Jaycees

Petitioner's Claim: That Minnesota's Human Rights Act was constitutional and required the Jaycees to admit women as regular members.

Chief Lawyer for Petitioner: Richard L. Varco Jr.

Chief Lawyer for Respondent: Carl D. Hall Jr.

Justices for the Court: William J. Brennan, Jr. (writing for the Court), Thurgood Marshall, Sandra Day O'Connor, Lewis F. Powell, Jr., William H. Rehnquist, John Paul Stevens, Byron R. White

Justices Dissenting: None (Harry A. Blackmun and Warren E. Burger did not participate)

Date of Decision: July 3, 1984

Decision: Minnesota's Human Rights Act was constitutional. Requiring the Jaycees to admit women as regular members did not violate the organization's freedom of association.

Significance: This was the first in a series of Supreme Court decisions that opened many all-male organizations to women.

FREEDOM OF ASSEMBLY

No women allowed

The Supreme Court often decides cases involving conflicting constitutional rights. In *Roberts v. U.S. Jaycees,* the U.S. Jaycees argued that the First Amendment freedom of association allowed the organization to refuse to admit women as regular members. (The freedom of association is the right to form organizations for political or social causes and to control who can be a member.) The state of Minnesota argued that it could force the Jaycees to admit women in order to stop sex discrimination. (Sex discrimination is unequal treatment of people based on their gender.) The Supreme Court had to choose between the freedom of association and the goal of ending sex discrimination.

As no photos are allowed in the Supreme Court, this is a line drawing of lawyer Richard Varco, Jr., defending the petitioner, Kathryn Roberts. Reproduced by permission of Richard R. Varco, Jr.

Future leaders in America

The U.S. Jaycees is a nonprofit organization with national offices in Tulsa, Oklahoma. State offices are also located throughout the country. Many cities and other communities also have local Jaycees organizations called chapters. As of 1999, the Jaycees' goal is to promote leadership

training and community involvement for young adults between twenty-one and thirty-nine years old.

Prior to 1984, however, the Jaycees' main goal was to promote community service and leadership by young men. Regular membership was only open to men between the ages of eighteen and thirty-five. The Jaycees developed training programs to teach young men how to be leaders in business and society. Men over thirty-five and women of all ages could only become associate members. Associate members paid membership fees but could not vote, hold office, or participate in Jaycees awards and training programs.

Rebellion in the ranks

In the early 1970s, two local chapters in Minnesota began to admit women as regular members. Minneapolis did so in 1974, and St. Paul began in 1975. Women became important members of both chapters and served on their boards of directors.

Because female membership violated the organization's rules, the U.S. Jaycees declared that all members of the Minneapolis and St. Paul chapters were forbidden from serving in the Jaycees' state or national offices. It also forbade those members from receiving awards or voting at the annual national convention. The U.S. Jaycees then announced that the national board of directors would meet to consider canceling Minneapolis and St. Paul's membership in the U.S. Jaycees.

The Minneapolis and St. Paul chapters filed complaints with the Minnesota Department of Human Rights. The Department of Human Rights was responsible for enforcing the Minnesota Human Rights Act, which made it illegal to deny people the benefits of using a public facility because of their gender. The Minneapolis and St. Paul Jaycees said they would be violating the Human Rights Act if they did not admit women as regular members.

The Department of Human Rights ruled in favor of the chapters. It said that the Jaycees is a public facility, and that excluding women from membership in a public facility was unlawful sex discrimination under the Minnesota Human Rights Act.

The U.S. Jaycees responded by suing Kathryn R. Roberts, the head of the Minnesota Department of Human Rights, in federal court in Minnesota. The U.S. Jaycees argued that by forcing the Jaycees to admit women, the Human Rights Act violated the First Amendment right to freedom of association. Specifically the Jaycees argued that under the First Amendment, its members had a right to exclude women to pursue its goal of developing leadership abilities and community involvement for young men. It also said it had a First Amendment right to support political and public causes of interest to young men. Forcing the Jaycees to admit women would interfere with those First Amendment rights.

The federal court ruled in favor of Roberts. On appeal, the Court of Appeals for the Eighth Circuit reversed and ruled in favor of the Jaycees. It said the Jaycees' right to determine its membership was protected by the First Amendment freedom of association. Roberts appealed to the U.S. Supreme Court.

Reversing discrimination

The U.S. Supreme Court reversed the Eighth Circuit's decision and ruled in favor of Roberts and the Minnesota Human Rights Act. Writing for the Court, Justice William J. Brennan, Jr. immediately noted the conflict between the freedom of association and the goal of ending sex discrimination. Resolving that conflict depended on the importance of the two rights.

Justice Brennan said that ending sex discrimination is a compelling state interest. A compelling state interest is an interest so important that the government may interfere with other, less important rights in order to serve that interest. Deciding the case, then, depended on the importance of the Jaycees' right to freedom of association.

To answer this question, Justice Brennan described two different kinds of freedom of association. He called the first one the freedom of intimate association. This freedom is the right to have close family relationships. Justice Brennan said this right is so important that it would win in a battle against the compelling state interest of ending sex discrimination.

The Jaycees, however, was not a small family, but rather a large organization. This meant that instead of exercising the freedom of intimate association, it was exercising the second kind of freedom, called the freedom of expressive association. The freedom of expressive association is the right to gather with people to speak, worship, or pursue goals as a group. Expressive association is of such importance that Justice Brennan said that the government may not control a group's reason for gathering or the goals it pursues.

WILLIAM J. BRENNAN, JR.

Justice William J. Brennan, Jr., who wrote the decision in *Roberts v. U.S. Jaycees,* graduated at the top of his class in Harvard Law School. After practicing law in Newark, New Jersey, he served as a judge on the New Jersey Superior Court and then the New Jersey Supreme Court. President Dwight D. Eisenhower nominated Brennan to the U.S. Supreme Court in 1956.

As a Supreme Court Justice who also was a Catholic Democrat, Brennan never stopped fighting for the rights of minorities and the politically weak citizens of America. He firmly believed that our Constitution guarantees "freedom and equality of rights and opportunities . . . to all people of this nation." Justice Brennan wrote decisions in favor of ending racial and gender discrimination, and protecting the freedom of speech and the rights of criminal defendants. Brennan retired from the Supreme Court in 1990 and passed away in July 1997.

The freedom of expressive association, however, is less important than the state's compelling interest in ending sex discrimination. Organizations that exclude women reinforce old ideas that women have fewer or different abilities and interests than men. Therefore, Justice Brennan concluded that under the Minnesota Human Rights Act the Jaycees could admit women as regular members without interfering with its freedom of association. Even with female members, the Jaycees still could pursue the goals of fostering community involvement and leadership for young men.

In time, the Jaycees committed itself to fostering development for young men and women alike. In fact, *Roberts* was the first of many Supreme Court cases to open all-male organizations to women. In 1987 in *Rotary International v. Rotary Club of Duarte,* the Supreme Court ruled that an organization of businesses devoted to public service had to admit women as members. Then in 1996 in ***United States v. Virginia,*** the Court ruled that all-male military colleges had to admit women as students. In this way, the Supreme Court has helped to create equal opportunities for men and women in America.

Suggestions for further reading

Hanmer, Trudy J. *Sexism and Sex Discrimination.* New York: Franklin Watts, 1990.

King, David C. *Freedom of Assembly.* Brookfield, CT: Millbrook Press, 1997.

Klinker, Philip A. *The First Amendment.* Englewood Cliffs, NJ: Silver Burdett Press, 1991.

Pascoe, Elaine. *Freedom of Expression: The Right to Speak Out in America.* Brookfield, CT: Millbrook Press, 1992.

The Supreme Court: Selections from the Four-Volume Encyclopedia of the American Constitution and Supplement. New York: Macmillan Library Reference USA, 1999.

The World Book Encyclopedia, 1997 ed., entry on "Jaycees." Chicago: World Book 1997.

The First Amendment says "Congress shall make no law . . . abridging the freedom . . . of the press." Under the Due Process Clause of the Fourteenth Amendment, states also must recognize freedom of the press.

When the United States adopted the First Amendment in 1791, the press meant printed books, newspapers, and pamphlets, also called handbills. With advances in technology, the press came to include the broadcast media of radio and television. In the 1990s the Internet expanded the press to include computer-based publications.

The freedom of the press protects the right to publish information and to express ideas in these various media. It is an important right in a free society. To make sure government is running properly, citizens need to be informed. People do not have the time or ability to watch everything the government does. The press serves this function by investigating and reporting on the government's activity. If the citizens do not like what they see, they can remove politicians from office and elect new ones to do a better job.

In 1787 future president Thomas Jefferson made the following remark about the importance of the freedom of the press: "Were it left to me to decide whether we should have a government without newspapers or newspapers without government, I should not hesitate for a moment to prefer the latter."

History of free press concerns

The United States adopted freedom of the press in reaction to the press's history in England and the American colonies. Even before the German Johannes Gutenberg invented the printing press in the fifteenth century, government and church leaders in England regularly banned handwritten books that threatened their power. After the invention of the printing press, the English government required printers to get a license from a government or church official before publishing anything. By the mid-sixteenth century, anyone found with a book that criticized the British government could be executed.

In 1585 Queen Elizabeth I of England created a new set of laws to control the press in her country. Printing could occur only at approved presses in Oxford, Cambridge, and London. All material to be printed had to be approved beforehand by the Archbishop of Canterbury or the Bishop of London. Violators faced imprisonment or destruction of their printing equipment. Although these laws expired in 1695, the British government continued to enforce laws against sedition. These laws prevented anyone from printing something that criticized the government, even if it was true.

Printing was introduced in the American colonies in 1639 in Cambridge, Massachusetts. By 1765 more than thirty newspapers were printed in the colonies. The press, however, faced controls similar to those in England. Many colonies had censorship laws controlling what could be published. They also had sedition laws to punish people for speaking against the government. In 1765 the British government passed the Stamp Act, which placed a tax on colonial newspapers. When the United States adopted the First Amendment in 1791, it was trying to prevent all of these practices from controlling the press in America.

Avoiding government censorship

Americans especially did not want the government to have censorship power, which is the power to control what is published. Censorship is sometimes called "prior restraint" because it keeps a publication from being printed. In the case of ***Near v. Minnesota*** (1931), the U.S. Supreme Court officially ruled that the First Amendment prohibits the government from using prior restraints. In *Grosjean v. American Press Co.* (1936), the Supreme Court also outlawed taxes that apply only to the press and not to businesses generally. Such taxes act as a form of prior restraint by making it more difficult for the press to report the news.

The Supreme Court, however, has recognized a number of exceptions to the rule against prior restraints. The government may ban the printing of obscene material, which is sexual material that is offensive. The Supreme Court says obscenity is not protected by the First Amendment because it has no value in the flow of information in society.

The government also may ban the publication of material that would harm national security. For example, the government may prevent people from printing material to start a violent revolution. During wartime, the government may prevent publishers from revealing information such as the location of U.S. troops and their battle plans.

In ***New York Times Co. v. United States*** (1971), however, the Supreme Court ruled that the federal government could not prevent newspapers from printing a report about the United States's involvement in the Vietnam War (1954-1975). Although the report would embarrass the federal government, the Court said printing the report would not harm national security enough to merit stopping the presses. It was an important case that strengthened the rule against censorship and prior restraints.

Punishment for publishing

Freedom of the press also limits the government's power to punish people after they publish something. As noted earlier, England and the American colonies had sedition laws that punished people for criticizing the government, even truthfully. The First Amendment was designed to prevent such laws.

However, Congress passed a Sedition Act in 1798. It prohibited anybody from speaking against the government. Many Democratic-Republican newspaper editors were convicted under the Sedition Act. (The Democratic-Republican Party, which has since become known simply as the Democratic Party, was opposed to the Federalist Party, which was more powerful at the time.) When Democratic-Republican President Thomas Jefferson took office in 1801, he pardoned, meaning excused, the violators, and the unpopular law expired. Since then, the Supreme

Court has said sedition laws like the Sedition Act of 1798 would violate freedom of the press.

The press, however, can be forced to pay damages when it commits libel. Libel is publishing false information that harms a person's reputation. The U.S. Supreme Court has created two sets of rules concerning libel laws, one for public figures and the other for private individuals.

Public figures are people who are well-known to the general population, such as celebrities, or who are involved in public business, such as politicians. In ***New York Times Company v. Sullivan*** (1964), the Supreme Court said that one of the press's most important functions is to report about public figures. The Court said libel laws might prevent the press from publishing important information for fear that it might be untrue. So the Supreme Court decided that public figures can sue for libel only when the press knows that it is printing untrue material. If the press prints false information by accident, public figures cannot sue.

Private individuals are different. They are people who are not known to the public. The public does not have a great interest in learning about private individuals, so the press does not need as much protection when reporting about them. In *Gertz v. Robert Welch, Inc.* (1974), the Supreme Court said that when the press prints an untrue statement about a private individual, the person can sue for libel even if the press did not know the material was untrue. The individual only must prove that the press was negligent, meaning careless, when it printed the false information.

Freedom to gather news

As shown above, the First Amendment protects the press's right to report the news. To report the news, however, the press must be able to investigate and gather it. Many Supreme Court cases involve news gathering.

Branzburg v. Hayes (1972) concerned some news reporters, called journalists, who interviewed drug users and gang members to write stories for their newspaper. The journalists promised not to reveal the names of the people they interviewed. The government, however, wanted the journalists to reveal the names to grand juries that were investigating criminal activity. (A grand jury is a group of people who decide whether the government has enough evidence to charge somebody with a crime.)

The journalists refused. They said freedom of the press gives them the privilege, or right, to keep secrets when they learn things while gathering the news. Without such a privilege, the journalists said they would not be able to get people to talk to them, and so would not be able to gather and report the news. The Supreme Court rejected this argument. It ruled that when journalists have knowledge of criminal activity, they must share it with grand juries just like every other citizen.

Criminal trials also create news gathering problems. The Sixth Amendment to the U.S. Constitution says criminal defendants have a right to a fair trial. Under the First Amendment, however, the press has a right to report criminal trials to inform the public about them. In some cases, the press's coverage of a trial can be so great that it hurts the defendant's Sixth Amendment right to a fair trial. For example, if people who are going to serve on the jury hear about the case from the press, they might make up their minds about whether the defendant is guilty before hearing the case as a juror. That would be unfair to the defendant.

Nebraska Press Association v. Stuart (1976) involved a criminal trial that was getting a lot of press coverage. To protect the defendant's right to a fair trial, the trial judge issued a "gag order." The order prevented the press from reporting about the trial. The press appealed the order all the way to the U.S. Supreme Court. This time the journalists won. The Supreme Court decided that a "gag order" is a prior restraint that violates the freedom of the press. The Court said there are many ways trial judges can protect the right to a fair trial without violating the freedom of the press. For example, judges can transfer trials to other communities, postpone trials until press coverage slows down, and be careful to select jurors who have not already made up their minds from listening to the press.

Television also has created news gathering issues. Do television reporters have a right to attend criminal trials and to televise them to the public? In *Richmond Newspapers, Inc. v. Virginia* (1980), the Court ruled that reporters do have a right to attend criminal trials. In *Chandler v. Florida* (1981), it said trial judges may allow reporters to televise trials if they make sure it does not interfere with the defendant's right to a fair trial. Because of this, the public sometimes gets to watch important trials on television as they happen.

Suggestions for further reading

Evans, J. Edward. *Freedom of the Press.* Minneapolis, MN: Lerner Publications Company, 1990.

Farish, Leah. *The First Amendment: Freedom of Speech, Religion, and the Press.* Hillside, NJ: Enslow Publishers, Inc., 1998.

Goldman, David J. *The Freedom of the Press in America.* Minneapolis, MN: Lerner Publications Company, 1967.

Klinker, Philip A. *The First Amendment.* Englewood Cliffs, NJ: Silver Burdett Press, 1991.

Pascoe, Elaine. *Freedom of Expression: The Right to Speak Out in America.* Brookfield, CT: Millbrook Press, 1992.

Schwartz, Bernard. *Freedom of the Press.* New York, NY: Facts on File, 1992.

Steins, Richard. *Censorship: How Does It Conflict with Freedom?* New York, NY: Twenty-First Century Books, 1995.

Zeinert, Karen. *Free Speech: From Newspapers to Music Lyrics.* Hillside, NJ: Enslow Publishers, Inc., 1995.

Zerman, Melvyn B. *Taking on the Press: Constitutional Rights in Conflict.* New York, NY: Crowell, 1986.

Near v. Minnesota
1931

Appellant: J.M. Near

Appellee: State of Minnesota, ex rel. Floyd B. Olson, County Attorney of Hennepin County

Appellant's Claim: That a state "gag law" preventing publication of his newspaper violated the First Amendment freedom of the press.

Chief Lawyers for Appellant: Weymouth Kirkland and T.E. Latimer

Chief Lawyers for Appellee: James E. Markham and Arthur L. Markve

Justices for the Court: Louis D. Brandeis, Oliver Wendell Holmes, Charles Evans Hughes (writing for the Court), Owen Josephus Roberts, Harlan Fiske Stone

Justices Dissenting: Pierce Butler, James Clark McReynolds, George Sutherland, Willis Van Devanter

Date of Decision: June 1, 1931

Decision: The law violated the freedom of the press.

Significance: This was the first time the Supreme Court declared that "prior restraints" on publication violated the First Amendment.

FREEDOM OF THE PRESS

True or false?

In 1925, Minnesota passed a law called the Minnesota Gag Law. The law allowed judges to stop the publication of any newspaper that created a scandal or defamed (lied about) a person. The law was designed to fight "yellow journalism," which was a trend in the newspaper industry in the 1920s to print exaggerated or false stories.

J.M. Near published a newspaper in Minneapolis, Minnesota, called *The Saturday Press.* Near's prejudice against Catholics, Jews, and African Americans showed through in *The Saturday Press.* The newspaper, however, also printed articles about corruption in city politics, and many of them were true.

From September through November 1927, *The Saturday Press* published a series of articles that said Minneapolis was being controlled by a Jewish gangster. The articles accused the city mayor, county attorney, and chief of police of accepting bribes and refusing to stop the gangster. On behalf of the state of Minnesota, the county attorney sued Near and *The Saturday Press.* He charged them with violating the Gag Law by publishing scandalous and defamatory (untrue) material that lied about public officials.

Near tried to get the lawsuit thrown out of court. He argued that the Gag Law violated the First Amendment freedom of the press, which says "Congress shall make no law . . . abridging the freedom . . . of the press." Under the Due Process Clause of the Fourteenth Amendment, states also must obey the freedom of the press.

The trial judge rejected Near's defense and decided that *The Saturday Press* was scandalous and defamatory. He issued an order preventing Near from publishing the newspaper in the future. Near appealed the order all the way to the U.S. Supreme Court.

No prior restraints

In a close decision, the Supreme Court voted 5–4 to declare the Minnesota Gag Law unconstitutional. Writing for the Court, Chief Justice Charles Evans Hughes started by confirming what the Court had decided six years earlier. The First Amendment freedom of the press is one of the liberties, or freedoms, protected by the Fourteenth Amendment from state interference. This means that all states, including Minnesota, must obey the freedom of the press.

Chief Justice Hughes went on to explain the meaning of the freedom of the press. He told the story of how publishers in England used to need approval from government or church officials before publishing books. Justice Hughes said that the First Amendment was designed to avoid such "prior restraints" on publication. America's founders did not want the government to have the power to stop a publisher from printing what the government did not like. In fact, America's founders thought it was important for the public to be informed about the government's bad deeds so the public could be aware of and fight any government corruption.

Justice Hughes decided that the Minnesota Gag Law violated the First Amendment. Preventing Near from printing *The Saturday Press* in the future was a prior restraint on publication. Justice Hughes said that if the newspaper lied about public officials, those officials could sue for libel. (Libel is the publication of false information that hurts a person's reputation.) The public, however, had a right to hear about government misconduct, and the First Amendment allowed *The Saturday Press* to print such stories.

Decency denied

For himself and three others, Justice Pierce Butler wrote a dissenting opinion, meaning he disagreed with the Court's decision. Justice Butler thought the freedom of the press only protects the right to print "what is true, with good motives and for justifiable ends." He did not think it gave publishers the right to print material that ruins another person's reputation.

In fact, Justice Butler said that the Minnesota Gag Law was not a "prior restraint." The law punished Near and *The Saturday Press* only after they printed defamatory (untrue) material. It told them they could not print such material again. Justice Butler said the Court's decision threatened peace by allowing publishers to print lies about anyone.

Near's Legacy

Near has had the effect that Justice Hughes predicted and that Justice Butler feared. On the good side, it has allowed the press to be a government watchdog. For example, in 1971, the Supreme Court used *Near* to rule that the federal government could not stop newspapers from printing an embarrassing report about the government's involvement in the Vietnam War.

FOUR HORSEMEN

The dissenters in *Near,* Justices Pierce Butler, James Clark McReynolds, George Sutherland, and Willis Van Devanter, often voted together. By convincing just one more justice to vote with them, they were able to control the result in many of Supreme Court cases. Because of this power, they were called the Four Horsemen. This name was a comparison to Notre Dame's undefeated football offense in 1924, and to the horsemen described in the Bible's prediction of the end of the world.

In the 1930s, the Four Horsemen frequently voted against laws passed by Congress to help America get out of the Great Depression. The Great Depression was a time when many Americans lost their jobs and had trouble providing food for their families. Despite the severity of the Great Depression, the Four Horsemen saw a greater danger from passing laws that violated the U.S. Constitution. In *Near,* however, they were unable to stop the Court from strengthening the freedom of the press.

Like Justice Butler feared, however, some "tabloid" publishers today abuse the freedom of the press by printing crazy stories about people with animal bodies and babies that weigh 1,000 pounds. When these tabloids print lies about actual people, like politicians or celebrities, the injured person must file a libel lawsuit to protect his reputation.

Suggestions for further reading

Cushman, Clare, ed. *The Supreme Court Justices: Illustrated Biographies, 1789-1993.* Washington, DC: Congressional Quarterly Inc., 1993.

Evans, J. Edward. *Freedom of the Press.* Minneapolis: Lerner Publications Company, 1990.

Farish, Leah. *The First Amendment: Freedom of Speech, Religion, and the Press.* Hillside, NJ: Enslow Publishers, Inc., 1998.

Goldman, David J. *The Freedom of the Press in America.* Minneapolis: Lerner Publications Company, 1967.

Klinker, Philip A. *The First Amendment.* Englewood Cliffs, NJ: Silver Burdett Press, 1991.

Pascoe, Elaine. *Freedom of Expression: The Right to Speak Out in America.* Brookfield, CT: Millbrook Press, 1992.

Schwartz, Bernard. *Freedom of the Press.* New York: Facts on File, 1992.

Steins, Richard. *Censorship: How Does It Conflict with Freedom?* New York: Twenty-First Century Books, 1995.

White, G. Edward. *American Judicial Tradition: Profiles of Leading American Judges.* New York: Oxford University Press, 1988.

Zeinert, Karen. *Free Speech: From Newspapers to Music Lyrics.* Hillside, NJ: Enslow Publishers, Inc., 1995.

Zerman, Melvyn B. *Taking on the Press: Constitutional Rights in Conflict.* New York: Crowell, 1986.

New York Times Company v. United States 1971

Petitioner: New York Times Company

Respondent: United States of America

Petitioner's Claim: That preventing newspapers from publishing a top secret report on the government's involvement in the Vietnam War violated the First Amendment.

Chief Lawyer for Petitioner: Alexander M. Bickel

Chief Lawyer for Respondent: Erwin N. Griswold, U.S. solicitor general

Justices for the Court: Hugo Lafayette Black, William J. Brennan, Jr., William O. Douglas, Thurgood Marshall, Potter Stewart, Byron R. White

Justices Dissenting: Harry A. Blackmun, Warren E. Burger, John Marshall Harlan II

Date of Decision: June 30, 1971

Decision: The freedom of the press prevented the federal government from stopping the newspapers.

Significance: The Supreme Court emphasized that "prior restraints" on publication are almost always illegal under the First Amendment.

Associate Justice Hugo Lafayette Black.
Courtesy of the Supreme Court of the United States.

Military conflict leading to the Vietnam War (1954–75) began even before World War II (1939–45). The people of Cambodia, Laos, and Vietnam were fighting to free themselves from French control. Beginning with President Harry Truman in 1945, America pro-mised to help France maintain control in the region. By 1969, America had over half a million troops fighting in the Vietnam War.

Public opinion about the war was mixed, with many people highly critical of America's involvement. By the mid-1960s, even some government officials began to question whether America should be involved. This led Secretary of Defense Robert McNamara to prepare a forty-seven volume report called "History of U.S. Decision-Making Process on Vietnam Policy." Many parts of the report were classified "TOP SECRET." They would come to be called the "Pentagon Papers."

Fighting against war

Daniel Ellsberg, an employee of the RAND corporation, helped prepare the report. Initially he was very much in favor of America's involvement in Vietnam. After spending some time in Vietnam and watching innocent civilians die, however, Ellsberg turned against the war. As he prepared the report for McNamara, Ellsberg decided that the public needed to learn how and why the federal government had involved America in what Ellsberg thought was an evil and unnecessary war.

In 1969, Ellsberg took eighteen volumes of the report from Washington, D.C., to Santa Barbara, California, where he rented a copy machine and copied them. Ellsberg then tried to convince some government officials to help him release the report to the public. When that failed, Ellsberg gave the report to the *New York Times* in March 1971.

After reviewing the report for three months, the *New York Times* printed its first article about the Pentagon Papers on June 13, 1971. The *Times* published more articles on June 14 and 15, and the *Washington Post* began printing articles on June 18.

Stop the presses

The federal government did not want the public to see the Pentagon Papers. It said that the report contained information that would hurt national security, including the continuing war effort in Vietnam. The federal government also was embarrassed for the public to learn the truth about America's involvement in Vietnam.

The government filed lawsuits in New York City and Washington, D.C. to stop the *Times* and the *Post* from printing their articles. The courts issued orders temporarily stopping the newspapers until the government could present its case. The government argued that the U.S. Constitution gave it the power to protect national security by permanently preventing the newspapers from printing the report. The newspapers said that being prevented from printing the report violated the First Amendment freedom of the press. Both cases were appealed to a court of appeals and finally to the U.S. Supreme Court.

No prior restraints

Less than three weeks after the cases began, the Supreme Court voted 6–3 in favor of the newspapers. The Court said that stopping the publications would violate the First Amendment freedom of the press. The Court could not agree on a reason for its decision. Therefore, the justices each wrote separate opinions sharing their views about the case.

Justices Hugo Lafayette Black and William O. Douglas wrote opinions describing the history of the First Amendment. They told how America's founders were afraid the federal government might use its powers to violate their freedoms of speech, religion, assembly, and the press. In 1789, future president James Madison drafted the First Amendment to protect those freedoms.

Madison knew that a free press would be especially important for helping the public keep its eye on the government. Without a free press, the public would never be able to learn about the government's bad deeds. As Justice Black wrote, "Open debate and discussion of public issues are vital to our national health." Therefore, America adopted the First Amendment to prevent the government from stopping the publication of embarrassing information. Because the federal government was trying to prevent the *Times* and the *Post* from publishing information, Justices Black and Douglas said that the First Amendment would not allow it.

Justices Potter Stewart and Byron R. White wrote different opinions. They both agreed that the Pentagon Papers contained information that probably would hurt national security. But they also agreed that the First Amendment prevented the government from stopping the newspapers from publishing the report. Justice White warned, however, that the First Amendment would not prevent the government from filing criminal charges if the newspapers violated criminal laws against revealing national defense secrets.

Speedy delivery dangerous

Justices Harry A. Blackmun, Warren E. Burger, and John Marshall Harlan II each wrote dissenting opinions, meaning they disagreed with the Court's decision. They said that the case was handled too quickly for the Court to consider it and make a proper ruling. (Most cases take years to get through the Supreme Court. Because of the serious nature of prior restraints, the courts resolved this case in just three weeks.) Justices Harlan and Blackmun also suggested that the Constitution allows the federal government to stop publications that will seriously damage national security.

Justice Blackmun's opinion ended on a very serious note. He pointed out that printing some of the secrets in the Pentagon Papers could result in "the death of soldiers, the destruction of alliances, the greatly increased difficulty of negotiation with our enemies, and the inability of our diplomats to negotiate" in Vietnam. Justice Blackmun warned that if the newspapers caused such damage by printing the Pentagon Papers, the American people would know who to blame.

ELLSBERG PROSECUTION

Daniel Ellsberg faced criminal charges for stealing the Pentagon Papers. On June 28, 1971, the federal government charged him with theft of federal property. On December 30, 1971, charges of spying under the federal Espionage Act were added. Anthony Russo, Jr., who helped Ellsberg steal the report, faced similar charges.

The trial occurred in federal court in Los Angeles, California, with Judge William Matthew Byrne Jr. presiding. The trial began in July 1972, but then halted when Judge Byrne learned that the federal government was illegally taping the defendants' secret conversations. A second trial began in January 1973. Before it ended, however, Judge Byrne learned that the government had broken into the office of Ellsberg's psychologist to steal Ellsberg's file. He also learned about more illegal taping. In disgust, Judge Byrne dismissed the entire case against Ellsberg and Russo on May 11, 1973.

Aftermath

American troop withdrawal from Vietnam quickened in 1971, when the Pentagon Papers were published. At the end of 1971 there were just 160,000 American troops in South Vietnam, compared to 335,000 at the beginning of the year. If public pressure helped quicken troop withdrawal, then the First Amendment served its purpose by allowing the newspapers to be watchdogs over the federal government.

Suggestions for further reading

Evans, J. Edward. *Freedom of the Press.* Minneapolis: Lerner Publications Company, 1990.

Farish, Leah. *The First Amendment: Freedom of Speech, Religion, and the Press.* Hillside, NJ: Enslow Publishers, Inc., 1998.

Goldman, David J. *The Freedom of the Press in America.* Minneapolis: Lerner Publications Company, 1967.

Herda, D.J. *New York Times v. United States: National Security and Censorship.* Hillside, NJ: Enslow Publishers, Inc., 1994.

Klinker, Philip A. *The First Amendment.* Englewood Cliffs, NJ: Silver Burdett Press, 1991.

Mikula, Mark and L. Mpha Mabunda, eds. *Great American Court Cases.* Vol. 1., *Individual Liberties.* Detroit: The Gale Group, 1999.

Moss, Joyce and George Wilson. *Profiles in American History: Significant Events and the People Who Shaped Them.* Vol. 8, *Civil Rights Movement to the Present.* Detroit: Gale Research, 1994.

Pascoe, Elaine. *Freedom of Expression: The Right to Speak Out in America.* Brookfield, CT: Millbrook Press, 1992.

Schwartz, Bernard. *Freedom of the Press.* New York: Facts on File, 1992.

Steins, Richard. *Censorship: How Does It Conflict with Freedom?* New York: Twenty-First Century Books, 1995.

Zeinert, Karen. *Free Speech: From Newspapers to Music Lyrics.* Hillside, NJ: Enslow Publishers, Inc., 1995.

Zerman, Melvyn B. *Taking on the Press: Constitutional Rights in Conflict.* New York: Crowell, 1986.

Branzburg v. Hayes
1972

Petitioner: Paul M. Branzburg.

Respondents: Judge John P. Hayes, et al.

Petitioner's Claim: That the First Amendment gives news reporters a privilege protecting the confidentiality of their sources of information.

Chief Lawyer for Petitioner: Edgar A. Zingman

Chief Lawyer for Respondents: Edwin A. Schroering, Jr.

Justices for the Court: Harry A. Blackmun, Warren E. Burger, Lewis F. Powell, Jr., William H. Rehnquist, Byron R. White

Justices Dissenting: William J. Brennan, Jr., William O. Douglas, Thurgood Marshall, Potter Stewart

Date of Decision: June 29, 1972

Decision: The First Amendment does not give news reporters a privilege to keep their sources secret from the government.

Significance: News reporters must share information about criminal activity with grand jury investigations just like every other citizen.

Protecting his informants

Paul Branzburg was a reporter for a Kentucky newspaper called the *Louisville Courier-Journal.* In 1969 the newspaper printed an article by Branzburg describing two people making hashish from marijuana; both are illegal drugs. In the article Branzburg said he promised the two peo-

Associate Justice Byron R. White.
Courtesy of the Library of Congress.

ple he would not reveal their identities.

In 1971 the newspaper printed another article by Branzburg on use of illegal drugs. He wrote the second article after spending two weeks watching and interviewing dozens of drug users in Frankfort, Kentucky. Again Branzburg promised not to reveal the identities of the drug users.

On both occasions Branzburg was called to testify before a Kentucky grand jury. (A grand jury is a group of people who review evidence presented by the state to determine if it has enough evidence to charge someone with a crime.) Branzburg refused to reveal the identities of the people he had interviewed. He said the First Amend-ment gave him a privilege, or right, to keep his sources confidential, meaning secret. Branzburg said that without the privilege, sources would not talk to him for fear they would be drawn into a grand jury investigation. If sources stopped talking to him, he would not be able to report the news. Branzburg said that would violate the First Amendment's guarantee of freedom of the press.

In both instances a state judge disagreed with Branzburg and ordered him to answer the grand jury's questions. Branzburg appealed to the Kentucky Court of Appeals, which denied his requests for protection. Branzburg then appealed to the U.S. Supreme Court. The Supreme Court agreed to consider his case along with two other cases. The other cases involved journalists who refused to testify before grand juries about their investigation and interviews of the Black Panther Party, a radical group that wanted to overthrow the federal government.

FREEDOM OF THE PRESS

Journalists are citizens too

The Supreme Court voted 5–4 against a reporter's privilege. Writing for the Court, Justice Byron R. White analyzed the importance of grand jury investigations and the freedom of the press.

Justice White said that under the U.S. Constitution, grand juries play the important role of reviewing evidence to determine if there is enough to charge someone with a crime. Grand juries cannot do this job properly unless they review all available evidence. Every citizen has a duty to share any evidence he or she has with the grand jury. Justice White said journalists are citizens too, so they do not deserve a special privilege. He supported this decision by referring to prior Supreme Court cases that decided the press must obey labor, business, and tax laws as well.

Justice White agreed that the freedom of the press is important. The First Amendment protects the press by saying, "Congress shall make no law . . . abridging the freedom . . . of the press." States must recognize this freedom under the Due Process Clause of the Fourteenth Amendment. Justice White said, however, that the main reason for the freedom of the press is to prevent government from controlling what is published. He said requiring news reporters to testify before grand juries does not stop them from printing their stories.

Justice White rejected the argument that journalists would not be able to investigate the news without a privilege to keep sources secret. Justice White said the press had operated successfully in the United States without such a privilege for almost 200 years.

Freedom no more?

Four justices dissented, meaning they disagreed with the Court's decision. Justice Potter Stewart wrote an opinion for himself and Justices William J. Brennan, Jr., and Thurgood Marshall. Justice Stewart said the Supreme Court's decision ignored evidence that journalists would lose confidential sources without a privilege. Losing sources would make it harder to report the news. Stewart said this infringes on the freedom of the press.

In Stewart's opinion, the government should be allowed to force journalists to testify before grand juries only when it can show three things: (1) that the reporter probably has information about an actual crime; (2) that the government cannot get the information from anywhere else; and (3) that the government's need for the information is more important than the freedom of the press.

REVEALING SOURCES

In *Branzburg* the media fought for the right to keep its sources secret. In *Cohen v. Cowles Media Co.,* it fought for the right to reveal its sources. Dan Cohen was the public relations director for a candidate for Minnesota governor in 1982. Cohen gave two Minnesota newspapers, the *Pioneer Press* and the *Star Tribune,* incomplete information about the opposing candidate. Although the newspapers promised to keep Cohen's name secret, they ended up printing his name as the source of the information. Cohen lost his job over the incident.

Cohen sued the Minnesota newspapers for fraud and breach of contract. The newspapers tried to get the case thrown out of court. They said the First Amendment guarantee of freedom of the press protected their right to print Cohen's name. The U.S. Supreme Court ruled in favor of Cohen, saying the media can be sued for breaking promises to keep sources secret.

Justice William O. Douglas also wrote a dissenting opinion. Unlike Stewart, Douglas did not think journalists could ever be forced to testify before a grand jury. Douglas said the press does the important job of keeping U.S. citizens informed about public issues. Without a privilege, the press would stop being a government watchdog. Eventually it would be controlled by the government, reporting only the news the government wanted it to report.

Suggestions for further reading

Evans, J. Edward. *Freedom of the Press.* Minneapolis, MN: Lerner Publications Company, 1990.

Farish, Leah. *The First Amendment: Freedom of Speech, Religion, and the Press.* Hillside, NJ: Enslow Publishers, Inc., 1998.

Goldman, David J. *The Freedom of the Press in America.* Minneapolis, MN: Lerner Publications Company, 1967.

Klinker, Philip A. *The First Amendment.* Englewood Cliffs, NJ: Silver Burdett Press, 1991.

Mikula, Mark, and L. Mpho Mabunda, eds. *Great American Court Cases:* Vol. I, *Individual Liberties.* Detroit, MI: Gale Group, 1999.

Pascoe, Elaine. *Freedom of Expression: The Right to Speak Out in America.* Brookfield, CT: Millbrook Press, 1992.

Schwartz, Bernard. *Freedom of the Press.* New York, NY: Facts on File, 1992.

Steins, Richard. *Censorship: How Does It Conflict with Freedom?* New York, NY: Twenty-First Century Books, 1995.

Zeinert, Karen. *Free Speech: From Newspapers to Music Lyrics.* Hillside, NJ: Enslow Publishers, Inc., 1995.

Zerman, Melvyn B. *Taking on the Press: Constitutional Rights in Conflict.* New York, NY: Crowell, 1986.

Nebraska Press Association v. Stuart 1976

Petitioners: Nebraska Press Association, et al.

Respondents: Judge Hugh Stuart, et al.

Petitioners' Claim: That a court order preventing the media from reporting about a criminal trial violated the First Amendment.

Chief Lawyer for Petitioners: E. Barrett Prettyman, Jr.

Chief Lawyer for Respondents: Harold Mosher, Assistant Attorney General of Nebraska

Justices for the Court: Harry A. Blackmun, William J. Brennan, Jr., Warren E. Burger (writing for the Court), Thurgood Marshall, Lewis F. Powell, Jr., William H. Rehnquist, John Paul Stevens, Potter Stewart, Byron R. White

Justices Dissenting: None

Date of Decision: June 30, 1976

Decision: The court order violated the First Amendment freedom of the press.

Significance: The Court said that in most cases, allowing the media to report criminal trials will not interfere with the defendant's Sixth Amendment right to a fair trial.

FREEDOM OF THE PRESS

Stop the press

On October 19, 1975, Erwin Simants was arrested and charged with murdering six members of the Kellie family in Sutherland, Nebraska. Sutherland was a small rural town with only 850 people.

The Simants case immediately received local, state, and national media coverage. Simants' attorney and the prosecuting attorney asked the Lincoln County Judge to issue a gag order to stop the media from reporting the case. Both attorneys were afraid that newspaper and television coverage would prevent Simants from getting a fair trial.

Press coverage of trials, such as at the Bruno Hauptmann trial in 1935, makes it hard to keep juries from making decisions about a case before hearing all the facts.
Courtesy of the National Archives and Records Administration.

The county judge issued the gag order. The next day members of the news media, including the Nebraska Press Association, asked the court to remove the gag order. The county court transferred the case to the state district court, where Judge Hugh Stuart heard the case. Judge Stuart issued his own gag order, preventing the media from reporting about a confession Simants made to the police, a note Simants wrote on the night of the murders, and charges that the murders occurred during a sexual attack.

The media appealed to the Nebraska Supreme Court, arguing that the gag order violated the First Amendment freedom of the press. The Nebraska Supreme Court disagreed and approved the gag order with a few changes. The Nebraska Press Association and the rest of the media appealed to the U.S. Supreme Court.

Freedom restored

With a unanimous decision, the Supreme Court ruled that the gag order violated the freedom of the press. Writing for the Court, Chief Justice Warren E. Burger said that the case involved a conflict between the freedom of the press and Simants' right to a fair trial. Burger's opinion analyzed both interests before making a decision.

The Sixth Amendment of the U.S. Constitution protects a criminal defendant's right to be tried by an "impartial jury." An impartial jury is one that can hear the case and determine guilt or innocence in a fair manner. States must protect this right under the Due Process Clause of the Fourteenth Amendment. (The Due Process Clause of the Fourteenth Amendment prevents state and local governments from violating certain rights related to life, freedom, and property.) Justice Burger admitted that press coverage can prevent a defendant from getting a fair trial. If jurors hear about confessions and other evidence through the newspapers and television, they might make up their minds before hearing the case in court, which would violate the Sixth Amendment right to a fair trial.

The First Amendment, however, protects the freedom of the press. States must also obey this freedom under the Due Process Clause of the Fourteenth Amendment. Justice Burger said that the main reason America adopted the First Amendment was to prevent the government from using prior restraints. A prior restraint happens when the government stops the media from printing or reporting certain information. Prior restraints are the worst kind of violation of the freedom of the press because they prevent the public from learning about public issues. A gag order, for example, is similar to a prior restraint because it stops the public from learning about a criminal trial.

Justice Burger said that the freedom of the press and the right to a fair trial are equally important. In fact, after the media circus surrounding the famous trial of Bruno Hauptmann in 1935, courts developed tools for making sure a defendant gets a fair trial even with media coverage. Courts can transfer cases to other communities or postpone trials until media coverage slows down. Judges can take care to select jurors who have not already made up their minds from press coverage. Judges also can ask the lawyers and court employees not to leak details that are not shared in open court.

Justice Burger said that if cases are handled this way, defendants can get a fair trial and the media can still exercise its right to report what happens in the courtroom. Justice Burger decided that it was not necessary to protect defendants by using gag orders that sacrifice the freedom of the press.

BRUNO HAUPTMANN TRIAL

Gag orders were one result of media coverage of the Bruno Hauptmann trial in 1935. Hauptmann was charged with the 1932 kidnapping and murder of the twenty–month–old son of Charles A. Lindbergh. In 1927, Lindbergh had become a national hero by being the first person to fly solo in an airplane across the Atlantic Ocean.

Because of Lindbergh's popularity, coverage of the Hauptmann trial in Fleming, New Jersey, became a media circus with a carnival atmosphere. Almost one thousand newspaper and broadcast journalists came to Fleming to cover the trial. To accommodate the press, the telephone company constructed a system large enough to serve a city of one million people. Press coverage attracted thousands of sightseers to Fleming, with the crowd reaching sixty thousand people on Sunday, January 6, 1935.

Hauptmann was convicted and executed for murdering Lindbergh's baby. Hauptmann's wife, however, insisted that her husband was not guilty, and some believe press coverage helped convict an innocent man.

Nebraska Press Association was one of a number of Supreme Court decisions protecting the press's right to cover criminal trials. Five years later in *Chandler v. Florida* (1981), the Supreme Court approved an experimental program in Florida that allowed television and photograph coverage inside the courtroom. During the 1980s, CourtTV began televising trials to viewers across the nation. With advances in technology, viewers someday may get live trial coverage over the Internet.

Suggestions for further reading

Evans, J. Edward. *Freedom of the Press.* Minneapolis: Lerner Publications Company, 1990.

Farish, Leah. *The First Amendment: Freedom of Speech, Religion, and the Press.* Hillside, NJ: Enslow Publishers, Inc., 1998.

Frost-Knappman, Elizabeth, Edward W. Knappman and Lisa Paddock, eds. *Courtroom Drama: 120 of the World's Most Notable Trials.* Vol. 2. Detroit: U•X•L, 1998.

Goldman, David J. *The Freedom of the Press in America.* Minneapolis: Lerner Publications Company, 1967.

Klinker, Philip A. *The First Amendment.* Englewood Cliffs, NJ: Silver Burdett Press, 1991.

Pascoe, Elaine. *Freedom of Expression: The Right to Speak Out in America.* Brookfield, CT: Millbrook Press, 1992.

Schwartz, Bernard. *Freedom of the Press.* New York: Facts on File, 1992.

Steins, Richard. *Censorship: How Does It Conflict with Freedom?* New York: Twenty-First Century Books, 1995.

Zeinert, Karen. *Free Speech: From Newspapers to Music Lyrics.* Hillside, NJ: Enslow Publishers, Inc., 1995.

Zerman, Melvyn B. *Taking on the Press: Constitutional Rights in Conflict.* New York: Crowell, 1986.

Hazelwood School District v. Kuhlmeier 1988

Petitioners: Hazelwood School District, et al.

Respondents: Three former students at Hazelwood East High School

Petitioners' Claim: That Principal Robert E. Reynolds did not violate the freedom of the press when he deleted two pages from *Spectrum,* a student newspaper.

Chief Lawyer for Petitioners: Robert P. Baine, Jr.

Chief Lawyer for Respondents: Leslie D. Edwards

Justices for the Court: Anthony M. Kennedy, Sandra Day O'Connor, William H. Rehnquist, Antonin Scalia, John Paul Stevens, Byron R. White

Justices Dissenting: Harry A. Blackmun, William J. Brennan, Jr., Thurgood Marshall

Date of Decision: January 13, 1988

Decision: Principal Reynolds did not violate the students' free press rights.

Significance: Public schools may control the contents of student newspapers that are part of classroom education.

Journalism I

During the 1982-1983 school year, students taking a Journalism II class at the Hazelwood East High School ran a student newspaper called *Spectrum.* It gave the students a chance to practice what they learned in Journalism I. Like most student newspapers, *Spectrum* featured stories about student life in and out of school. Over 4,500 students, school personnel, and other people in St. Louis County, Missouri, read *Spectrum.* The May 13, 1983, issue of *Spectrum* was supposed to contain two controversial articles. One article described the experiences of three students who were pregnant. *Spectrum* used different names for the three girls to protect their privacy. In the article, the pregnant girls commented on their sexual activity and use or non-use of birth control. The second article described the way divorce affected students at Hazelwood East High School. In the article, one student blamed his father for his parents' divorce. He said his father did not spend enough time with the family, argued about everything, and always was out of town on business or out late playing cards with his friends.

Hazelwood School District v. Kuhlmeier

Principal Robert E. Reynolds holds up a copy of the Spectator. *The Court decided in favor of a principal's right to censor school papers.* Reproduced by permission of the Corbis Corporation.

FREEDOM OF THE PRESS

Bad Principles

Principal Robert E. Reynolds reviewed each issue of *Spectrum* before it was published. When he reviewed the May 13 issue three days before publication, he did not like the articles on pregnancy and divorce. Reynolds thought it was too easy to identify the girls and their boyfriends in the article on pregnancy. He also thought the article would give young students a bad message about casual sex. As for the article on divorce, Principal Reynolds thought it was unfair, and failed to give the father a chance to tell his side of the story. Reynolds did not think there was enough time to rearrange *Spectrum* to delete the two articles. He decided to delete the entire two pages on which the articles appeared. Those pages contained four other articles that Reynolds would have allowed if there had been time to layout the paper again.

Many students did not learn about Reynolds's decision until after *Spectrum* was published with two missing pages. Three students, including Kuhlmeier, were furious. They believed Principal Reynolds had violated their freedom of the press. The First Amendment protects this freedom by saying, "Congress shall make no law . . . abridging [limiting] the freedom of . . . the press." Under the Due Process Clause of the Fourteenth Amendment, state and local governments, including public schools, must obey the freedom of the press. Kuhlmeier and two other journalism students sued Principal Reynolds and the Hazelwood School District in federal district court. The court ruled in favor of the school, saying Principal Reynolds acted reasonably to protect privacy for the pregnant girls and the divorced father. The Court of Appeals for the Eighth Circuit, however, reversed. It said public schools may not violate the freedom of the press except to protect education.

Principal Reynolds and the Hazelwood School District took the case to the U.S. Supreme Court.

Freedom of the Principal

With a 6-3 decision, the Supreme Court reversed and ruled in favor of Principal Reynolds and the school district. Writing for the Court, Justice Byron R. White began by saying students do not shed their free press rights at the schoolhouse gate. The rest of his opinion, however, limited those rights. Justice White said the First Amendment does not protect students in school as much as adults in public. Schools do not have to allow speech that disagrees with the school's educational mission. When

LOVELL V. CITY OF GREEN

In 1938, Alma Lovell was convicted for handing out religious pamphlets in the city of Griffin, Georgia. The pamphlets described the religion of Jehovah's Witnesses, a form of Christianity. A city law made it illegal to distribute any written material without getting permission from the city manager. Lovell had not asked for permission before handing out her pamphlets. The U.S Supreme Court reversed Lovell's conviction. It said the United States adopted the freedom of the press to prevent censorship by the government. Censorship happens when the government controls what can and cannot be published and read. The Griffin city law was illegal censorship under the First Amendment. The Court did not reach the same result in *Hazelwood.* It said students in school have less freedom under the First Amendment than adults in public. Under *Hazelwood,* a school may censor a student newspaper to make sure the newspaper agrees with the school's educational mission.

a school pays to publish a student newspaper as part of a regular class, it can make sure the newspaper teaches the students what they are supposed to learn about journalism. This means the school may prevent the newspaper from containing poor grammar and bad research. As one purpose of school is to teach students how to be mature members of society, schools also may prevent student newspapers from containing profanity, vulgar language, and material that is inappropriate for young students. A school violates the freedom of the press only when its censorship does not serve the school's educational mission. The Court decided that Principal Reynolds acted reasonably when he deleted two pages from *Spectrum.* The article on pregnancy failed to protect privacy for the pregnant girls and their boyfriends. The topic of teenage sex was inappropriate for 14-year-old freshmen and their even younger brothers and sisters at home. Principles of good journalism said the students should have given the father a chance to tell his side of the story on divorce. In short, Principal Reynolds was allowed to delete the articles because they disagreed with the principles taught in the journalism classes and the sexual values taught by the school system. Because Reynolds did not think he had time to save the other four articles on those two pages, deleting them was reasonable too. Reynolds did not violate the freedom of the press.

Stop the Thought Police

Three justices dissented, meaning they disagreed with the Court's decision. Justice William J. Brennan, Jr., wrote a dissenting opinion. He said the students who published *Spectrum* in Journalism II expected a civics lesson. Part of that lesson should have been about free press rights under the First Amendment. Only by teaching students those rights can schools prepare them to be members of American society. Brennan said allowing schools to control student newspapers is like allowing the "thought police" to "strangle the free mind at its source."

Suggestions for further reading

Evans, J. Edward. *Freedom of the Press.* Minneapolis: Lerner Publications Company, 1990.

Farish, Leah. *The First Amendment: Freedom of Speech, Religion, and the Press.* Hillside, NJ: Enslow Publishers, Inc., 1998.

Fuller, Sarah Betsy. *Hazelwood v. Kuhlmeier: Censorship in School Newspapers.* Hillside, NJ: Enslow Publishers, Inc., 1998.

Goldman, David J. *The Freedom of the Press in America.* Minneapolis: Lerner Publications Company, 1967.

Klinker, Philip A. *The First Amendment.* Englewood Cliffs, NJ: Silver Burdett Press, 1991.

Pascoe, Elaine. *Freedom of Expression: The Right to Speak Out in America.* Brookfield, CT: Millbrook Press, 1992.

Schwartz, Bernard. *Freedom of the Press.* New York: Facts on File, 1992.

Steins, Richard. *Censorship: How Does It Conflict with Freedom?* New York: Twenty-First Century Books, 1995.

Zeinert, Karen. *Free Speech: From Newspapers to Music Lyrics.* Hillside, NJ: Enslow Publishers, Inc., 1995.

Zerman, Melvyn B. *Taking on the Press: Constitutional Rights in Conflict.* New York: Crowell, 1986.

Hustler Magazine v. Falwell 1988

Petitioners: Hustler Magazine, Inc., et al.

Respondent: Reverend Jerry Falwell

Petitioners' Claim: That the First Amendment prevented Jerry Falwell from recovering damages for emotional distress caused by a fake advertisement about him in *Hustler* Magazine.

Chief Lawyer for Petitioners: Alan L. Issacman

Chief Lawyer for Respondent: Norman Roy Grutman

Justices for the Court: Harry A. Blackmun, William J. Brennan, Jr., Thurgood Marshall, Sandra Day O'Connor, William H. Rehnquist (writing for the Court), Antonin Scalia, John Paul Stevens, Byron R. White

Justices Dissenting: None (Anthony M. Kennedy did not participate)

Date of Decision: February 24, 1988

Decision: Falwell was not allowed to recover damages for emotional distress.

Significance: For a public figure to recover damages for emotional distress, he must prove that the publisher knew or should have known it was printing something false.

In the public eye

FREEDOM OF THE PRESS

The First Amendment protects the freedom of the press in the United States. It allows people to publish newspapers, magazines, and books that explore important issues for the public. America's founders believed that the ability to share ideas is one of the most important parts of freedom. Publishers often write about public figures—people such as politicians and celebrities who are well known to the public. Sometimes publishers harm a public figure's reputation by writing things that are not true. This is called libel. When libel happens, the public figure can sue the publisher to recover money for his damages. In ***New York Times v. Sullivan*** (1964), however, the U.S. Supreme Court said a public figure can recover for libel only if he proves that the publisher knew he was printing a false statement. Otherwise, publishers would be afraid to print stories they thought were true because the stories might contain an error. That would violate the freedom of the press. In *Hustler Magazine v. Falwell,* the Court had to decide whether a public figure can recover damages when he is injured by a parody. A parody is a funny article, cartoon, or other item that is not meant to be true. It simply explores a public topic with humor.

Hustler *Magazine owner Larry Flynt and Reverend Jerry Falwell putting their differences aside to share a laugh.* Reproduced by permission of Archive Photos, Inc.

Hustler Magazine v. falwell

Funny pages

Reverend Jerry Falwell is a Baptist minister in Virginia with national television and radio programs. In addition to being a religious leader, Falwell is a political activist who works to support Christian issues. One of those issues is fighting against pornography—the publication of photographs about sex. Falwell's activities make him a public figure recognized across the nation. Larry C. Flynt is the publisher of *Hustler Magazine. Hustler* contains sexually graphic photographs. It also contains articles on issues of national concern. *Hustler's* pictures and articles often offend the Christian values preached by Reverend Falwell. Around November 1983, a liquor company called Campari was printing advertisements with celebrities describing the first time they drank Campari. That month, *Hustler* printed a fake advertisement called "Jerry Falwell talks about his first time." The ad contained a fake interview with Falwell and claimed that Falwell only preaches when he is drunk. The bottom of the ad said it was an "ad parody - not to be taken seriously."

No laughing matter

The parody did not amuse Jerry Falwell. He sued *Hustler* and Larry Flynt in federal district court for invasion of privacy, libel, and emotional distress. The court threw out the claim for invasion of privacy but allowed the jury to decide the claims for libel and emotional distress. A person causes emotional distress when he purposely does something outrageous that is indecent or immoral. The jury decided in favor of *Hustler* and Flynt on the claim for libel. The jury thought the ad parody was obviously fake. That meant it could not hurt Falwell's reputation. On the claim for emotional distress, however, the jury found in Falwell's favor and awarded him $150,000. *Hustler* and Flynt appealed. They argued that under *New York Times v. Sullivan,* they could not be punished unless they purposefully lied about Falwell. Because the ad parody was fake, *Hustler* and Flynt said the freedom of the press protected their right to print it. The United States Court of Appeals disagreed and ruled in favor of Falwell, so *Hustler* and Flynt took the case to the U.S. Supreme Court.

Parodies protected

With a unanimous decision, the Supreme Court reversed and ruled in favor of *Hustler* and Flynt. Writing for the Court, Chief Justice William

JOHN PETER ZENGER

Before the United States of America was born, the colony of New York had a law against seditious libel. The law made it a crime to criticize the government, even if the criticism was true. In the 1730s, John Peter Zenger ran a newspaper called the *New-York Weekly Journal.* Zenger's newspaper printed many articles that criticized New York and its governor, William Cosby. In 1734, Cosby had Zenger arrested and thrown in jail for seditious libel. Zenger stayed in jail for ten months until his trial on August 4, 1735. Zenger's lawyer was a popular Philadelphia attorney and Pennsylvania politician named Andrew Hamilton. At trial, Hamilton admitted that Zenger published articles that criticized Governor Cosby. He said, however, that Zenger was innocent because the criticism was true. The judge ruled that whether the articles were true did not matter under the crime of seditious libel. In closing arguments, Hamilton still asked the jury not to convict Zenger for publishing the truth. The jury came back with a verdict of not guilty. It was a victory for free speech and free press, which the United States protected fifty-seven years later in the First Amendment.

H. Rehnquist said the heart of the First Amendment is the "importance of the free flow of ideas and opinions on matters of public interest and concern." Such matters often involve public figures. Free talk about public issues and figures is "essential to the common quest for truth." Rehnquist described a little history of political cartoons. Political cartoons make fun of politicians and other public figures but are not always true. Rehnquist said such cartoons have helped the public discuss important presidents such as Abraham Lincoln, Theodore Roosevelt, and Franklin D. Roosevelt. Without political cartoons, discussion of political issues would suffer. That would violate the freedom of the press. Under the First Amendment, then, publishers are allowed to print parodies about public figures. A public figure can sue for damages only when a publisher harms his reputation with lies. Because *Hustler's* ad parody was not meant to be taken seriously, it was not a lie and had not injured Falwell's reputation. *Hustler* and Flynt did not have to pay Falwell for his emotional distress.

Suggestions for further reading

Dictionary of American History. New York: Charles Scribner's Sons, 1976.

Evans, J. Edward. *Freedom of the Press.* Minneapolis: Lerner Publications Company, 1990.

Farish, Leah. *The First Amendment: Freedom of Speech, Religion, and the Press.* Hillside, NJ: Enslow Publishers, Inc., 1998.

Goldman, David J. *The Freedom of the Press in America.* Minneapolis: Lerner Publications Company, 1967.

Klinker, Philip A. *The First Amendment.* Englewood Cliffs, NJ: Silver Burdett Press, 1991.

Kross, Jessica, ed. *American Eras, 1600-1754: The Colonial Era.* Detroit: Gale Research, 1998.

Morris, Richard Brandon, ed. *Encyclopedia of American History: Bicentennial Edition.* New York: Harper & Row, Publishers, Inc., 1976.

Pascoe, Elaine. *Freedom of Expression: The Right to Speak Out in America.* Brookfield, CT: Millbrook Press, 1992.

Schwartz, Bernard. *Freedom of the Press.* New York: Facts on File, 1992.

Steins, Richard. *Censorship: How Does It Conflict with Freedom?* New York: Twenty-First Century Books, 1995.

Zeinert, Karen. *Free Speech: From Newspapers to Music Lyrics.* Hillside, NJ: Enslow Publishers, Inc., 1995.

Zerman, Melvyn B. *Taking on the Press: Constitutional Rights in Conflict.* New York: Crowell, 1986.

Privacy is something cherished by almost all Americans. It is the right to live life without the government prying into what we do—the right to be let alone. Privacy allows us to develop into individuals with our own thoughts, beliefs, hopes, and dreams. It permits us to decide how to live our lives in our own homes. Privacy allows adults to decide who to marry, whether to have children, and how to raise a family. The right to privacy restricts how the government can investigate our lives.

Surprisingly, the words "privacy" and "right to privacy" do not appear in the U.S. Constitution. Instead, certain parts of the Constitution protect specific kinds of privacy. For example, the freedoms of expression and religion in the First Amendment protect the right to have private thoughts and ideas. The Fourth Amendment says the government may not arrest a person or search his house without good reasons. The Fifth Amendment says a criminal defendant does not have to testify against himself at trial. That means he can keep private any information about the crime he is charged with committing.

These Amendments, however, do not say Americans have a general right to privacy. Where, then, does the right of privacy come from? The

Supreme Court developed it through decades of interpreting the U.S. Constitution.

Developing the right of privacy

The first Americans to mention the right to privacy were Boston lawyers named Louis D. Brandeis and Samuel D. Warren. In 1890, they published an article called "The Right to Privacy." Brandeis and Warren said Americans needed protection from newspapers that invaded privacy by exposing private lives to the public. As they do today, newspapers then often wrote embarrassing or humiliating articles about people. Brandeis and Warren said Americans should be allowed to sue newspapers to protect their privacy.

In 1916, Brandeis became a justice on the U.S. Supreme Court. Twelve years later in *Olmstead v. United States* (1928), he wrote a famous dissenting opinion (which means he disagreed with the Court's decision in the case). Justice Brandeis said the Constitution was written to protect privacy to help Americans pursue happiness:

> **The makers of our Constitution ... sought to protect Americans in their beliefs, their thoughts, their emotions and their sensations. They conferred, as against government, the right to be let alone—the most comprehensive of the rights of man and the right most valued by civilized men.**

Almost four more decades passed before the Supreme Court recognized a general right of privacy. In between, some justices wrote opinions supporting such a right. In *Public Utilities Commission v. Pollak* (1952), Justice William O. Douglas said "the right to be let alone is indeed the beginning of all freedoms." Then in *Poe v. Ulman* (1961), Justice John Marshall Harlan II referred to a Connecticut law that interfered with marriage as "an intolerable invasion of privacy."

In ***Griswold v. Connecticut*** (1965), the Supreme Court finally recognized a right to privacy in the U.S. Constitution. The case involved a Connecticut law that made it illegal for married couples to use contraceptives, or birth control. (Contraceptives prevent a woman from getting pregnant when she has sexual intercourse.) Nothing in the Constitution specifically says married couples have a right to use birth control. The Court, however, said the law interfered with "the right of privacy in marriage." In other words, privacy for married couples in America allows them to decide whether to use contraceptive devices.

Since *Griswold,* the Court has had to decide what the right of privacy protects. The issue arises in cases involving marriage, sexual reproduction, abortion, family life, the right to die, and right to have information kept private. Sometimes the Supreme Court recognizes the right to privacy in these cases, but other times it does not.

Marriage

As *Griswold* made clear, marriage is one of the relationships protected by the right of privacy. That is because families are an important part of the American way of life. People growing up often dream of the day when they will have their own family. Settling down with a family is one way Americans pursue happiness in life.

Many privacy cases, then, have been about the family. Two years after *Griswold,* for example, the Supreme Court decided ***Loving v. Virginia*** (1967). *Loving* involved a Virginia law that made it illegal for people of different races to marry each other. The Lovings were a white man and black woman who were convicted under this law. The Lovings appealed their convictions and won. The Supreme Court said marriage is one of the "basic civil rights of man." Laws that prevent people of different races from marrying each other violate the right to privacy and are unconstitutional.

Other marriage cases have included *Zablocki v. Redhail* (1978) and *Boddie v. Connecticut* (1971). In *Zablocki,* the Supreme Court said laws that make it financially difficult for poor people to get married violate the right to privacy. Logically, the freedom to marry also must include the freedom to end a marriage. In *Boddie,* then, the Court struck down laws that make it financially difficult for poor people to get a divorce.

Sexual reproduction

As privacy protects marriage, it also protects the decision whether or not to have children. As described above, the Court in *Griswold* said the government may not prevent married couples from using contraceptive devices. In ***Eisenstadt v. Baird*** (1972), the Court said unmarried couples also have a privacy right to use contraceptives. Then in *Carey v. Population Services International* (1977), the Court said the government may not prevent people under sixteen years old from using birth control. Taken together, these decisions protect every American's right to determine whether or not to have children.

Some people believe these decisions also protect a couple's right to engage in sexual relations, whether or not they are trying to have children. The question soon arose whether the right to privacy protects homosexual relations. (Homosexuals are people who have sexual relations with members of the same sex.) Many states have laws that make homosexual relations a crime.

In ***Bowers v. Hardwick*** (1986), the U.S. Supreme Court said laws that make homosexual relations a crime do not violate the right of privacy. The Court said the right of privacy protects traditional relationships in America, which means marriage, family, and sexual reproduction by a man and a woman. Homosexuals, then, are still struggling to get the Supreme Court to recognize their right to privacy.

Abortion

If privacy protects the right to avoid getting pregnant by using birth control, does it protect a right to end pregnancy by having an abortion? This is one of the most fiercely debated questions in the United States. Abortion rights activists say women, whose bodies are the ones affected by pregnancy, have a constitutional right to have an abortion. They say the medical risks and long term consequences of having a baby give women this right. Opponents of abortion say an unborn fetus is a living person with a right to life. For them, abortion is murder.

In the landmark decision of ***Roe v. Wade*** (1973), the Supreme Court said privacy protects the right to have an abortion until the fetus, the unborn, can live outside the mother's womb. At that point, the state can protect the unborn's life by preventing abortion unless it is necessary to save the mother's life. After *Roe,* people continue to argue, sometimes violently, about whether abortion should be legal.

Family life

After people marry and have children, they spend many years raising their families, trying to make them as healthy, safe, and happy as possible. The right to privacy allows people to make many family decisions. For example, in *Pierce v. Society of Sisters* (1925), the Supreme Court said parents do not have to send their children to public schools. As long as parents make sure their children get a good education, they can send their children to public or private schools, or teach them at home.

Another privacy case about family life was ***Moore v. City of East Cleveland*** (1977). East Cleveland had a law that required people living in a house to belong to one family. The law defined a family as a mother and father and their parents and children. Cleveland enforced the law by convicting Inez Moore, a woman who lived in a house with her unmarried son and two grandchildren, who were cousins. Moore said the law violated her right of privacy and the Supreme Court agreed. The Court said Americans are allowed to live with family members outside the traditional "nuclear" family of mother, father, and children.

The right to die

The right of privacy lets Americans decide how to live. Does it also protect a right to die? If a person has only six painful months to live while dying from cancer, does she have a right to end her life to avoid the pain. Can a family shut off the life support system for someone who will be in a coma for the rest of her life?

The last question was the issue in ***Cruzan v. Director, Missouri Department of Health*** (1990). After an automobile accident in 1983, Nancy Cruzan was alive but unable to move, speak, or communicate—with almost no hope of recovery. Believing Nancy would not want to live like that, her family decided to shut off her life support system. The State of Missouri would not allow it, so Nancy's family took the case to the U.S. Supreme Court.

Although the Supreme Court decided in Missouri's favor, it also said Americans have a right to refuse unwanted medical treatment, even if it will result in death. In other words, the right of privacy includes a right to die. Nancy's family was allowed to remove the life support system only after coming up with more evidence that Nancy would not want to live that way.

The right to die came up again in ***Washington v. Glucksberg*** (1997). Washington, like most states, had a law making it illegal to help someone end her life. A group of physicians and terminally ill patients filed a lawsuit saying the law interfered with the right to die. They argued that people who are dying from painful illnesses have a right to end their lives with dignity rather than suffer until death. The Supreme Court disagreed.

It said the right to die in *Cruzan* was a right to refuse medical treatment. The right of privacy does not include a right to be killed with medical assistance.

Private information

The end of the twentieth century has been called the beginning of the Information Age. Computers store vast amounts of information about people. Americans naturally are concerned about private information becoming available to the public. They also fear invasion of privacy by governmental agents trying to investigate criminal activity. At the same time, the government needs to investigate and catch criminals to bring them to justice.

To a certain degree, Americans are protected by privacy laws. The federal Omnibus Crime Control and Safe Streets Act of 1968 regulates the government's use of wiretapping to listen to telephone conversations. The Privacy Protection Act of 1974 and the Freedom of Information Act require the government to be fair when it collects, uses, and discloses private information. Sometimes, however, people file lawsuits saying the government has gone too far with an investigation.

That was the case in ***Watkins v. United States*** (1957). In the 1950s, Congress was investigating communist activity in the United States. Communists were members of a political party that wanted to overthrow the federal government. John T. Watkins, a labor union official, was called before Congress to testify about known communists. Watkins, however, refused to identify people who used to be, but no longer were, members of the Communist party. Watkins was convicted of contempt of Congress for refusing to answer such questions, but the Supreme Court reversed his conviction. The Court said Congress does not have unlimited power to investigate the private lives of American citizens.

Right to privacy cases came into the Information Age in ***Whalen v. Roe*** (1977). New York State had a computer system that stored the names and addresses of patients who received prescription medicines and drugs. The system was designed to control the illegal use of such drugs. Patients filed a lawsuit saying the computer system violated their right to privacy. The patients were afraid they would be called drug addicts if the public got access to the prescription information.

The U.S. Supreme Court said the computer system did not violate the right of privacy because the law required New York to keep the prescription information secret. As computers become more powerful and store ever increasing amounts of information, Americans need to work harder to protect their right to privacy.

Suggestions for further reading

Dolan, Edward F. *Your Privacy: Protecting It in a Nosy World.* New York: Cobblehill Books, 1995.

Hoobler, Dorothy, and Thomas Hoobler. *Your Right to Privacy.* New York: Franklin Watts, 1986.

Wawrose, Susan C. *Griswold v. Connecticut: Contraception and the Right of Privacy.* New York: Franklin Watts, 1996.

Watkins v. United States
1957

Petitioner: John T. Watkins

Respondent: United States of America

Petitioner's Claim: That convicting him for refusing to answer questions before a Congressional committee violated the U.S. Constitution.

Chief Lawyer for Petitioner: Joseph L. Rauh, Jr.

Chief Lawyer for Respondent: J. Lee Rankin, U.S. Solicitor General

Justices for the Court: Hugo Lafayette Black, William J. Brennan, Jr., William O. Douglas, Felix Frankfurter, John Marshall Harlan II, Earl Warren

Justices Dissenting: Tom C. Clark (Harold Burton and Charles Evans Whittaker did not participate)

Date of Decision: June 17, 1957

Decision: The Supreme Court reversed Watkins's conviction. It said Congress went beyond its powers by asking Watkins to reveal the names of former Communists.

Significance: Congress does not have unlimited power to investigate the private lives of American citizens.

During most of the twentieth century, communism competed with the American system of capitalism for world domination. Under communism, the government owns all property so that people can share it equally. Under capitalism, individuals own property and can accumulate as much as they want for themselves. Communists believe that workers under capitalism suffer to make business and property owners wealthy. Capitalists believe that people under communism suffer to make government officials wealthy and powerful.

In 1917, the Communist Party took control of the government in Russia. In 1922, Russia and other communist countries in Asia combined to form the Union of Soviet Socialist Republics ("USSR"). The USSR's goal was to spread communism throughout the world, by force and violence if necessary. After World War II ended in 1945, Soviet troops helped communist governments take control in Eastern Europe.

Congress investigates

In the United States, some members of the Communist Party wanted to overthrow the federal government and replace it with communism. Because the Communist Party was successful in the USSR and Eastern Europe, many Americans feared it would succeed in the United States, too. Communism became very unpopular in the United States. "Better

Joseph L. Rauh, Jr. defended John Watkins's right to privacy all the way to the Supreme Court, and won. Reproduced by permission of the Corbis Corporation.

dead than red" became a popular saying, referring to the color of the USSR's flag. If a person became known as a communist, he often faced threats and punishment from employers, neighbors, and the government.

In 1938, the U.S. House of Representatives formed a committee to investigate communism and other "un-American" activities. It became known as the House Un-American Activities Committee ("HUAC"). Generally, Congressional committees are allowed to do three things. They may investigate government misconduct, study whether current laws are working, and determine if the United States needs new laws.

HUAC, however, seemed to be doing something different. It seemed to be trying to get rid of American communists by exposing them to the public. In fact, a HUAC report said the committee's job was simply "to expose people and organizations attempting to destroy [the United States]." American communists believed this violated the First Amendment, which protects the right to belong to any political organization.

HUAC questions Watkins

John T. Watkins was a labor union official. Labor unions fight for workers' rights. The Communist Party believes that people should share wealth equally. Because the groups share similar philosophies, many people associated with labor unions also were members of the Communist Party. Two people testified before HUAC that Watkins was a member of the Communist Party. In April 1954, Watkins himself testified before HUAC. Watkins admitted that he helped the Communist Party between 1942 and 1947 by giving it money, signing petitions, and attending conferences. Watkins said he had a disagreement with the Communist Party in 1947 that prevented him from helping it again.

HUAC then read a list of people to Watkins and asked whether any of them had ever been members of the Communist Party. Watkins refused to name people who used to be members but no longer were. Watkins said he did not believe Congress had the right to expose people because of their past activities.

The United States filed criminal charges against Watkins for his refusal to answer HUAC's questions. Watkins argued that HUAC's questions violated the First Amendment, especially the freedoms of speech and association. The trial court disagreed, found Watkins guilty, and placed him on probation. The Court of Appeals for the District of

Columbia affirmed (approved) Watkins' conviction, so Watkins took the case to the U.S. Supreme Court.

The right to privacy

On June 17, 1957, the Supreme Court decided four cases, including *Watkins,* in favor of alleged communists. That day became known as "Red Monday." In *Watkins,* Chief Justice Earl Warren wrote a long opinion that analyzed Congress's power to investigate and the limitations on that power.

Justice Warren said Congress's power to make laws also includes the power to conduct investigations. Congress may investigate government misconduct, the working of existing laws, and the need for new laws. Congress, however, has "no general authority to expose the private affairs of individuals" or "to punish those investigated."

When Congress investigates a person, it must obey his constitutional rights. Under the First Amendment, those rights include the freedoms of speech and association. Because speech stems from beliefs, the freedom of speech includes the right to believe. The freedom of association protects the right to belong to political groups, even the Communist Party.

Justice Warren described these freedoms as a "right to privacy." He said forcing someone to reveal his or other people's unpopular beliefs or associations, such as membership in the Communist Party, could result in hateful attacks by the public. That violates the privacy protected by the First Amendment. As Justice Warren put it, "there is no congressional power to expose for the sake of exposure."

Congress created HUAC to investigate "un-American" activity. Justice Warren said that term was too hard to define and it allowed HUAC to investigate things outside Congress's three main investigational powers. The committee's vague purpose made it impossible for Watkins to know whether the questions about former communists were within Congress' power, or an abuse of that power. Convicting Watkins for refusing to answer such questions was unfair under the U.S. Constitution, so his conviction had to be reversed.

Fighting communism

Justice Tom C. Clark dissented, meaning he disagreed with the Court's decision. Justice Clark believed communism was dedicated to over-

FEDERAL BUREAU OF INVESTIGATION

In *Watkins,* the Supreme Court said the executive branch of government is the one with power to investigate criminal activity. Within the executive branch, the Federal Bureau of Investigation ("FBI") handles that job. Like Congress in *Watkins,* however, the FBI often is accused of violating the right to privacy.

In fact, when Congress investigated the FBI in the mid-1970s, it found several instances of misconduct. Although the FBI is supposed to work solely for the country, it also did personal political work for Presidents Roosevelt, Kennedy, Johnson, and Nixon. For example, in 1964 the FBI investigated the staff of President Johnson's political opponent, Barry Goldwater.

Congress also learned about an FBI program called Cointelpro. Between 1956 and 1971, the FBI used Cointelpro to investigate Americans involved in unpopular activities, such as communism, socialism, and the civil rights movement. The FBI's tactics under Cointelpro included illegal wiretapping, kidnapping, and burglary. The Senate called these tactics "degrading to a free society."

throwing the federal government, by violence and force, if necessary. He said Congress was allowed to investigate what kinds of laws it needed to fight communism, and citizens were required to share information they had related to HUAC's investigation. Clark said, "There is no general privilege of silence." He feared the Court's decision would prevent Congress from doing its job for the United States.

Impact

The Red Monday decisions angered conservative Americans. Senator William Jenner tried to pass a law eliminating the Supreme Court's power to review cases involving communists. The law was not enacted, and the Court voted in favor of convicting communists in some future cases. The Red Scare of communism calmed down by the end of the

1950s, and HUAC later abandoned its investigations. Contrary to Justice Clark's concerns, *Watkins* has not hurt Congress' ability to conduct investigations. Congress simply may not violate the right to privacy protected by the First Amendment when it investigates individual citizens.

Suggestions for further reading

Davis, James Kirkpatrick. *Spying on America: The FBI's Domestic Counter-Intelligence Program.* New York: Praeger, 1992.

Dolan, Edward F. *Your Privacy: Protecting It in a Nosy World.* New York: Cobblehill Books, 1995.

Hoobler, Dorothy, and Thomas Hoobler. *Your Right to Privacy.* New York: Franklin Watts, 1986.

King, David C. *Freedom of Assembly.* Brookfield, CT: Millbrook Press, 1997.

Weber, Michael L. *Our Congress.* Brookfield, CT: Millbrook Press, 1994.

Griswold v. Connecticut 1964

Appellants: Charles Lee Buxton and Estelle T. Griswold

Appellee: State of Connecticut

Appellants' Claim: That Connecticut's birth control law violated the U.S. Constitution.

Chief Lawyer for Appellants: Thomas I. Emerson

Chief Lawyer for Appellee: Joseph B. Clark

Justices for the Court: William J. Brennan, Jr., Tom C. Clark, William O. Douglas (writing for the Court), Arthur Goldberg, John Marshall Harlan II, Earl Warren, Byron R. White

Justices Dissenting: Hugo Lafayette Black, Potter Stewart

Date of Decision: May 11, 1964

Decision: Laws that prevent married couples from using birth control violate marital privacy.

Significance: The U.S. Constitution protects a general right of privacy for Americans.

In 1879, Connecticut passed a law making it a crime for anyone, even married couples, to use birth control drugs or devices. (Birth control prevents a woman from getting pregnant when she has sexual intercourse.) The law also made it a crime to give someone medical information and advice about birth control. Connecticut said it enacted the law to prevent married people from having sexual relations outside marriage.

Birth control laws became very unpopular among some Americans. Children are expensive to care for. Without birth control, poor people found it difficult to control the size of their families. Women also faced serious health risks and even death from having too many pregnancies or from having abortions when they could not afford another child. (Abortion ends a pregnancy before the fetus, or unborn child, is born.)

Around 1960, several women filed a lawsuit to challenge Connecticut's law. They said they needed to use birth control for health reasons, but could be convicted for doing so. The courts in Connecticut ruled against the women, so they appealed to the U.S. Supreme Court.

In *Poe v. Ullman* (1961), the Supreme Court decided not to decide the case. It said Connecticut's law was "dead words" and "harmless empty shadows" because Connecticut never tried to enforce it. Justice John Marshall Harlan II wrote a dissenting opinion, saying he believed the Court should strike down the law. Harlan foreshadowed what the Court would do a few years later in *Griswold* by saying the law was an "unjustifiable invasion of privacy."

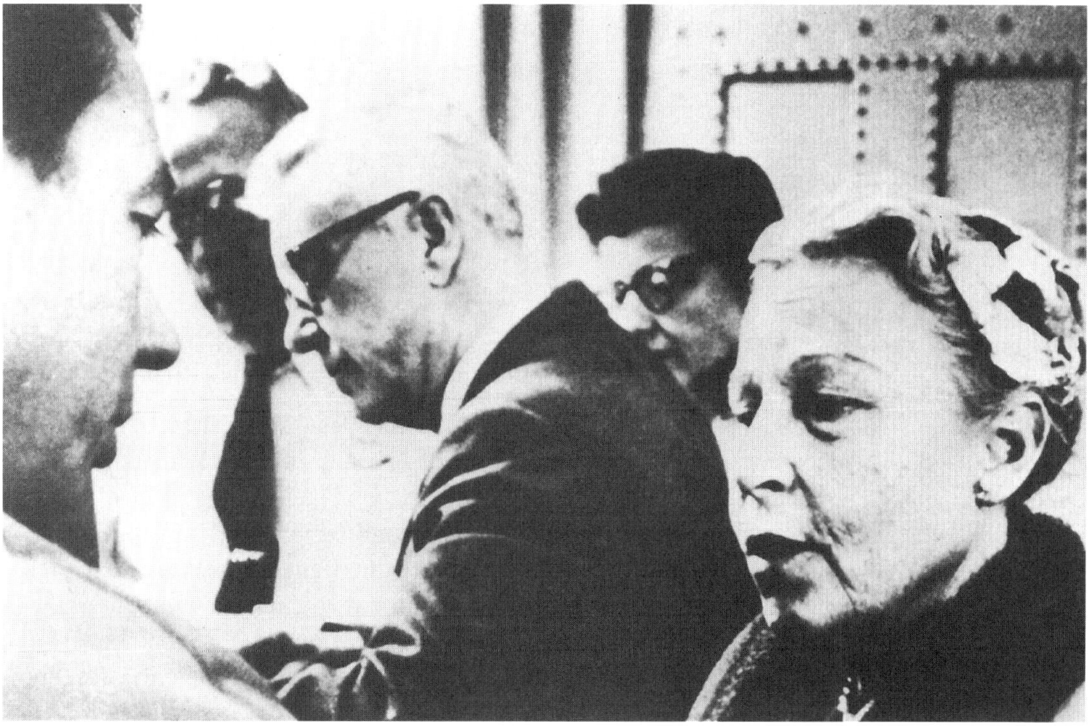

Estelle Griswold fought for her right to marital privacy. Reproduced by permission of the Corbis Corporation.

RIGHT TO PRIVACY

Griswold tests dead law

Estelle T. Griswold was executive director of the Planned Parenthood League of Connecticut. (Planned Parenthood is an organization that educates the public about birth control.) Dr. Charles Lee Buxton was chairman of Yale University's obstetrics department. On November 1, 1961, four months after the Supreme Court's decision in *Poe,* Griswold and Buxton opened a birth control clinic in New Haven, Connecticut. Referring to the Supreme Court's decision in *Poe,* Buxton said he believed it was now legal for doctors to prescribe birth control for patients in Connecticut.

Nine days later, Griswold and Buxton were arrested and their clinic was closed. At the trial on January 2, 1962, police detectives testified that they entered the clinic on its third day of operation and met Estelle Griswold. She told them the facility was a birth control clinic and offered information and devices.

Griswold and Buxton's attorney argued that Connecticut's law violated the freedom of speech by preventing doctors from counseling patients about birth control. The trial judge rejected this argument. Griswold and Buxton were found guilty and fined $100 each. Both the Appellate Division and the State Supreme Court of Errors affirmed (approved) the convictions, saying the law was valid under Connecticut's police power to protect public health and safety. Griswold and Buxton appealed to the U.S. Supreme Court.

Leave me alone

With a 7–2 decision, the Supreme Court reversed Griswold and Buxton's convictions. Writing for the Court, Justice William O. Douglas said Connecticut's birth control law violated the constitutional right of privacy. In a concurring opinion, Justice Arthur Goldberg quoted former Justice Louis Brandeis, who called the right of privacy "the right to be let alone."

Griswold was a landmark decision because the U.S. Constitution does not actually mention a right of privacy. Justice Douglas found the right in what he called the "penumbras" of many constitutional amendments. (Penumbra is a body of rights implied in a civil constitution.) For example, the First Amendment protects the right to have private thoughts and to receive information. The Fourth Amendment protects the right to be safe from unfair arrests. The Fifth and Fourteenth Amendments say the government cannot violate the right to liberty, meaning freedom, without following fair procedures.

MARGARET SANGER

On October 16, 1916, Margaret Sanger opened the first birth control clinic in the United States in Brooklyn, New York. Sanger was a nurse who worked with poor people. She saw many poor women die, some from having too many children and others from having abortions when they could not afford another child. Sanger opened the clinic to teach women about birth control to save their lives. The clinic charged ten cents for each consultation, making it affordable for poor people.

In New York, the Comstock law made it illegal to distribute birth control information. Nine days after she opened the clinic, Sanger was arrested for violating the Comstock law. Sanger yelled at the policewoman who arrested her, saying, "You dirty thing. You are not a woman. You are a dog." The police dragged Sanger into a patrol wagon. As Sanger was taken away, a woman chased after the wagon yelling, "Come back! Come back and save me!" This strengthened Sanger's courage to fight the law.

Sanger was found guilty and sentenced to thirty days in prison. After serving her time, Sanger returned to educating women about birth control and fighting to make it legal in America. She enjoyed victory in 1936 when the U.S. Supreme Court struck down the Comstock law and the American Medical Association decided doctors should give birth control devices to their patients.

Justice Douglas said taken together, these Amendments protect privacy in the United States of America. That means the Constitution protects a general right of privacy. Douglas decided marriage is one relationship protected by the right of privacy. He said marital privacy is "older than the Bill of Rights — older than our political parties, older than our school system." Because Connecticut's law invaded marital privacy by preventing married couples from using birth control, it was unconstitutional.

Out of thin air

Justices Hugo Lafayette Black and Potter Stewart dissented, meaning they disagreed with the Court's decision. Justice Black agreed that Connecticut's law was offensive, and Justice Stewart called it silly, but both said the law did not violate the U.S. Constitution. They disagreed that the Constitution contains a general right of privacy. Justice Stewart said if Connecticut's citizens did not like the law, they should ask the legislature to change it. Justice Black added that if Americans wanted a right of privacy in the U.S. Constitution, they should ask the states to add it by constitutional amendment. He said, "That method of change was good for our Fathers, and being somewhat old-fashioned I must add it is good enough for me."

Impact

Eight years after *Griswold,* the Supreme Court said the right of privacy allows unmarried people to use birth control. In 1977, it said the right prevents states from banning birth control for people under sixteen. In the landmark decision of ***Roe v. Wade*** (1972), the Court said privacy protects a woman's right to have an abortion. Taken together, these decisions mean the right of privacy lets Americans decide whether or not to have children.

In *Roe v. Wade,* the Court also clarified that the right of privacy comes from the protection of "liberty" in the Fourteenth Amendment, not from the "penumbras" of other amendments.

Suggestions for further reading

Chesler, Ellen. *Woman of Valor: Margaret Sanger and the Birth Control Movement in America.* New York: Simon & Schuster, 1992.

Dolan, Edward F. *Your Privacy: Protecting It in a Nosy World.* New York: Cobblehill Books, 1995.

Hoobler, Dorothy, and Thomas Hoobler. *Your Right to Privacy.* New York: Franklin Watts, 1986.

Moss, Joyce, and George Wilson. *Profiles in American History: Significant Events and the People Who Shaped Them.* Vol. 6. Detroit: Gale Research, 1994.

Wawrose, Susan C. *Griswold v. Connecticut: Contraception and the Right of Privacy.* New York: Franklin Watts, 1996.

Whalen v. Roe
1977

Appellant: Robert P. Whalen, New York Commissioner of Health

Appellees: Richard Roe, et al.

Appellant's Claim: That a New York computer system that stored information about prescription drug users was constitutional.

Chief Lawyer for Appellant: A. Seth Greenwald, Assistant Attorney General of New York

Chief Lawyer for Appellees: Michael Lesch and H. Miles Jaffee

Justices for the Court: Harry A. Blackmun, William J. Brennan, Jr., Warren E. Burger, Thurgood Marshall, Lewis F. Powell, Jr., William H. Rehnquist, John Paul Stevens (writing for the Court), Potter Stewart, Byron R. White

Justices Dissenting: None

Date of Decision: February 22, 1977

Decision: New York's computer system was reasonable and did not violate the right of privacy.

Significance: The government may collect and store vast amounts of private information on computers.

In 1970, New York State was concerned about the abuse of prescription drugs. Prescription drugs are drugs that doctors use to treat patients for illness, pain, and other medical conditions. Each doctor fills out a piece of paper called a prescription, which the patient then gives to a pharmacist. The pharmacist, in turn, sells the drug to the patient.

New York formed a commission to study the state's drug control laws. The commission learned that it was impossible to stop people from using stolen prescription drugs. There also was no way to stop unethical doctors and pharmacists from giving patients more drugs than they needed. Finally, there was no way to stop patients from going to more than one doctor to get many prescriptions for the same drug. All of these problems made it easy for people to abuse prescription drugs by using more than they needed.

Associate Justice John Paul Stevens.
Courtesy of the Supreme Court of the United States.

Fighting drug abuse

Because drug abuse can injure health, ruin life, and even cause death, New York passed a new law to correct these problems. The new law created five drug schedules. Schedule I was for drugs, such as heroin, that had no legal medical uses. Drugs in schedules II through V had valid medical uses but tended to be abused.

Schedule II drugs were prescription drugs with the most serious abuse problems. Under the new law, prescriptions for schedule II drugs had to be written on a form that produced three copies. On the form, the doctor writing the prescription had to record her name, the name of the pharmacist, the drug and amount being prescribed, and the name, address, and age of the patient. The physician kept one copy of the form, the pharmacist kept the second copy, and the third copy went to the New York State Department of Health in Albany, New York.

The Department of Health sorted, coded, and recorded the forms on a log. The Department then recorded the data from the forms onto magnetic tapes for computer processing. Under the law, the Department kept the written forms in a locked vault for five years and then destroyed them. It designed the computer system so outside computers could not access the data. The law made it a crime for the Department of Health to disclose private information about patients to the public. By storing this information in computer records, New York hoped to prevent illegal drug use by monitoring prescriptions.

Fighting for the right of privacy

A few days before New York's law went into effect, patients who used schedule II drugs filed a lawsuit in federal district court to challenge the law. They argued that the law violated the right of privacy by storing private information about them in government computers.

The patients were worried that they would be called drug addicts if their private information was shared with the public. They said that fear would discourage people from getting schedule II drugs. In fact, the evidence showed that one adult and one child already had stopped getting schedule II drugs because of that fear. A doctor even said he completely stopped prescribing schedule II drugs because his patients were horrified by the new law.

The district court ruled in favor of the patients. It said liberty under the Fourteenth Amendment protects the right of privacy in America. Privacy, in turn, protects the relationship between doctors and patients. Because New York's law interfered with that relationship by discouraging patients from getting schedule II drugs from their doctors, it was unconstitutional. New York appealed the case to the U.S. Supreme Court.

Privacy not threatened

With a unanimous decision, the Supreme Court reversed and ruled in favor of New York. Writing for the Court, Justice John Paul Stevens considered whether New York's law was reasonable, and whether it violated the right of privacy.

JACOBSEN v. MASSACHUSETTS (1905)

In 1796, a British doctor discovered a vaccine for smallpox, which was a deadly disease. In 1902, Cambridge, Massachusetts, passed a law forcing everyone in the city to receive a smallpox vaccination. Henning Jacobsen refused to be vaccinated and was charged with violating the law. At his trial, Jacobsen offered evidence that the vaccination did not really protect people against smallpox. He also offered evidence that he and his son experienced harmful reactions to vaccinations. The trial court rejected Jacobsen's evidence and convicted him.

Jacobsen appealed to the U.S. Supreme Court. He argued that forcing him to be injected with a vaccine violated his liberty under the Fourteenth Amendment. Jacobsen said it violated the "right of every freeman to care for his own body and health" and was "nothing short of an assault upon his person." The Supreme Court rejected these arguments and affirmed Jacobsen's conviction. The Court said liberty does not prevent the government from deciding how people should take care of their health.

In 1980, the World Health Organization said the vaccine had eliminated smallpox from the Earth. Vaccinations, however, are contrary to some people's religious and moral beliefs. In addition, some doctors say vaccinations do more harm than good. For example, vaccinations may be responsible for mysterious medical conditions, such as multiple sclerosis, that doctors have been unable to understand or cure. Today, many states allow people to refuse to be vaccinated for medical, religious, and moral reasons.

Justice Stevens decided New York's law was reasonable. Drug abuse was a valid health concern. New York could discourage drug abuse by keeping track of what patients were using. The computer database would help New York investigate drug violations, which Justice Stevens said was a valid exercise of New York's police power to protect the health of its citizens.

As for the right of privacy, Justice Stevens said it has two parts: the desire to keep private information secret, and the freedom to make individual health decisions. Justice Stevens said New York's law did not violate either interest. The law required the Department of Health to keep all private information secret. Prescription forms were stored in a locked vault and then destroyed after five years. The computer system was secure from outside computers. In short, New York's law protected privacy.

The law also did not violate the freedom to make individual health decisions. Patients still were allowed to use schedule II drugs if necessary. By the time of the district court's decision, over 100,000 schedule II prescriptions had been filled under the law. That meant the law was not stopping people from getting schedule II drugs. Again, the fear of being branded as a drug addict was unreasonable because the law protected each patient's private information.

Justice Stevens said the Court realized the privacy risk caused by storing vast amounts of personal information on government computers. He said the result might be different if the law did not protect private information, or if someone shared such information with the public by accident or on purpose. New York's law, which did not have such problems, was constitutional.

Suggestions for further reading

Dolan, Edward F. *Your Privacy: Protecting It in a Nosy World.* New York: Cobblehill Books, 1995.

Hoobler, Dorothy, and Thomas Hoobler. *Your Right to Privacy.* New York: Franklin Watts, 1986.

Mikula, Mark, and L. Mpho Mabunda, eds. *Great American Court Cases.* Vol. 1. Detroit: The Gale Group, 1999.

FREEDOM OF RELIGION AND THE ESTABLISHMENT CLAUSE

"The Star-Spangled Banner" says the United States of America is the "land of the free." One of the most cherished freedoms in America is the freedom of religion. It protects our right to worship as we choose or not to worship at all.

Religion has served many purposes for humanity. In prehistoric times it explained natural events and created order out of a chaotic world. Although science does this today, people continue to use religion as a shelter from the horrors of the world. Religion helps communities develop moral values for their children. Some people use places of worship just to socialize with fellow human beings.

During the seventeenth and eighteenth centuries, many people fled Europe to find religious freedom in the American colonies. In Europe most people were forced to follow a religion selected by the government and to pay taxes to support it. In this way, the Church of England had been that country's official religion since the sixteenth century. This restricted people who wanted to follow a different sect of Christianity or another religion. People who tried to follow other religions were punished with imprisonment and sometimes death.

The American colonists, however, did not enjoy true religious freedom. Most of the original colonies established their own official religions. Some colonists fell into the same habits of persecution that they left behind in England. Puritans, for example, who were greatly persecuted in England, were intolerant of other religions in Massachusetts.

After the colonies revolted against England in 1776, became the United States, and established a federal government with the U.S. Constitution in 1789, Congress drafted the Bill of Rights. Although the Constitution defined and limited the powers of the federal government, it did not protect the rights of American citizens. The Bill of Rights, which consists of the first ten amendments to the Constitution, does just that. Mindful of the history of religious oppression by the Church of England and the early American colonies, Congress used the First Amendment to protect religious freedom in America. The First Amendment says, "Congress shall make no law respecting an establishment of religion, or prohibiting the free exercise thereof."

The First Amendment, indeed the whole Bill of Rights, talks only about protecting American rights from action by the federal government. While some states included freedom of religion in their state constitutions, state governments did not have to obey the First Amendment regarding freedom of religion. After the American Civil War (1861-1865), however, the states adopted the Fourteenth Amendment to the U.S. Constitution in 1868. The Due Process Clause in the Fourteenth Amendment says, "No State shall ... deprive any person of life, liberty, or property, without due process of law." Interpreting the "liberty" portion of the Due Process Clause, the U.S. Supreme Court has decided that state governments also must obey most of the Bill of Rights, including the First Amendment's guarantee of freedom of religion.

The United States's recognition of religious freedom, however, wasn't as simple as adopting the First Amendment. When the states ratified the Bill of Rights in 1791, almost every American practiced some form of Protestant Christianity. When these Americans thought of religious tolerance, they did not think of Roman Catholicism, Buddhism, Islam, Judaism, or any of the world's other religions. Only through centuries of immigration has religious diversity flourished in the United States. That has been the true test of the strength of the nation's commitment to freedom of religion.

Free Exercise Clause

The First Amendment contains two clauses addressing religious freedom. The Free Exercise Clause, discussed here, prevents the government from "prohibiting the free exercise" of religion. The Establishment Clause, discussed below, prevents the government from making laws "respecting an establishment of religion."

What is the "free exercise" of religion? Certainly, it means the government cannot tell Americans what religious beliefs to have. But "exercise" means more than belief. The First Amendment also protects the right to engage in religious activity. For example, in *Pierce v. Society of Sisters* (1925), the U.S. Supreme Court overturned an Oregon law that required all children to attend public schools instead of private, religious schools.

The question becomes: How strong is the guarantee of freedom of religion? It surely does not, for instance, give Americans the right to make human sacrifices. In other words, religious freedom is not absolute, or unlimited. Cases under the Free Exercise Clause involve balancing the freedom to engage in religious activity against the government's right to pass laws for the health, safety, and general welfare of its citizens.

For example, in ***Reynolds v. United States*** (1879), members of the Church of Jesus Christ of Latter Day Saints, also called Mormons, challenged federal laws that prohibited polygamy. Polygamy is the practice of having more than one spouse. Male Mormons claimed that having more than one wife was a part of their religion protected by the First Amendment. The U.S. Supreme Court disagreed, saying that the Free Exercise Clause does not allow people to disobey laws that protect the general welfare of society.

Similarly, in *Jacobsen v. Massachusetts* (1905), the Court said Seventh-Day Adventists had to obey state laws requiring vaccinations, or shots, to protect against deadly viruses. In *Employment Division v. Smith* (1990), the Court said Oregon could prevent Native Americans from using peyote, a hallucinogenic drug, in their sacramental ceremonies.

When deciding if a law violates the right to freedom of religion, the U.S. Supreme Court says the law may not discriminate by treating religions differently. The Court itself, however, has reached conflicting results in different cases. In *Braunfeld v. Brown* (1961), the Court upheld a Philadelphia, Pennsylvania, law that required businesses to close on Sundays. An Orthodox Jewish businessman said the law interfered with his religion because he had to open his store on Sundays in order to close it on Saturdays for religious worship. The Supreme Court disagreed, saying the law made his religious observance more difficult, but not impossible. In *Shervert v. Verner* (1963), however, the Court said a Seventh-Day Adventist who was fired for refusing to work on Saturdays could not be denied unemployment compensation benefits (money to help people who lose their jobs).

Establishment Clause

The Establishment Clause prevents the government from making laws "respecting an establishment of religion." In 1802 President Thomas Jefferson wrote a letter in which he mentioned the need to maintain "a wall of separation" between church and state. Establishment Clause cases have adopted this language. They stand for the idea that religion and government must remain separate.

Keeping government and religion separate obviously means that government may not declare an official religion, such as the Church of England. It also means that government may not interfere in religious business. For example, in *Watson v. Jones* (1872), the Court ruled that a dispute within the Presbyterian Church could not be resolved in the courts, but only by church officials. In *Kedroff v. St. Nicholas Cathedral* (1952), which involved the Russian Orthodox Church, the Court said the federal government could not interfere even if church authority was being exercised by a foreign country that was hostile to the United States.

The more difficult Establishment Clause cases involve government assistance or approval of religion. These cases usually involve public and private schools or governmental holiday displays.

School prayer, for instance, has been a subject of heated debate in the United States. Polls suggest that most Americans want some form of prayer to be allowed in public schools. In ***Engel v. Vitale*** (1962), however, the Supreme Court said the Establishment Clause prevents public schools from using even a nondenominational prayer, one that does not come from a specific religion. Clearly, then, public schools also may not have readings from Bibles or other religious texts.

Public school curricula also have been the subject of Establishment Clause cases. In ***Epperson v. Arkansas*** (1968), the Supreme Court considered a state law that outlawed the teaching of evolution, the scientific theory that humans descended from monkey-like ancestors. The Court said prohibiting the teaching of evolution violated the Establishment Clause because it was designed to promote creationism, a religious belief that humans were created directly by God. As of 1999, states continued to wrestle with laws requiring schools to teach creationism, evolution, and both or neither.

Financial aid to schools also creates Establishment Clause controversies. In ***Everson v. Board of Education*** (1947), the Court said government cannot pass laws that "aid one religion, aid all religions, or prefer one religion over another." In *Everson,* however, the Court approved a state law that provided bus money to parents of children attending all schools, including private Catholic schools. The Court said because the law helped children get to school on public buses, it benefited education, not religion. Eventually the Court said that while the government may not aid religion, it also may deny to religious organizations commonly available public services, such as those related to health and safety.

This confusion led the Court in ***Lemon v. Kurtzman*** (1971) to adopt a three-part test for determining when a law violates the Establishment Clause. Under the Lemon test, a law is valid if it (1) has a secular, or non-religious, purpose; (2) has a main effect that neither advances nor restricts religion; and (3) does not foster excessive entanglement, or mixing, between religion and government.

Unfortunately, this test also is confusing and has produced conflicting results, especially in the area of governmental holiday displays. In ***County of Allegheny v. American Civil Liberties Union*** (1989), the Court considered challenges to two holiday displays. One, appearing in a county courthouse in Pittsburgh, Pennsyvania, displayed a Christian nativity scene with a message that said "Glory to God in the Highest." The other, appearing in front of a city-county governmental building in Pittsburgh, displayed a Christmas tree and a Jewish menorah, or candelabrum.

In a split decision, the Court decided that the first display violated the Establishment Clause by endorsing Christianity. The Jewish menorah, however, did not endorse religion because it was displayed with a Christmas tree, which conveyed a secular, non-religious holiday message. The result probably offended some Christians. The suggestion that the menorah did not convey a religious message probably offended some Jews. The case illustrates the difficulty of fairly enforcing the guarantee of freedom of religion.

Suggestions for further reading

Evans, J. Edward. *Freedom of Religion.* Minneapolis, MN: Lerner Publications Company, 1990.

Farish, Leah. *The First Amendment: Freedom of Speech, Religion, and the Press.* Hillside, NJ: Enslow Publishers, Inc., 1998.

Gay, Kathlyn. *Church and State: Government and Religion in the United States.* Brookfield, CT: Millbrook Press, 1992.

Hirst, Mike. *Freedom of Belief.* New York, NY: Franklin Watts, 1997.

Kleeberg, Irene Cumming. *Separation of Church and State.* New York: Franklin Watts, 1986.

Klinker, Philip A. *The First Amendment.* Englewood Cliffs, NJ: Silver Burdett Press, 1991.

Moskin, Marietta D. *In the Name of God: Religion in Everyday Life.* New York, NY: Atheneum, 1980.

Sherrow, Victoria. *Freedom of Worship.* Brookfield, CT: Millbrook Press, 1997.

Reynolds v. United States
1879

Petitioner: George Reynolds

Respondent: United States

Petitioner's Claim: The Morrill Act, which made practice of polygamy a crime, violated his First Amendment right to freedom of religion.

Chief Lawyers for Petitioner: George W. Biddle and Ben Sheeks

Chief Lawyers for Respondent: Charles Devens, U.S. Attorney General, and Samuel F. Phillips, U.S. Solicitor General

Justices for the Court: Joseph P. Bradley, Nathan Clifford, Stephen Johnson Field, John Marshall Harlan I, Ward Hunt, Samuel Freeman Miller, William Strong, Noah Haynes Swayne, Morrison Remick Waite

Justices Dissenting: None

Date of Decision: May 5, 1879

Decision: Polygamy was not protected by freedom of religion.

Significance: The Mormons, a religious group who settled Utah, permitted its men to practice polygamy. In *Reynolds v. U.S.*, the Supreme Court found that laws banning polygamy were constitutional. They did not violate the Mormons' right to free exercise of their religion. This still remains the most important legal case to address the issue of polygamy.

FREEDOM OF RELIGION AND THE ESTABLISHMENT CLAUSE

The Morrill Anti-Bigamy Act is passed

George Reynolds's religion allowed for the practice of polygamy.
Reproduced by permission of the Utah State Historical Society.

In the middle of the nineteenth century, after a long trek westward, the Mormons settled the land that became the state of Utah. The Mormons were followers of a religious prophet named Joseph Smith. Their religion was called the Church of Jesus Christ of Latter-Day Saints. They held a variety of beliefs. The most controversial belief was that a man could have two or more wives, a practice known as polygamy.

Many people in the United States had known about the Mormon practice of polygamy since 1852. Most Americans were traditional Christians who believed in monogamy—having only one spouse. Until the Mormons arrived, however, there were no federal laws against bigamy or polygamy. The government left the Mormons alone for many years, but in 1862, President Abraham Lincoln signed the Morrill Anti-Bigamy Act into law. The Morrill Act outlawed polygamy throughout the United States in general and in Utah in particular. The government did not do much to enforce the law at that time because it was concerned with the Civil War.

Congress strengthens anti-bigamy law

Congress again took up the issue of Mormon polygamy after the Civil War ended. The Morrill Act was strengthened when the Poland Law was passed in 1874. The Poland Law increased the powers of the federal courts in the territory of Utah. Because federal judges were not appointed by local politicians, they were usually non-Mormons who were more aggressive about enforcing the anti-bigamy law.

Mormon leader Brigham Young's advisor, George Q. Cannon, was a territorial delegate to Congress. Together, Young and Cannon decided to challenge the federal government in court. They were confident that if the government tried any Mormons for bigamy, the United States Supreme Court would throw out the convictions. Their belief was based on the First Amendment right to free exercise of religion. They arranged to bring a "test case" to court. They chose Young's personal secretary, George Reynolds, to act as the defendant. Reynolds was a devout Mormon and practicing polygamist.

Young and Cannon were successful. The government indicted (charged) Reynolds with bigamy in October of 1874. However, the first trial failed because of jury selection problems. The government indicted Reynolds again in October of 1875.

Federal prosecutors charged that Reynolds was married to both Mary Ann Tuddenham and Amelia Jane Schofield. The prosecutors had little trouble proving that Reynolds lived with both women. However, they did have some trouble serving Schofield with a subpoena. (A subpoena is a legal document ordering a person to appear in court.) The following dialogue is taken from questions the prosecution asked the deputy marshal sent to serve the subpoena on Schofield:

> **Question: State to the court what efforts you have made to serve it. Answer: I went to the residence of Mr. Reynolds, and a lady was there, his first wife, and she told me that this woman was not there; that that was the only home that she had, but that she hadn't been there for two or three weeks. I went again this morning, and she was not there. Question: Do you know anything about her home, where she resides? Answer: I know where I found her before. Question: Where? Answer: At the same place.**

Judge White gave instructions to the jury after more evidence was presented that Reynolds had two wives. The instructions completely destroyed Reynolds's defense that the First Amendment protected his practice of polygamy allowed by his Mormon faith.

The jury found Reynolds guilty on December 10, 1875. On July 6, 1876, the territorial Supreme Court affirmed (maintained) his sentence. Reynolds then appealed to the U.S. Supreme Court. On November 14 and 15, 1878, his lawyers, George W. Biddle and Ben Sheeks, argued before the highest court in the land that Reynolds's conviction must be overturned on the basis of the First Amendment.

The Supreme Court destroys the Mormons' hopes

On January 6, 1879, the Supreme Court upheld the trial court's decision. The Court based its decision on historic American cultural values, namely that from the earliest times polygamy was considered an offense against society. Most civilized countries considered marriage a "sacred obligation," and a civil contract usually regulated by law. Therefore, the Court ruled that the First Amendment did not protect polygamy. Reynolds's sentence of two years in prison and a $500 fine remained.

The Court's decision rocked the Mormons. Initially, they vowed to resist the Court's ruling. Later, however, they seemed to accept their fate. In 1890, Mormon leader Wilford Woodruff issued a document called the Manifesto. The Manifesto ended "any marriages forbidden by the law of the land." After 1890, most Mormons abandoned the practice of polygamy.

The *Reynolds* case is still the leading Supreme Court case on the issue of polygamy. In 1984, a U.S. District Court considered the case of Utah policeman Royston Potter, who was fired from his job because of bigamy. District Court Judge Sherman Christensen rejected Potter's First Amendment defense. The U.S. Tenth Circuit Court of Appeals upheld this ruling. In October 1985, the U.S. Supreme Court refused to hear Potter's appeal. By refusing to hear cases like Potter's, the Court has effectively decided to keep *Reynolds* as the law of the land.

Many legal scholars have criticized the Supreme Court for not altering or overturning its opinion in *Reynolds*. It has been more than a century since the decision was handed down. During that time, the Court has greatly expanded First Amendment protection of free exercise of religion. In the 1960s and early 1970s, the Court increased the Constitution's protection for the civil rights of women, minorities, and other classes of persons whose equality under the law had not been a part of the old "common law" on which *Reynolds* was based. As of 2000, however, the Supreme Court has not reconsidered the ruling it gave in *Reynolds*.

FIGHTS OVER POLYGAMY

The Mormon practice of polygamy had been controversial for almost as long as the religion existed in the United States. In 1857, 2,500 Army troops were sent into Utah to install a governor to replace Mormon leader Brigham Young. Mormons responded angrily. The result was the "Utah War." During this war, Mormons killed 120 people passing through Utah on their way to California.

For years, Utah was refused statehood because of its approval of polygamy. The controversy spread to the Mormon community itself. In 1873, Ann Eliza Webb Young made history by moving out of the home owned by her husband, Brigham Young, and demanding a divorce. She became a nationwide crusader against polygamy. The battle continued throughout the 1880s and 1890s. Over 1,000 Mormons were fined or imprisoned for polygamy. It wasn't until Mormons themselves outlawed the practice of polygamy that Utah's application for statehood was accepted, on January 4, 1896.

Suggestions for further reading

Cannon, George Quayle. *A Review of the Decision of the Supreme Court of the United States, in the Case of Geo. Reynolds vs. the United States.* Salt Lake City, UT: Deseret News Printing, 1879.

Casey, Kathryn. "An American Harem." *Ladies Home Journal* (February 1990): pp. 116–121.

Embry, Jessie L. *Mormon Polygamous Families: Life in the Principle.* Salt Lake City, UT: University of Utah Press, 1987.

Firmage, Edwin Brown. *Zion in the Courts: A Legal History of the Church of Jesus Christ of Latter-Day Saints, 1830–1900.* Urbana, IL: University of Illinois Press, 1988.

Foster, Lawrence. *Religion and Sexuality: The Shakers, the Mormons, and the Oneida Community.* Urbana, IL: University of Illinois Press, 1984.

Johnson, John W., ed. *Historic U.S. Court Cases, 1960–1990: An Encyclopedia.* New York, NY: Garland Publishing, 1992.

Wagoner, Richard S. *Mormon Polygamy: A History.* Salt Lake City, UT: Signature Books, 1989.

Cantwell v. Connecticut 1940

Appellants: Newton Cantwell, Jesse Cantwell, Russell Cantwell

Appellee: State of Connecticut

Appellants' Claim: That a state law requiring a public official to approve a religion before its members can make door-to-door solicitations violates the First Amendment right to freedom of religion.

Chief Lawyer for Appellants: Hayden C. Covington

Chief Lawyers for Appellee: Edwin S. Pickett and Francis A. Pallotti

Justices for the Court: Hugo Lafayette Black, William O. Douglas, Felix Frankfurter, Charles Evans Hughes, James Clark McReynolds, Frank Murphy, Stanley Forman Reed, Owen Josephus Roberts (writing for the Court), Harlan Fiske Stone

Justices Dissenting: None

Date of Decision: May 20, 1940

Decision: The state law violated the freedom of religion. The Supreme Court said a state may control the time, place, and manner of solicitation only if it does not treat religions differently.

Significance: The Court made it clear that states must recognize the freedom of religion as laid out in the Free Exercise Clause of the First Amendment.

FREEDOM OF RELIGION AND THE ESTABLISHMENT CLAUSE

Exercising religion

Associate Justice Owen Josephus Roberts.
Courtesy of the Supreme Court of the United States.

One of the freedoms protected by law in the United States is the right to choose and speak about one's religious beliefs. The First Amendment of the U.S. Constitution protects this freedom by preventing Congress from passing any laws that prohibit, or ban, the "free exercise" of religion. This portion of the First Amendment is called the Free Exercise Clause.

One of the greatest tests of freedom of religion in America comes when different religions clash. Centuries ago, before the United States declared independence from England, the British government took care of this problem by outlawing all religions except the official Church of England. The Free Exercise Clause was written to prevent the U.S. government from having such power over religion. *Cantwell v. Connecticut* tested the strength of this freedom in the United States.

Spreading the faith

Newton Cantwell and his two sons, Jesse and Russell, were Jehovah's Witnesses living in Connecticut in the 1930s. Jehovah's Witnesses is a form of Christianity that believes the end of the world is near. Its members spend much of their time preaching to others to gain new members before the end arrives.

Newton Cantwell and his sons went from door to door in a neighborhood in New Haven, Connecticut, preaching their faith. Most of the people in the neighborhood were Roman Catholic. The Cantwells had books about the Jehovah's Witnesses religion and portable record players with records that described the books. The Cantwells asked people to listen to the records and buy the books. When people refused, the Cantwells asked for a donation of money to support the Jehovah's Witnesses.

On one occasion Jesse Cantwell stopped on the street to talk to two men, both of whom were Catholic. The men were angry to hear that the Jehovah's Witnesses's material spoke badly of Catholics, calling them "Enemies." One of the men wanted to hit the Cantwells, and both told the Cantwells to leave them alone. The Cantwells left immediately.

The police arrested the Cantwells and charged them with violating many Connecticut laws. The trial court convicted, or found them guilty, of breaking two of the laws. The first law said members of a religion could not solicit donations, that is, ask for money, without first getting a license from the state secretary of public welfare. The law allowed the secretary to refuse to give a license to anyone he did not think had a real religion. The Cantwells had not received a license. The second law prohibited a breach of the peace. The trial court said the Cantwells violated this law by angering the Catholic men on the street.

The Cantwells appealed to the state supreme court. They said convicting them of crimes for trying to spread their religion violated the First Amendment right to freedom of religion. The supreme court disagreed and affirmed, or approved, most of the convictions, so the Cantwells appealed to the U.S. Supreme Court.

Limiting the freedom of religion

In a decision agreed on by all nine justices, the Supreme Court overturned the convictions. The Court began by rejecting Connecticut's argument that the First Amendment applies only to the federal government and not to state governments. The Court noted that the Fourteenth Amendment of the U.S. Constitution prevents state governments from taking away a person's liberty, or freedom, in an unlawful manner. According to the Court, one of the freedoms protected by the Fourteenth Amendment is the freedom of religion. That means state governments must recognize the First Amendment right to freedom of religion.

JEHOVAH'S WITNESSES

Jehovah's Witnesses is a form of Christianity that began in Allegheny, Pennsylvania, in 1872. Its members believe that God should be called Jehovah, and that God's followers should be called Witnesses. They got this from the Old Testament Book of Isaiah, which says "Ye are my witnesses, saith Jehovah, and I am God."

Jehovah's Witnesses refuse to follow laws that they believe conflict with the Bible. This has led many Jehovah's Witnesses to challenge laws before the U.S. Supreme Court.

For example, Jehovah's Witnesses obey the Bible's command to spread its teachings by trying to convince others to join the organization. This led to the case of *Cantwell v. Connecticut,* in which Jehovah's Witnesses who went door to door in a mostly Catholic neighborhood were convicted for unlawful solicitation. The Supreme Court overturned the convictions because the state law violated the First Amendment right to freedom of religion. Jehovah's Witnesses' refusal to say the pledge of allegiance in school led to the case of ***West Virginia State Board of Education v. Barnette.*** In this case the Supreme Court decided that being forced to say the pledge of allegiance violated the First Amendment right to freedom of speech.

The Court decided that convicting the Cantwells violated their freedom of religion. The freedom to exercise religion has two parts. One is the freedom to believe, and the other is the freedom to act on that belief. The freedom of religious belief is absolute, meaning the government cannot tell a person what to believe and what not to believe.

The freedom of religious action, however, is not absolute. The government may regulate religious activity for the safety and general well-being of society. The Court said that as long as it does not discriminate against any religion (meaning treat religions differently), Connecticut may pass laws affecting the time, place, and manner in which a person may engage in religious activity, including solicitation.

The Connecticut law did not pass this test. It discriminated by giving the secretary of public welfare the power to give a license to some religions and not to others. The Court said that kind of power was the exact evil the Free Exercise Clause was designed to prevent.

Similarly, the conviction for breach of the peace violated the freedom of religion. The Cantwells did not pose a danger to society by preaching their religion on the street, where they had a right to be. Convicting people for breach of the peace when they peacefully try to spread their religion is unconstitutional under the First Amendment.

Cantwell's legacy

The Bill of Rights protects U.S. citizens from having their rights violated by the federal government. In 1940 it still wasn't clear whether state and local governments had to recognize the individual rights contained in the Bill of Rights. *Cantwell* was part of an important trend that, today, requires state and local governments to recognize almost all of the freedoms laid out in the Bill of Rights, including the First Amendment guarantee of freedom of religion.

Suggestions for further reading

Evans, J. Edward. *Freedom of Religion.* Minneapolis, MN: Lerner Publications Company, 1990.

Farish, Leah. *The First Amendment: Freedom of Speech, Religion, and the Press.* Hillside, NJ: Enslow Publishers, Inc., 1998.

Gay, Kathlyn. *Church and State: Government and Religion in the United States.* Brookfield, CT: Millbrook Press, 1992.

Hirst, Mike. *Freedom of Belief.* New York, NY: Franklin Watts, 1997.

Klinker, Philip A. *The First Amendment.* Englewood Cliffs, NJ: Silver Burdett Press, 1991.

Sherrow, Victoria. *Freedom of Worship.* Brookfield, CT: Millbrook Press, 1997.

Minersville School District v. Gobitis 1940

Petitioners: Minersville School District, et al.

Respondents: Walter Gobitis, et al.

Petitioners' Claim: That requiring school students to say the pledge of allegiance does not violate the First Amendment freedom of religion.

Chief Lawyer for Petitioners: Joseph W. Henderson

Chief Lawyers for Respondents: George K. Gardner and Joseph R. Rutherford

Justices for the Court: Hugo Lafayette Black, William O. Douglas, Felix Frankfurter (writing for the Court), Charles Evans Hughes, James Clark McReynolds, Frank Murphy, Stanley Forman Reed, Owen Josephus Roberts

Justices Dissenting: Harlan Fiske Stone

Date of Decision: June 3, 1940

Decision: The Court upheld the law requiring students to salute the flag.

Significance: In 1940, while America was being pulled into World War II, the Supreme Court made national loyalty more important than the freedom of religion. Three years later, however, the Court decided that forcing students to say the pledge of allegiance violates the First Amendment freedom of speech.

Minersville School District v. Gobitis

Freedom of religion in America suffered a loss in *Minersville School District v. Gobitis*. The case began around 1940 in Minersville, Pennsylvania, where the school board required teachers and students to salute the American flag each day.

Lillian and William Gobitis were Jehovah's Witnesses who refused to salute the flag. Jehovah's Witnesses is a form of Christianity that makes obedience to the Bible more important than following the laws of government. Jehovah's Witnesses believe that saluting the American flag violates the Bible's command not to worship anyone or anything except God.

The Minersville school district expelled the Gobitis children from school for their refusal to salute the flag. Their parents enrolled them in private school, but it cost too much for the family to afford. The Gobitis family decided to send the children back to public school, and their father filed a lawsuit to prevent the Minersville school district from forcing the children to say the pledge of allegiance. Mr. Gobitis got the order he wanted from the trial court, so Minersville appealed to the U.S. Supreme Court.

Country before religion

In an 8–1 decision, the U.S. Supreme Court reversed and ruled in favor of the school district. Writing for the Court, Justice Felix Frankfurter said the case was a battle between the freedom of religion and the power of government.

Justice Frankfurter agreed that the freedom of religion is important, and is protected by the First Amendment of the U.S. Constitution, which says that the federal government "shall make no law ... prohibiting the free exercise [of religion]." State and local governments have to obey the First Amendment freedom of religion under the Due Process Clause of the Fourteenth Amendment. The Due Process Clause prevents states from unlawfully taking away a person's life, liberty (or freedom), and property. School boards, such as the Minersville school district, are part of local government. Therefore, they must obey the freedom of religion.

Justice Frankfurter also agreed that the freedom of religion includes the right to choose one's religious beliefs and to reject others. He said that the First Amendment prevents the government from interfering with a person's religious beliefs.

Justice Frankfurter said, however, that the freedom of belief does not excuse people from obeying laws that relate to their duties as American citizens. One of those duties is to have a sense of national unity, which is respect for America as a country of people dedicated to freedom. Justice Frankfurter said that national unity is the government's most important goal. He went so far as to say that without national unity, America would fall apart and be unable to protect the freedom of religion.

When balancing the freedom of religion against the government's interest in creating national unity, the Court decided in favor of national unity. The Court said that school boards could force students to say the pledge of allegiance without violating their freedom of religion.

Where's the freedom of belief?

Justice Harlan Fiske Stone wrote a dissenting opinion, which means that he disagreed with the Court's decision. Justice Stone believed that forcing students to say a pledge that was against their religious beliefs was the very evil the First Amendment was designed to prevent. It was the same as forcing students to say something that they did not believe.

In Justice Stone's opinion, state governments could encourage national unity without interfering with religion by requiring students to study American history. He said that learning about American government and the rights protected under the U.S. Constitution would "tend to inspire patriotism and love of country." Forcing students to say a pledge that offended their religion might destroy national loyalty.

Freedom restored

Historians say *Minersville* was the result of patriotism surrounding World War II. The *Minersville* decision, however, did not last long. Three years later in ***West Virginia State Board of Education v. Barnette*** (1943), Jehovah's Witnesses from West Virginia challenged another school board that forced them to salute the American flag. In that case, the Supreme Court decided that the law violated the First Amendment freedom of speech, which is the right to speak one's mind.

The Supreme Court, however, still rules against the freedom of religion to protect the general welfare of society. For example, in *Employment Division v. Smith* (1990), the Court said that Oregon could prevent Native Americans from using peyote, a drug, in their sacramental ceremonies.

THE PLEDGE OF ALLEGIANCE

The Pledge of Allegiance was written in 1892 to celebrate the 400th anniversary of Christopher Columbus's discovery of America. As published that year in a magazine called *The Youth's Companion,*it said, "I pledge allegiance to my Flag and to the Republic for which it stands—one Nation indivisible—with liberty and justice for all." Later these words were changed three times to write the pledge as it is today. The most controversial change came in 1954, when Congressman Louis Rabaut suggested adding the words "under God" to the pledge. Opponents said the change would violate the separation of church and state. Congress, however, voted to approve the change, and children across America now begin each school day by pledging allegiance to "one Nation under God."

Suggestions for further reading

Evans, J. Edward. *Freedom of Religion.* Minneapolis: Lerner Publications Company, 1990.

Gay, Kathlyn. *Church and State: Government and Religion in the United States.* Brookfield, CT: Millbrook Press, 1992.

Kleeberg, Irene Cumming. *Separation of Church and State.* New York: Franklin Watts, 1986.

Klinker, Philip A. *The First Amendment.* Englewood Cliffs, NJ: Silver Burdett Press, 1991.

Stevens, Leonard A. *Salute! The Case of the Bible vs. the Flag.* New York: Coward, McCann & Geoghegan, Inc., 1973.

Swanson, June. *I Pledge Allegiance.* Minneapolis: Carolrhoda Books, 1990.

Everson v. Board of Education 1947

Petitioner: Arch R. Everson

Respondent: Board of Education of Ewing Township

Petitioner's Claim: That a New Jersey law allowing school boards to pay parents for transporting their children to schools, both public and religious, violated the constitutional separation of church and state.

Chief Lawyers for Petitioner: Edward R. Burke and E. Hilton Jackson

Chief Lawyer for Respondent: William H. Speer

Justices for the Court: Hugo Lafayette Black (writing for the Court), William O. Douglas, Frank Murphy, Stanley Forman Reed, Fred Moore Vinson

Justices Dissenting: Harold Burton, Felix Frankfurter, Robert H. Jackson, Wiley Blount Rutledge

Date of Decision: February 10, 1947

Decision: The New Jersey law was constitutional. It treated all children equally, and it served the general welfare of society by supporting education, not religion.

Significance: The Court's decision defined the meaning of the First Amendment separation of church and state.

Thomas Jefferson first made the observation that church and state should be separated as if by a wall.
Courtesy of the Library of Congress.

Combating religious persecution

When the United States of America declared its independence in 1776, some of its founders wanted to escape the religious persecution that had been widespread in Europe. (Religious persecution is punishment for religious beliefs.) Most Europeans, including British citizens under the Church of England, were forced to be loyal to a state-approved religion. Loyalty meant paying taxes to support the official religion and refusing to follow a different religion. Penalties for violators included fines, jail, torture, and even death.

The United States's earliest leaders fought to keep the country free of these evils. In 1779 future president Thomas Jefferson drafted a Bill for Establishing Religious Freedom in Virginia. In it he wrote "that to compel a man to furnish contributions of money for the propagation [spreading] of opinions which he disbelieves, is sinful and tyrannical."

Six years later, with Jefferson's bill still not enacted, the Virginia legislature tried to pass a law to raise taxes to support Virginia's official church. Future president James Madison expressed his opposition to the law by writing an essay called "Memorial and Remonstrance." In it Madison wrote about the persecution that happens under government-supported religions. Madison's essay helped to defeat the tax bill and to pass Jefferson's Bill for Establishing Religious Freedom in 1786.

FREEDOM OF RELIGION AND THE ESTABLISHMENT CLAUSE

Three years later, as a member of the United States's first Congress under the new U.S. Constitution, Madison drafted the First Amendment for the Bill of Rights. (The Bill of Rights, adopted in 1791, contains the first ten amendments to the U.S. Constitution.) The First Amendment says "Congress shall make no law respecting an establishment of religion, or prohibiting the free exercise thereof." The first part of the amendment, called the Establishment Clause, prevents the government from establishing an official religion or supporting one religion over others. The second part, called the Free Exercise Clause, prevents the government from interfering with a person's right to choose his religious beliefs. The two clauses clashed in *Everson v. Board of Education.*

Fighting taxes for religion

In the 1940s, New Jersey passed a law allowing local school districts to make rules for transporting children to and from school. Following this law, the Board of Education of Ewing Township passed a law to pay parents the money they spent to send their children to public or Catholic Catholicism schools on public buses. The money to pay the parents came from taxes paid by all citizens.

Arch Everson, a resident and taxpayer in Ewing Township, filed a lawsuit. He argued that using tax dollars to help children get to Catholic schools violated the Establishment Clause. The trial court agreed, ruling that the New Jersey and Ewing Township laws were unconstitutional. On appeal, the highest court in New Jersey reversed the decision, ruling that the laws did not violate the Establishment Clause. Everson appealed to the U.S. Supreme Court.

Protecting the freedom of religion

The Supreme Court voted 5–4 to uphold the New Jersey and Ewing Township laws. Writing for the Court, Justice Hugo Lafayette Black discussed the history of religious persecution in Europe and the American colonies. He explained how the First Amendment was designed to avoid such persecution by keeping religion and government separate:

> **The 'establishment of religion' clause of the First Amendment means at least this: Neither a state nor the Federal Government can set up a church. Neither can pass laws which aid one religion, aid all religions, or prefer one religion over another.**

> **Neither can force nor influence a person to go to or to remain away from church against his will or force him to profess a belief or disbelief in any religion. No person can be punished for entertaining or professing religious beliefs or disbeliefs, for church attendance or non-attendance. No tax in any amount, large or small, can be levied to support any religious activities or institutions, whatever they may be called, or whatever form they may adopt to teach or practice religion. Neither a state nor the Federal Government can, openly or secretly, participate in the affairs of any religious organizations or groups and vice versa. In the words of Jefferson, the clause against establishment of religion by law was intended to erect 'a wall of separation between Church and State.'**

This language made it seem as if the Court would rule against the New Jersey laws. After all, Everson had argued that using tax money to send children to Catholic school was aiding religion. The Court said the Establishment Clause prevented the government from passing laws to aid religion.

Justice Black, however, said the tax was not being used to support the Catholic Church. It was being used to transport children to both public and Catholic schools. Black said transportation to school was a public service for the general good of society because it supported education. To give that service to public school children and not Catholic school children would be like giving police protection only to public school children. Justice Black said that would violate the Free Exercise Clause by interfering with the right to attend Catholic school instead of public school. He wrote that the First Amendment requires the government to treat different religions equally and not to treat individual religions unfairly.

Lowering the wall of separation

Four justices dissented, meaning they disagreed with the decision by the majority of the Court. Two of them wrote dissenting opinions. Justice Robert H. Jackson said helping children attend Catholic schools was helping them to become Catholic adults. In that way, the law aided religion and violated the separation of church and state.

Justice Jackson also believed that the Ewing Township law discriminated against other religions. (Discrimination means treating people differently based on some characteristic, such as their religion.) The township law helped only children in public or Catholic schools. It did not pay bus fares for children going to other private schools or to religious schools that were not Catholic. In Jackson's opinion, this was like a law that gave police protection to children going to public and Catholic schools, but not Protestant schools.

Justice Wiley Blount Rutledge also wrote a dissenting opinion. He analyzed James Madison's historical fight against state-supported religions. Justice Rutledge said that when Madison wrote the First Amendment, one of his biggest goals was to outlaw state taxation to support religion. Rutledge believed the New Jersey and Ewing Township laws violated the First Amendment by supporting religion with tax dollars. Rutledge said they were no different from laws using taxes to send children to Sunday school. Rutledge feared that the Court's decision was a wrecking ball that would knock down the wall of separation between church and state.

The battle continues

More than fifty years after the Court's decision in *Everson,* school districts still struggle with the separation of church and state. School districts that want to improve education choices for poor children have created voucher programs. Poor children may use the vouchers to pay to attend private schools instead of public schools. Some of these programs allow the children to use the vouchers to attend religious schools. Because school districts use tax money to cover the cost of the vouchers, some people think they are violating the separation of church and state by aiding religion. The issue may be the subject of another Supreme Court case.

Suggestions for further reading

Evans, J. Edward. *Freedom of Religion.* Minneapolis, MN: Lerner Publications Company, 1990.

Farish, Leah. *The First Amendment: Freedom of Speech, Religion, and the Press.* Hillside, NJ: Enslow Publishers, Inc., 1998.

Gay, Kathlyn. *Church and State: Government and Religion in the United States.* Brookfield, CT: Millbrook Press, 1992.

THOMAS JEFFERSON BUILDS THE WALL

Thomas Jefferson, author of the Declaration of Independence and third president of the United States of America, believed freedom of religion was a basic right of every human being. For Jefferson, protecting that right meant preventing government from being involved in religion. In a letter in 1802 to the Danbury Baptist Association, President Jefferson wrote of the importance of maintaining a "wall of separation between church and state."

The "wall of separation" language does not appear in the U.S. Constitution or the First Amendment. The U.S. Supreme Court, however, uses the language to understand the Establishment Clause in the First Amendment. That clause prevents the government from "respecting an establishment of religion."

Controversy over the "wall of separation" language erupted in 1998. Library of Congress scholar James H. Hutson analyzed Jefferson's letter to the Danbury Baptist Association. Hutson said Jefferson did not mean for the "wall of separation" language to be used to understand or apply the First Amendment Establishment Clause. Instead, Hutson said Jefferson only meant to win support from religious groups in New England. Some people think the "wall of separation" language is making it impossible for the government to pass laws that many Americans want, such as allowing prayer in schools.

Hirst, Mike. *Freedom of Belief.* New York, NY: Franklin Watts, 1997.

Kleeberg, Irene Cumming. *Separation of Church and State.* New York, NY: Franklin Watts, 1986.

Klinker, Philip A. *The First Amendment.* Englewood Cliffs, NJ: Silver Burdett Press, 1991.

Sherrow, Victoria. *Freedom of Worship.* Brookfield, CT: Millbrook Press, 1997.

Engel v. Vitale
1962

Petitioner: Steven L. Engel, et al.

Respondent: William J. Vitale, et al.

Petitioner's Claim: That a New York school district violated the First Amendment by requiring a short prayer to be read before class each morning.

Chief Lawyer for Petitioner: William J. Butler

Chief Lawyer for Respondent: Bertram B. Daiker

Justices for the Court: Hugo Lafayette Black (writing for the Court), William J. Brennan, Jr., Tom C. Clark, William O. Douglas, John Marshall Harlan II, Earl Warren

Justices Dissenting: Potter Stewart (Felix Frankfurter and Byron R. White did not participate)

Date of Decision: June 25, 1962

Decision: Official prayers in public schools are unconstitutional because they violate the separation of church and state.

Significance: The decision prevents public school teachers from leading their students in any religious activity.

Preventing an official religion

For some of the people who left England in the seventeenth and eighteenth centuries to colonize America, the reason was a desire to escape the Church of England. The Church of England was an official church supported by the British government. The British government required its citizens to worship in the Church of England and to say prayers from the Book of Common Prayer. People who followed other religions or said other prayers violated criminal laws and were punished.

The founders of the United States did not want the government to have religious power. They wanted U.S. citizens to be free to choose their own religion. The First Amendment in the Bill of Rights protects this freedom. (The Bill of Rights, adopted in 1791, contains the first ten amendments to the U.S. Constitution.) The First Amendment says, "Congress shall make no law respecting an establishment of religion, or prohibiting the free exercise thereof."

The first part of this amendment, called the Establishment Clause, prevents the government from establishing an official religion or supporting one religion over others. It has been described as creating a "wall of separation between church and state." Although the First Amendment only refers to the federal government, state governments must obey it under the Due Process Clause of the Fourteenth Amendment.

First graders pause for a moment of silent prayer in South Carolina. Reproduced by permission of the Corbis Corporation.

FREEDOM OF RELIGION AND THE ESTABLISHMENT CLAUSE

Prayers in public schools

In the 1960s the school board of New Hyde Park, New York, required all classes to read a short prayer with their teacher before school each day. The prayer said, "Almighty God, we acknowledge our dependence on Thee, and we beg Thy blessings upon us, our parents, our teachers and our Country." The prayer did not come from a specific religion. Students who did not want to say the prayer could either remain silent or leave the room. Teachers could not embarrass students who chose not to participate.

The parents of ten students filed a lawsuit to challenge the prayer. They said it violated the First Amendment guarantee of separation of church and state. The school district disagreed. It said the prayer did not establish an official state religion because it was nondenominational, meaning it did not come from a specific religion. The school district also said the prayer did not violate the Establishment Clause because students could choose not to participate.

The trial court ruled in favor of the school district. The New York Court of Appeals affirmed, which means it approved the trial court's ruling. Steven Engel and the other parents appealed to the U.S. Supreme Court.

Raising the wall of separation

In a 6–1 decision, the Supreme Court ruled against the school district's prayer. Writing for the Court, Justice Hugo Lafayette Black said the school district admitted that the prayer was religious activity. He explained that under the Establishment Clause, "it is no part of the business of government to compose official prayers for any group of the American people to recite as a part of a religious program carried on by government."

Justice Black supported this decision by analyzing history. He told the story of power struggles in England over what prayers to include in the Book of Common Prayer. He also described people who were punished for refusing to say those prayers or to attend the official Church of England. He explained how people who were forced to follow a particular religion came to hate both religion and the government. According to Justice Black, the First Amendment's Establishment Clause was meant to avoid such problems in the United States.

Justice Black rejected the arguments that the prayer was voluntary and nondenominational. He said the Establishment Clause prevents the government from conducting religious activity of any kind.

MILDRED ROSARIO

Mildred Rosario was a sixth grade teacher in the Bronx, New York. On June 8, 1998, as Rosario's students came to class, the principal used the school intercom to ask for a moment of silence for Christopher Lee, a fifth grader who had drowned.

After the silence, a student asked Rosario where Lee was. Rosario said he was in heaven. Rosario's students then asked questions about God and heaven. After giving the students a chance to leave the room Rosario answered the questions. Then she touched her students' foreheads and said a prayer.

After a student complained, the school board fired Rosario. Some people said Rosario clearly violated the law as laid out in the *Engel* ruling and the separation of church and state by praying with her public school students. Others thought Rosario simply was trying to help her children deal with the death of a fellow student. One student complained, "We talk about guns and condoms and they give us condoms to have safe sex on the streets. But we can't talk about the one who made us."

Ignoring the nation's religious heritage?

Justice Potter Stewart wrote a dissenting opinion, which means he disagreed with the Court's decision. Stewart thought the Court raised the wall of separation too high. In fact, said Stewart, the language "wall of separation" appears nowhere in the U.S. Constitution or the First Amendment. It comes from a letter that President Thomas Jefferson wrote to the Danbury Baptist Association in 1802.

In Stewart's opinion, the Establishment Clause only prevents the government from setting up an official religion, like the Church of England. Stewart said that a simple, nondenominational, voluntary school prayer does not establish a state religion. Instead, it allows students to participate in the United States's spiritual heritage.

Stewart described the nation's spiritual heritage as a history of recognizing God's influence in our daily lives. He said presidents from

George Washington to John F. Kennedy had asked for God's blessing when accepting the job of U.S. president. At the beginning of each day in the Supreme Court, the official Crier says, "God save the United States and this Honorable Court." Both the Senate and the House of Representatives open each day with a prayer led by a chaplain or other religious person.

In Stewart's opinion, the Court's decision meant that "the Constitution permits judges and Congressmen and Presidents to join in prayer, but prohibits school children from doing so."

Suggestions for further reading

Evans, J. Edward. *Freedom of Religion.* Minneapolis, MN: Lerner Publications Company, 1990.

Farish, Leah. *The First Amendment: Freedom of Speech, Religion, and the Press.* Hillside, NJ: Enslow Publishers, Inc., 1998.

Gay, Kathlyn. *Church and State: Government and Religion in the United States.* Brookfield, CT: Millbrook Press, 1992.

Hirst, Mike. *Freedom of Belief.* New York, NY: Franklin Watts, 1997.

Kleeberg, Irene Cumming. *Separation of Church and State.* New York, NY: Franklin Watts, 1986.

Klinker, Philip A. *The First Amendment.* Englewood Cliffs, NJ: Silver Burdett Press, 1991.

Sherrow, Victoria. *Freedom of Worship.* Brookfield, CT: Millbrook Press, 1997.

World Book Encyclopedia, 1997 ed., entry on "Religious Education." Chicago, IL: World Book, 1997.

Epperson v. Arkansas 1968

Appellants: Susan Epperson, et al.

Appellee: State of Arkansas

Appellants' Claim: That an Arkansas law that forbade her from teaching the theory of evolution to public school students was unconstitutional.

Chief Lawyer for Appellant: Eugene R. Warren

Chief Lawyer for Appellee: Don Langston, Assistant Attorney General of Arkansas

Justices for the Court: Hugo Lafayette Black, William J. Brennan, Jr., William O. Douglas, Abe Fortas (writing for the Court), John Marshall Harlan II, Thurgood Marshall, Potter Stewart, Earl Warren, Byron R. White

Justices Dissenting: None

Date of Decision: November 12, 1968

Decision: The Arkansas law violated the First Amendment separation of church and state.

Significance: The decision emphasized that governments may not favor one religion over others.

FREEDOM OF RELIGION AND THE ESTABLISHMENT CLAUSE

Evolution v. religion

Clarence Darrow was one of the lawyers in the famous Scopes Monkey Trial, which laid the foundation for Epperson *almost 45 years later.* Courtesy of the Library of Congress.

The theory of evolution, developed by Charles Darwin in the mid-nineteenth century, has created a problem regarding freedom of religion in the United States. Evolution teaches that all living creatures, including humans, evolved, that is, descended, from lower species of life. According to evolution, humans are related to gorillas, chimpanzees, and other ape-like animals.

Many religions, including Christianity, teach a different theory called creationism. This theory, found in the Bible's Book of Genesis, says God created humans as they are today. For some people who believe in creationism, evolution is an attack on their religious beliefs. When evolution began to be taught in public schools in the early twentieth century, some people feared it would turn their children away from Christianity. It angered them that their taxes were supporting public schools that might do this. These people passed laws to prevent teachers from giving lessons on evolution.

The most famous anti-evolution law was the one passed in Tennessee in 1925. It prevented instructors from teaching any theory that denied the story of creation as put forth in the Bible. When John T. Scopes was charged with violating the law, the Tennessee Supreme Court said the law was a valid exercise of the state's power to control what is taught in public schools. The U.S. Supreme Court did not consider the issue until forty-three years later, in *Epperson v. Arkansas.*

Challenging anti-evolution laws

The state of Arkansas passed its own anti-evolution law in 1928. Unlike the one in Tennessee, Arkansas's law did not mention the Bible. It simply made it unlawful for any public school to teach, or to use a textbook that teaches, that humans evolved from lower species of animals. A teacher who violated the law could be fired.

Susan Epperson was a high school biology teacher in Little Rock, Arkansas, in 1965. Up until then, the biology textbook approved by the local school board did not mention evolution. That year, however, the school board approved a new textbook that had a whole chapter on evolution. Epperson did not like the anti-evolution law, but she was worried that she could be fired if she used the textbook.

Epperson filed a lawsuit against the state of Arkansas to challenge the anti-evolution law. The trial court decided in Epperson's favor. It said the law violated the First Amendment right to freedom of speech by preventing teachers from speaking about evolution. The Supreme Court of Arkansas reversed this decision. Like the Tennessee Supreme Court in the Scopes case, the Supreme Court of Arkansas said the anti-evolution law was a valid exercise of the state's power to control what is taught in public schools. Epperson appealed to the U.S. Supreme Court.

Saving science

In a unanimous decision, the U.S. Supreme Court reversed the Arkansas court's ruling and struck down the anti-evolution law. Writing for the Court, Justice Abe Fortas said the anti-evolution law violated the separation of church and state required by the Establishment Clause in the First Amendment. That clause says, "Congress shall make no law respecting an establishment of religion." Although the First Amendment refers only to the federal government, states must obey it under the Due Process Clause of the Fourteenth Amendment.

Fortas said the Establishment Clause means government must remain neutral about religion. Quoting from another case, ***Everson v. Board of Education,*** Fortas said, "Neither [a State nor the Federal Government] can pass laws which aid one religion, aid all religions, or prefer one religion over another."

Fortas said the anti-evolution law favored the Christian theory of creationism found in the Bible's Book of Genesis. Because the law was

THE SCOPES "MONKEY TRIAL"

Evolution was the subject of the famous trial of John T. Scopes in Dayton, Tennessee, in 1925. Scopes taught a lesson on evolution to his high school class on April 24 of that year. Two months earlier, Tennessee had passed a law making it a crime "to teach any theory that denies the story of the divine creation of man as taught in the Bible" and "to teach instead that man has descended from a lower order of animals."

Tennessee charged Scopes with violating the anti-evolution law. Because the theory of evolution teaches that humans are related to ape-like ancestors, the case became known as the "monkey trial." Scopes's legal team included famous trial lawyer Clarence Darrow. By defending Scopes, Darrow fought for the right to teach science in public schools. Prosecutor William Jennings Bryan, who represented the state of Tennessee, said the case was a battle between evolution and Christianity. He said, "If evolution wins in Dayton, Christianity goes."

Christianity won as the jury found Scopes guilty of violating the law. Although the Tennessee Supreme Court reversed Scopes's conviction on a legal technicality, it said the anti-evolution law was legal. It would be another forty-three years before the U.S. Supreme Court, in *Epperson,* ruled against anti-evolution laws like the one in Tennessee.

designed to favor a religion, it violated the Establishment Clause and was unconstitutional.

What about the freedom of religion?

Justice Hugo Lafayette Black wrote a concurring opinion, meaning he agreed with the Court's decision. Justice Black, however, disagreed with the reason for the Court's decision. Black thought the anti-evolution law was too vague, meaning it was too difficult to understand.

Justice Black did not think the law violated the Establishment Clause. In fact, he said that forcing states to allow schools to teach evolution violated the right to freedom of religion. It forces students who believe in creationism to learn about an anti-religious theory. Apparently Justice Black's solution would be to keep both creationism and evolution out of public schools.

The battle continues

This battle between religion and science in public schools did not end after *Epperson.* In 1987 in *Edwards v. Aguillard,* the Supreme Court struck down a law that required public schools to teach creationism along with evolution. It said the law violated the Establishment Clause. In 1999 Kansas deleted evolution from state tests to discourage schools from teaching the subject. Alabama and Nebraska passed laws allowing teachers to discuss theories other than evolution, which probably meant creationism. New Mexico passed a law saying schools could teach only evolution. With the controversy still alive, the issue may be headed for the Supreme Court once again.

Suggestions for further reading

Blake, Arthur. *The Scopes Trial: Defending the Right to Teach.* Brookfield, CT: Millbrook Press, 1994.

Evans, J. Edward. *Freedom of Religion.* Minneapolis, MN: Lerner Publications Company, 1990.

Farish, Leah. *The First Amendment: Freedom of Speech, Religion, and the Press.* Hillside, NJ: Enslow Publishers, Inc., 1998.

Frost-Knappman, Elizabeth, Edward W. Knappman, and Lisa Paddock. *Courtroom Drama: 120 of the World's Most Notable Trials. Vol. 3.* Detroit, MI: UXL, 1998.

Gay, Kathlyn. *Church and State: Government and Religion in the United States.* Brookfield, CT: Millbrook Press, 1992.

Hirst, Mike. *Freedom of Belief.* New York, NY: Franklin Watts, 1997.

Kleeberg, Irene Cumming. *Separation of Church and State.* New York, NY: Franklin Watts, 1986.

Klinker, Philip A. *The First Amendment.* Englewood Cliffs, NJ: Silver Burdett Press, 1991.

McGowan, Tom. *The Great Monkey Trial: Science Versus Fundamentalism in America.* New York, NY: Franklin Watts, 1990.

Moss, Joyce and George Wilson. *Profiles in American History: Significant Events and the People Who Shaped Them.* Vol. 6, *Immigration to Women's Rights and Roles.* Detroit, MI: UXL, 1994.

Sherrow, Victoria. *Freedom of Worship.* Brookfield. CT: Millbrook Press, 1997.

Lemon v. Kurtzman
1971

Appellant: Alton J. Lemon, et al.

Appellee: David H. Kurtzman, Superintendent of Public Instruction of Pennsylvania, et al.

Appellant's Claim: That Rhode Island and Pennsylvania violated the First Amendment by paying the salaries of teachers of secular (non-religious) subjects in private, religious schools.

Chief Lawyer for Appellant: Henry W. Sawyer III

Chief Lawyer for Appellee: J. Shane Cramer

Justices for the Court: Hugo Lafayette Black, Harry A. Blackmun, William J. Brennan, Jr., Warren E. Burger (writing for the Court), William O. Douglas, John Marshall Harlan II, Thurgood Marshall (Rhode Island cases only), Potter Stewart, Byron R. White (Pennsylvania case only)

Justices Dissenting: Byron R. White (Rhode Island cases only)

Date of Decision: June 28, 1971

Decision: State laws allowing such payments violate the First Amendment separation of church and state.

Significance: The decision announced the "Lemon Test," a three-part test for determining whether a law violates the Establishment Clause in the First Amendment.

FREEDOM OF RELIGION AND THE ESTABLISHMENT CLAUSE

In 1925, the U.S. Supreme Court decided that Americans have a constitutional right to send their children to private schools. Many private schools in America are religious. The question arose whether states can give money to private, religious schools to help them operate

Chief Justice Warren E. Burger.
Courtesy of the Supreme Court of the United States.

Answering this question depends on the Establishment Clause of the First Amendment. The clause says, "Congress shall make no law respecting an establishment of religion." Although the First Amendment refers to the federal government, state and local governments must obey it under the Due Process Clause of the Fourteenth Amendment. The Due Process Clause prevents states and local governments from violating a person's right to life, liberty (or freedom), and property.

According to the Supreme Court, the Establishment Clause means government may not pass laws which "aid one religion, aid all religions, or prefer one religion over another." Some people think that this means states cannot give any help to religious schools, because that would be aiding religion. Over the years, however, the Supreme Court decided that states could give general help to religious schools if they give the same help to all schools, public and private. For example, states may help religious schools with bus transportation, school lunches, health services, and secular (non-religious) textbooks. The Supreme Court drew the line, however, in *Lemon v. Kurtzman.*

Tough times

The *Lemon* case involved two different laws, one in Rhode Island and the other in Pennsylvania. The laws allowed Rhode Island and Pennsylvania to help pay the salaries of teachers of secular (non-religious) subjects in religious schools. Both states passed the laws because it was becoming more expensive to operate private schools, and the states wanted to help such schools with their costs.

Alton J. Lemon was a resident and taxpayer in Pennsylvania. He and others filed lawsuits in federal court to challenge the two laws. They said that the laws violated the First Amendment Establishment Clause by aiding the religions that operated the private schools, most of which were Roman Catholic. The federal court dismissed Lemon's case, or threw it out of court, because it did not think Lemon had a valid complaint. Lemon appealed to the U.S. Supreme Court.

The Lemon Test

The Supreme Court ruled in Lemon's favor, deciding that both laws violated the First Amendment Establishment Clause. Writing for the Court, Chief Justice Warren E. Burger admitted that the Establishment Clause does not require a total separation of church and state. Some interaction is allowed, which explains why the states may give general help to religious schools, such as bus transportation and school lunches.

Justice Burger said, however, that there must be a limit to the amount of interaction between government and religion. Justice Burger announced a three-part test for determining if a law is valid under the Establishment Clause. First, the state must have a secular (non-religious) reason for passing the law. Second, the law's main effect must neither help nor hurt religion. Third, the law must not require excessive entanglement, or interaction, between government and religion.

The Court decided that both laws failed under the third part of the Lemon test. The laws allowed the states to help pay the salaries of teachers of secular subjects. To make sure those teachers taught only secular subjects and not religion, the state would have to supervise the schools and the teachers. Justice Burger said that state supervision of religious schools would involve too much interaction between government and religion.

Justice Burger finished his opinion by emphasizing that the Court's decision was not meant to be hostile toward religion or religious schools.

CHIEF JUSTICE WARREN E. BURGER

Warren E. Burger served as the chief justice of the U.S. Supreme Court from 1969 to 1986. Born in St. Paul, Minnesota, Burger attended the University of Minnesota and then graduated in 1931 from the St. Paul College of Law (now Mitchell College of Law). After practicing law for twenty-two years, Burger served as assistant U.S. attorney general under President Dwight D. Eisenhower from 1953 to 1956. He then served on the United States Court of Appeals for the District of Columbia Circuit from 1956 to 1969. President Richard M. Nixon selected Burger to be chief justice in 1969.

On the Supreme Court, Burger was a conservative justice, meaning his decisions usually favored the politics of Republicans instead of Democrats. For example, Justice Burger frequently voted in favor of limiting the power of the Supreme Court and giving more power to state courts. Justice Burger generally supported police and prosecutors instead of people charged with crimes. He also voted in favor of individual property rights and individual freedoms. As in *Lemon v. Kurtzman,* he favored a strong separation of church and state. In one of the Court's most famous decisions, ***Roe v. Wade*** (1973), Justice Burger voted in favor of a woman's constitutional right to have an abortion.

Instead, it was meant to protect religion from becoming controlled by government. He said that under the First Amendment, "religion must be a private matter for the individual, the family, and the institutions of private choice, and that while some involvement and entanglement are inevitable, lines must be drawn."

Where's the freedom of religion?

Justice Byron R. White wrote a dissenting opinion, disagreeing with part of the Court's decision. Justice White said that paying teachers of secular subjects was the same as giving religious schools secular textbooks and other benefits that public schools receive. To deny such help to religious schools was a form of discrimination against religion, which Justice White suggested is not allowed under the First Amendment.

The battle continues

As of 1999, states still struggle with the separation of church and state. Some states that want to improve education choices for poor children have created voucher systems. Poor children may use the vouchers to attend private schools instead of public schools. These programs sometimes allow children to use the vouchers to attend religious schools. Some people think this violates the separation of church and state by aiding religion. The issue may be the subject of another Supreme Court case.

Suggestions for further reading

Evans, J. Edward. *Freedom of Religion.* Minneapolis: Lerner Publications Company, 1990.

Farish, Leah. *The First Amendment: Freedom of Speech, Religion, and the Press.* Hillside, NJ: Enslow Publishers, Inc., 1998.

Gay, Kathlyn. *Church and State: Government and Religion in the United States.* Brookfield, CT: Millbrook Press, 1992.

Hirst, Mike. *Freedom of Belie.f* New York: Franklin Watts, 1997.

Kleeberg, Irene Cumming. *Separation of Church and State.* New York: Franklin Watts, 1986.

Klinker, Philip A. *The First Amendment.* Englewood Cliffs, NJ: Silver Burdett Press, 1991.

Sherrow, Victoria. *Freedom of Worship.* Brookfield, CT: Millbrook Press, 1997.

The Supreme Court: Selections from the Four-Volume Encyclopedia of the American Constitution and Supplement. New York: Macmillan Library Reference USA, 1999.

World Book Encyclopedia, 1997 ed., entry on "Burger, Warren Earl." Chicago: World Book, 1997.

Wisconsin v. Yoder
1972

Petitioner: State of Wisconsin

Respondents: Jonas Yoder, Wallace Miller, Adin Yutzy

Petitioner's Claim: That requiring Amish parents to send their children to public school until sixteen years old did not violate the First Amendment freedom of religion.

Chief Lawyer for Petitioner: John W. Calhoun

Chief Lawyer for Respondents: William B. Ball

Justices for the Court: Harry A. Blackmun, William J. Brennan, Jr., Warren E. Burger (writing for the Court), Thurgood Marshall, Potter Stewart, Byron R. White

Justices Dissenting: William O. Douglas (Lewis F. Powell Jr. and William H. Rehnquist did not participate)

Date of Decision: May 15, 1972

Decision: The Amish parents did not have to obey the Wisconsin law because it interfered with their religion.

Significance: The decision provided a test for balancing the state interest in education against the individual freedom of religion.

The Amish are Christians who first came to America in the mid-1700s. Their religion is based on an agricultural way of life. This means they worship God by farming in small communities of Amish people. On their farms and in their homes and daily lives, most Amish people refuse to use tractors, cars, electricity, and appliances, such as washing machines. Instead they use horses to plow their fields and gas lanterns to light their homes. To wash their clothes they use their hands. The Amish reject modern technology and conveniences in favor of living in harmony with nature and the land. This is an important part of their religion.

The Amish came to America seeking freedom of religion. Freedom of religion is the right to follow the religion of one's choice. The First Amendment of the U.S. Constitution protects this right. It says, "Congress shall make no law respecting an establishment of religion, or prohibiting the free exercise thereof." The second part of this amendment, called the Free Exercise Clause, prevents the government from interfering with a person's right to choose his religious beliefs. Although the First Amendment only refers to the federal government, state governments must obey it under the Due Process Clause of the Fourteenth Amendment. The Due Process Clause prevents states and local governments from violating certain rights related to life, freedom, and property.

School days

Most Amish children only go to school through the eighth grade. They spend the rest of their school days learning how to be part of the Amish community. For boys this usually means learning to be farmers or craftsmen. For girls it means learning to work around the farm and to take care of the home.

State governments, however, want to make sure that children go to school. Educated children can grow up to be working adults. Working adults help states remain strong by earning a living and by paying taxes to the state.

In the 1960s, the state of Wisconsin had a law that forced parents to send their children to public school until they reached sixteen years of age. Three Amish parents refused to obey the Wisconsin law. They kept their fourteen and fifteen-year-old children, who had completed the eighth grade, home from public school to learn how to live as Amish people.

Wisconsin filed criminal charges against the Amish parents, charging them with violating the school attendance law. At trial, the parents argued that the law violated the First Amendment freedom of religion. They said that in high school, their children would learn about worldly values such as money, science, and competition. They would be taught to go to college instead of staying in the Amish community. At the same time, they would not learn the skills they needed to live on a farm as Amish people.

The trial court rejected the parents' defense, found them guilty, and fined them five dollars each. It said that Wisconsin's interest in education was more important than the freedom of religion. The parents appealed to the Supreme Court of Wisconsin. It reversed the trial court's decision and ruled in favor of the Amish. It said that Wisconsin had failed to prove that its interest in education was more important than the freedom of religion. Wisconsin appealed to the U.S. Supreme Court.

The land of the free

In a 6–1 decision, the U.S. Supreme Court ruled in favor of the Amish. Writing for the Court, Chief Justice Warren E. Burger said that Wisconsin obviously had an interest in education, but that interest was not necessarily more important than the freedom of religion. To decide which was more important, Justice Burger used a three-part test.

First he decided if the Amish's religious beliefs were sincere. The answer to that question was "yes." Even Wisconsin agreed to this. For over three hundred years, the Amish had lived in agricultural communities where they worshiped God by living a simple, country lifestyle. They were not making it up to try to avoid school.

Second, Justice Burger decided whether the Wisconsin law interfered with the Amish religion. The answer to that question was also "yes." Attendance at high school would teach Amish children values that would not work in the Amish religious community. In fact, Justice Burger said that if Amish children were forced to go to high school, the Amish way of life might disappear. This would be the worst kind of interference with the freedom of religion.

The third part of the test was balancing Wisconsin's interest in education against the Amish's freedom of religion. Wisconsin argued that education was more important because without it, children would not grow up to be working adults. Justice Burger rejected this argument. Looking at the evidence in the case, he saw that Amish children attended school through the eighth grade, were trained on Amish farms, and grew up to be hard working adults in Amish communities. The one or two years of school they missed by not going until age sixteen did not hurt them or the State of Wisconsin. Therefore, the Court decided that the Amish's religious freedom was more important than Wisconsin's

AMISH EDUCATION

Although Amish children do not attend high school, their parents understand the importance of a basic education. Amish children complete grades one through eight, usually in a private school run by the Amish community. Many of these schools have twenty-five to thirty-five pupils in one room, with one teacher who teaches all eight grades.

The school day begins with a prayer and a Bible reading. Religion, however, is not formally taught. Instead, the students study subjects that most young school children study, such as reading, arithmetic, spelling, grammar, penmanship, history, and geography. Most Amish children also learn both English and German. They learn German because many Amish religious books are written in German.

There are some things missing from the one room Amish schoolhouse. Most Amish children do not study science or sex education. They also do not have official sports, dances, or clubs. They learn to cooperate instead of to compete with each other. Although Amish students are taught obedience and respect, playful pranks and giggles are common in the schoolhouse.

interest in requiring one to two years of additional education past the eighth grade.

Shame on the Court?

Justice William O. Douglas wrote a dissenting opinion, which means he disagreed with the Court's decision. Justice Douglas thought the Court was wrong for two reasons. First, Justice Douglas said the Court did not ask whether the Amish children wanted to go to high school instead of join the Amish community. He emphasized that children have constitutional rights just like adults. If the children want to get a public education and then go to college, they should be allowed to do so. Justice Douglas did not think the Court's decision gave Amish children that choice.

Second, Justice Douglas said that the Free Exercise Clause protects religious beliefs, but not religious actions. If religious activity is harmful, the state can stop it. (For example, people are not allowed to engage in human sacrifices and say it's protected by the freedom of religion.) Justice Douglas said that refusing to send children to school until age sixteen is harmful to the children. He feared that the Court's decision would eventually allow people to do even more harmful things in the name of religious freedom.

Suggestions for further reading

Evans, J. Edward. *Freedom of Religion.* Minneapolis: Lerner Publications Company, 1990.

Farish, Leah. *The First Amendment: Freedom of Speech, Religion, and the Press.* Hillside, NJ: Enslow Publishers, Inc., 1998.

Gale Encyclopedia of Multicultural America, 1995 ed., entry on "Amish." Detroit: Gale Research, 1995.

Gay, Kathlyn. *Church and State: Government and Religion in the United States.* Brookfield, CT: Millbrook Press, 1992.

Hirst, Mike. *Freedom of Belief.* New York: Franklin Watts, 1997.

Israel, Fred L. *The Amish.* New York: Chelsea House Publishers, 1996.

Klinker, Philip A. *The First Amendment.* Englewood Cliffs, NJ: Silver Burdett Press, 1991.

Sherrow, Victoria. *Freedom of Worship.* Brookfield, CT: Millbrook Press, 1997.

County of Allegheny v. American Civil Liberties Union 1989

Petitioners: County of Allegheny, et al.

Respondents: American Civil Liberties Union (ACLU), et al.

Petitioners' Claim: That government holiday displays with a Christian nativity scene and a Jewish menorah did not violate the First Amendment guarantee of separation of church and state.

Chief Lawyer for Petitioners: Peter Buscemi

Chief Lawyer for Respondents: Roslyn M. Litman

Justices for the Court: (Ruling against the Christian nativity scene) Harry A. Blackmun (writing for the Court), William J. Brennan, Jr., Thurgood Marshall, Sandra Day O'Connor, John Paul Stevens. (Ruling in favor of the Jewish menorah) Harry A. Blackmun (writing for the Court), Anthony M. Kennedy, Sandra Day O'Connor, William H. Rehnquist, Antonin Scalia, Byron R. White

Justices Dissenting: (Voting in favor of the Christian nativity scene) Anthony M. Kennedy, William H. Rehnquist, Antonin Scalia, Byron R. White. (Voting against the Jewish menorah) William J. Brennan, Jr., Thurgood Marshall, John Paul Stevens

Date of Decision: July 3, 1989

Decision: By different votes, the Court banned the Christian nativity scene but allowed the Jewish menorah.

Significance: The Court said that government may not sponsor holiday displays that support religion.

FREEDOM OF RELIGION AND THE ESTABLISHMENT CLAUSE

'Tis the season

Associate Justice Harry A. Blackmun. Reproduced by permission of Archive Photos, Inc.

Thanksgiving in November marks the beginning of a holiday season that leads to Christmas, Chanukah, New Year's Day, and other holidays. People of many religions celebrate the season with festive holiday displays.

In Allegheny County, Pennsylvania, the county courthouse celebrated the season by displaying a créche donated by a Roman Catholic organization called the Holy Name Society. A créche is a nativity scene that displays the events surrounding the birth of Jesus Christ. In 1986 the créche had figures of Jesus, Mary, and Joseph, plus shepherds, animals, and wise men. The créche also had a sign for the Holy Name Society (a Catholic group) and a message that said "Glory to God in the Highest."

One block from the courthouse was the City-County Building, which had government offices for both Allegheny County and the city of Pittsburgh, Pennsylvania. During the holiday season, Pittsburgh decorated the entrance to its side of the building with a 45-foot-tall Christmas tree. Beginning in 1982, Pittsburgh added an 18-foot menorah to the display. A menorah is a candleholder that is used to celebrate the Jewish holiday of Chanukah. In 1986 the display had a sign with the following message: "During this holiday season, the city of Pittsburgh salutes liberty. Let these festive lights remind us that we are the keepers of the flame of liberty and our legacy of freedom."

Celebrating holidays or establishing religion?

Not everyone approved of the holiday displays. On December 10, 1986, the Pittsburgh office of the American Civil Liberties Union (ACLU) joined seven residents in filing a lawsuit. They wanted to stop Allegheny County from displaying the créche and Pittsburgh from displaying the menorah. The ACLU said the displays, because they were sponsored by government, violated the Establishment Clause of the First Amendment.

The First Amendment says, "Congress shall make no law respecting an establishment of religion, or prohibiting the free exercise thereof." The first part of this amendment is called the Establishment Clause. It prevents the federal government from supporting religion or favoring one religion over others. State and local governments must obey the Establishment Clause under the Due Process Clause of the Fourteenth Amendment.

The United States adopted the First Amendment to avoid the situation that existed in England before the American Revolution. England had an official religion called the Church of England. British citizens were forced to pay taxes to support the Church of England, to attend its services, and to say prayers approved by the government. The United States's founders did not want anybody to be forced to support an official religion.

In its lawsuit, the ACLU argued that the holiday displays by Allegheny County and Pittsburgh violated the Establishment Clause. The ACLU said the créche showed government support of Christianity and the menorah showed support of Judaism. The trial court ruled in favor of the governments. It said the displays did not support religion, but only celebrated the holiday season. The ACLU appealed to the Third Circuit Court of Appeals. That court reversed the decision and ruled in favor of the ACLU. It said that both displays supported religion, in violation of the Establishment Clause. Allegheny County and Pittsburgh appealed to the U.S. Supreme Court.

A mixed ruling

The Supreme Court reached a decision that confused some observers. It said the créche violated the Establishment Clause, but the menorah with the Christmas tree did not.

Writing for the Court, Justice Harry A. Blackmun explained that the Establishment Clause prevents governments from supporting religion or favoring one religion over others. Justice Blackmun reviewed a similar Supreme Court case called *Lynch v. Donnelley.* That case involved a créche that was part of a large holiday display in the city of Pawtucket, Rhode Island. In *Lynch* the Supreme Court ruled that the créche did not violate the Establishment Clause because it was part of a large display that was secular, which means not religious. The display involved in *Lynch* was secular because it also had Santa Claus, reindeer, a Christmas tree, carolers, and a large banner that said "Seasons Greetings."

Justice Blackmun used the result in *Lynch* to decide *County of Allegheny.* He said the créche displayed by Allegheny County in front of the county courthouse obviously supported Christianity. It had figures showing the events of the birth of Jesus Christ. The scene was not surrounded by any secular, or non-religious, figures. Finally, it had a sign for a Catholic organization and another sign that said "Glory to God in the Highest." Justice Blackmun said that on the whole, the créche showed support for Christianity, and so violated the Establishment Clause.

As for the menorah and the Christmas tree displayed by Pittsburgh, Justice Blackmun admitted that the menorah was a religious object for the Jewish holiday of Chanukah. He decided, however, that Chanukah is both a religious and a secular holiday. Some Jews who are not religious still celebrate Chanukah, just like some people who are not religious still celebrate Christmas. Blackmun said that together, the Christmas tree, the menorah, and the sign about liberty celebrated the secular, non-religious aspects of Christmas and Chanukah. They did not support Christianity or Judaism, and so did not violate the Establishment Clause.

A chorus of opinions

Many justices wrote their own opinions, both agreeing and disagreeing with the decision by the Court. Justice Sandra Day O'Connor agreed that the créche violated the Establishment Clause and the menorah did not. She disagreed, however, that the menorah next to the Christmas tree was not a religious symbol. Instead, Justice O'Connor said that side by side, the Christmas tree and the menorah supported the freedom of religion, which is the right to choose religious beliefs. They did not show government support for one religion over another.

Justice William J. Brennan, Jr. also wrote his own opinion. Justice Brennan believed that both the créche and the menorah violated the Establishment Clause. He said the créche obviously supported

AMERICAN CIVIL LIBERTIES UNION

The American Civil Liberties Union (ACLU) is an organization that defends civil liberties. Civil liberties are the individual rights found in the Bill of Rights, which contains the first ten amendments to the U.S. Constitution. They include the freedom of speech, the freedom of religion, and the right to have a jury trial when accused of a crime.

The ACLU defends civil liberties in three ways. It educates people so they will know their civil liberties. It asks Congress to pass laws that protect civil liberties. When the ACLU thinks there has been a serious violation of somebody's civil liberties, it files a lawsuit to correct the violation.

Since the ACLU was founded in 1920, it has participated in many important and controversial cases, often taking unpopular stands. In 1930 it organized a team of lawyers to defend John T. Scopes, who faced criminal charges in Tennessee for teaching the theory of evolution. In 1954 it participated in the landmark case of ***Brown v. Board of Education,*** in which the U.S. Supreme Court outlawed segregation, the practice of separating racial groups in different public schools. In 1977 the ACLU defended the right of American Nazis to march peacefully in Skokie, Illinois.

When asked how it can defend a group like the Nazis, ACLU officials said the organization defends the right of people to express their views, not the views that they express.

Christianity and the menorah obviously supported Judaism. Putting the menorah next to a Christmas tree did not take away from its religious message. In Brennan's opinion, the Establishment Clause prevents government support for any religion, and both displays violated the clause.

Justice Anthony M. Kennedy had the opposite opinion. He did not think either display violated the Establishment Clause. Justice Kennedy said the Establishment Clause was designed to prevent the government from setting up an official religion, such as the Church of England. He said it was not designed to prevent the government from recognizing that religion plays an important role in the lives of Americans. Justice Kennedy pointed out that Congress begins every day with a prayer. The Supreme Court crier opens every session by saying "God save the United States and this honorable Court." U.S. money even has "In God We Trust" written on it. Kennedy believed the holiday displays simply recognized the role of religion in the holiday season. They did not force U.S. citizens to follow a specific religion.

Suggestions for further reading

Evans, J. Edward. *Freedom of Religion.* Minneapolis, MN: Lerner Publications Company, 1990.

Farish, Leah. *The First Amendment: Freedom of Speech, Religion, and the Press.* Hillside, NJ: Enslow Publishers, Inc., 1998.

Gay, Kathlyn. *Church and State: Government and Religion in the United States.* Brookfield, CT: Millbrook Press, 1992.

Hirst, Mike. *Freedom of Belief.* New York, NY: Franklin Watts, 1997.

Kleeberg, Irene Cumming. *Separation of Church and State.* New York: Franklin Watts, 1986.

Klinker, Philip A. *The First Amendment.* Englewood Cliffs, NJ: Silver Burdett Press, 1991.

Sherrow, Victoria. *Freedom of Worship.* Brookfield, CT: Millbrook Press, 1997.

Lee v. Weisman
1992

Petitioners: Robert E. Lee, et al.

Respondent: Daniel Weisman

Petitioners' Claim: That nonsectarian (not associated with a specific religion) prayers at public graduation ceremonies do not violate the First Amendment separation of church and state.

Chief Lawyer for Petitioners: Charles J. Cooper

Chief Lawyer for Respondent: Sandra A. Blanding

Justices for the Court: Harry A. Blackmun, Anthony M. Kennedy (writing for the Court), Sandra Day O'Connor, David H. Souter, John Paul Stevens

Justices Dissenting: William H. Rehnquist, Antonin Scalia, Clarence Thomas, Byron R. White

Date of Decision: June 24, 1992

Decision: Prayers at public school graduation ceremonies violate the Establishment Clause of the First Amendment.

Significance: The decision ended an American tradition that dates back to 1868.

When American colonists left England in the seventeenth and eighteenth centuries, some were escaping the Church of England. The Church of England was an official church supported by the British government. The British government required its citizens to worship in the Church of England and to say approved prayers from its Book of Common Prayers.

If people followed other religions or said other prayers, they violated criminal laws and were punished.

America's founders did not want the government to have religious power. They wanted every American to be free to choose his or her own religion. The First Amendment in the Bill of Rights protects this freedom. (The Bill of Rights, adopted in 1791, contains the first ten amendments to the U.S. Constitution.) The First Amendment says, "Congress shall make no law respecting an establishment of religion, or prohibiting the free exercise thereof."

FREEDOM OF RELIGION AND THE ESTABLISHMENT CLAUSE

The first part of this amendment, called the Establishment Clause, prevents the government from establishing an official religion or supporting one religion over others. It has been described as creating a "wall of separation between church and state." Although the First Amendment only refers to the federal government, state and local governments must obey it under the Due Process Clause of the Fourteenth Amendment. The Due Process Clause prevents state and local governments from unlawfully taking away a person's right to life, liberty (or freedom) or property.

The decision in Lee v. Weisman *eliminated the long-time tradition of prayers at public high school graduations.* Reproduced by permission of Jeffrey Meyers.

Religion in public schools

Lee v. Weisman

Because state and local governments run public schools, the schools must also obey the Establishment Clause. The U.S. Supreme Court has decided that the Establishment Clause prohibits public schools from using official prayers or Bible readings during the school day. In 1992, the Court had to decide the fate of prayers at public school graduation ceremonies.

For many years, middle and high schools principals in Providence, Rhode Island, invited religious leaders to say short prayers at their graduation ceremonies. The school system even had a pamphlet telling religious leaders to make the prayers nonsectarian, meaning general instead of from a specific religion. The prayers were a simple yet meaningful way for graduating students to acknowledge God's role in helping them get through school and prepare for life as an adult.

In 1989, Deborah Weisman was ready to graduate from the Nathan Bishop Middle School of Providence. The school planned to have Rabbi Leslie Gutterman say two short, nonsectarian prayers at the ceremony. Deborah and her father, Daniel Weisman, did not want to hear any prayers at graduation. Four days before the ceremony, Daniel Weisman filed a lawsuit to prevent the school from using any prayers. He argued that prayers at public school ceremonies violated the separation of church and state that was required by the Establishment Clause.

The trial court denied Weisman's request because there was not enough time to consider it, and Rabbi Gutterman prayed at Deborah's ceremony. The court, however, agreed to decide whether Providence schools could use prayers at future graduation ceremonies, such as when Deborah graduated from high school. The court decided against the prayers, and middle school principal, Robert E. Lee, appealed to the U.S. Court of Appeals for the First Circuit. That court also ruled against the prayers, and Lee appealed to the U.S. Supreme Court.

Pomp and circumstance

In a close decision, the Supreme Court voted 5–4 against the prayers. Writing for the Court, Justice Anthony M. Kennedy admitted that for many Americans, God's role in life should be mentioned at a ceremony as important as graduation. Justice Kennedy said, however, that public schools must obey the First Amendment Establishment Clause.

Justice Kennedy reviewed earlier Supreme Court cases involving prayer in school. In one of the most famous, ***Engel v. Vitale*** (1962), the

RELIGION IN SCHOOL

The separation of church and state faces constant opposition from Americans who want religion in public schools. With drugs, guns, and crime becoming bigger school problems, some Americans think religion in school would be a good thing.

This led the U.S. House of Representatives in June 1998 to consider a constitutional amendment called the Religious Freedom Amendment. The amendment would have allowed prayer in public schools, but it failed to receive the votes it needed to pass. Over the following year, America watched in horror as school shootings, such as the one at Columbine High School in Colorado, became regular news items. The House of Representatives responded by passing a bill, or proposed law, in June 1999 to allow states to post the Ten Commandments in public schools.

The House's bill created a lot of controversy. Some Americans argued that the bill was necessary to stop the spread of violence. Some politicians called the Ten Commandments the basis of American civilization. Others said that posting them in public schools would violate the First Amendment separation of church and state. They asked whose Ten Commandments should be posted, the Catholic, Protestant, or Jewish version?

Supreme Court said that the Establishment Clause prohibits schools from using nonsectarian prayers at the beginning of each day, even if they are voluntary. The Court ruled that because the Establishment Clause prevents the government from favoring religion, prayers in school were not acceptable.

Using the result in *Engel,* Justice Kennedy said that prayers at public school graduation ceremonies also violated the Establishment Clause. Although students do not have to attend graduation to get their diplomas, the graduation ceremony is one of life's most important events. Students should not be forced to listen to prayers at such ceremonies. It did not matter that Rabbi Gutterman said prayers that were nonsectarian. Justice

Kennedy said that the purpose of the Establishment Clause is to prevent the government from favoring any religion, whether specific or nonsectarian.

Death of a tradition

Justice Antonin Scalia wrote a dissenting opinion, meaning he disagreed with the Court's decision. Justice Scalia said that the Establishment Clause prevents the government from setting up an official religion or forcing people to follow a particular religion. In Justice Scalia's opinion, it does not prevent the government from continuing the American tradition of using nonsectarian prayers at public celebrations.

Justice Scalia described the history of this tradition. The Declaration of Independence mentions God's role in life. Most presidents starting with George Washington have said a short prayer when accepting the nation's highest job. Many of them have declared a national day of Thanksgiving, a day for offering thanks to God for everything we have in America. Justice Scalia also explained that Congress opens each session with a short prayer, and the Supreme Court crier begins each session by saying "God save the United States and this honorable Court."

For Justice Scalia, saying a short, nonsectarian prayer at graduation is part of an American tradition. In fact, looking at the prayers Rabbi Gutterman said at Deborah Weisman's graduation, Scalia said, "they are so characteristically American they could have come from the pen of George Washington or Abraham Lincoln himself."

Suggestions for further reading

Evans, J. Edward. *Freedom of Religion.* Minneapolis: Lerner Publications Company, 1990.

Farish, Leah. *The First Amendment: Freedom of Speech, Religion, and the Press.* Hillside, NJ: Enslow Publishers, Inc., 1998.

Gay, Kathlyn. *Church and State: Government and Religion in the United States.* Brookfield, CT: Millbrook Press, 1992.

Hirst, Mike. *Freedom of Belief.* New York: Franklin Watts, 1997.

Kleeberg, Irene Cumming. *Separation of Church and State.* New York: Franklin Watts, 1986.

Klinker, Philip A. *The First Amendment.* Englewood Cliffs, CT: Silver Burdett Press, 1991.

Lawton, Kim A. "Do Students Have a Prayer?" *Christianity Today,* June 21, 1993.

Mitchell, Alison and Frank Bruni. "Guns and Schools." *New York Times,* June 18, 1999.

Seelye, Katharine Q. "House Rejects School Prayer Amendment to Constitution." *New York Times,* June 5, 1998.

Sherrow, Victoria. *Freedom of Worship.* Brookfield, CT: Millbrook Press, 1997.

Church of Lukumi Babalu Aye, Inc. v. City of Hialeah 1993

Petitioner: Church of Lukumi Babalu Aye, Inc.

Respondent: City of Hialeah

Petitioner's Claim: That city laws prohibiting animal sacrifices during religious ceremonies violated the First Amendment freedom of religion.

Chief Lawyer for Petitioner: Douglas Laycock

Chief Lawyer for Respondent: Richard G. Garrett

Justices for the Court: Harry A. Blackmun, Anthony M. Kennedy (writing for the Court), Sandra Day O'Connor, William H. Rehnquist, Antonin Scalia, David H. Souter, John Paul Stevens, Clarence Thomas, Byron R. White

Justices Dissenting: None

Date of Decision: June 11, 1993

Decision: The laws violated the freedom of religion.

Significance: The decision is a recent reminder that laws may not target religious activity with unfair treatment.

Santería is a religion that developed among African slaves in Cuba in the 1800s and then spread to the United States in 1959. Santeros, as the followers are called, combine a traditional African religion with Roman Catholicism. They use Catholic saints to worship African spirits called *orishas*. Santeros believe orishas help them follow their destiny, and that orishas need animal sacrifices to live. This means animal sacrifices are an important part of the Santería religion. Santeros usually worshiped in private because in Cuba they were persecuted, or punished, for practicing their religion.

Associate Justice Anthony M. Kennedy.
Reproduced by permission of Archive Photos, Inc.

In April 1987, a Santería church called the Church of Lukumi Babalu Aye leased land in the city of Hialeah, Florida. The church planned to build a house of worship, school, cultural center, and museum. The president of the church, Ernesto Pichardo, said that the church's goal was to bring the practice of the Santería faith, including animal sacrifices, into the open.

Some people in Hialeah did not want Santeros to practice animal sacrifices in the city. They said animal sacrifices were offensive to human morals and a cruelty to animals. They also said animal sacrifices would create health hazards in the city. The Hialeah city council passed laws, called ordinances, prohibiting animal sacrifices for religious ceremonies.

The church filed a lawsuit against the city. It argued that the city ordinances violated the Free Exercise Clause in the First Amendment by preventing Santeros from practicing their religion. The Free Exercise Clause prevents the government from enacting laws that prohibit the "free exercise" of religion.

The trial court ruled against the church. It said that even if the laws interfered with the Santería religion, the laws were valid because they served the health and general well-being of the city. The U.S. Court of Appeals for the Eleventh Circuit affirmed, meaning approved, the trial court's decision, and the church appealed to the U.S. Supreme Court.

No religious persecution in America

With a unanimous decision, the Supreme Court reversed the Eleventh Circuit's decision and ruled in favor of the Church of Lukumi Babalu Aye. Writing for the Court, Justice Anthony M. Kennedy said that the Free Exercise Clause prevents the City of Hialeah from stopping religious practice. For a law to be valid under the Free Exercise Clause, it must satisfy two tests. First, it must be neutral, meaning it must apply to everyone and not just to a religion. Second, it must serve an important government interest while restricting religion as little as possible.

Hialeah's ordinances failed under both tests. The ordinances were not neutral as they did not apply generally to everyone. People still could kill animals for food. Jewish people could kill animals to make kosher food. Sportsmen were allowed to fish and hunt for animals to kill. The

Santerians practice a religion that combines a Cuban form of voodoo with Roman Catholicism. Reproduced by permission of Archive Photos, Inc.

SANTERÍA

Santeríaa is a religion with its roots in Africa. In the nineteenth century, the Yoruba people from West Africa were brought to Cuba to work as slaves in the sugar industry. In Cuba they combined their African religion with Roman Catholicism to create Santería, a Spanish word that means "the way of the saints." Santeros use figures of Catholic saints to worship Yoruba spirits called orishas. Santeros believe orishas help them follow a destiny God has chosen. During a revolution in Cuba in 1959, many Santeros left the island to settle in Venezuela, Puerto Rica, and the United States. As of 1999, Santeros in the United States live mainly in southern Florida and New York City.

only people who were not allowed to kill animals were Santeros during religious ceremonies. Laws that treat religion unfairly are not neutral.

The ordinances also failed to restrict religion as little as possible to serve a valid governmental interest. The city said its main reason for passing the laws was to protect the city from health hazards. The Court said that the city could do that by requiring the Santeros to dispose of sacrificed animals in a safe and healthy manner. The city did not have to ban sacrifices altogether in order to keep the city healthy. After all, people slaughtered cattle and hogs to eat, yet still kept the city healthy.

Because the laws were not neutral, and because they restricted the Santería religion too much, the Court ruled that the laws were unconstitutional under the First Amendment. The Church of Lukumi Babalu Aye was allowed to practice its religion, including animal sacrifices, without being punished by the government.

Suggestions for further reading

Evans, J. Edward. *Freedom of Religion.* Minneapolis: Lerner Publications Company, 1990.

Farish, Leah. *The First Amendment: Freedom of Speech, Religion, and the Press.* Hillside, NJ: Enslow Publishers, Inc., 1998.

Gay, Kathlyn. *Church and State: Government and Religion in the United States.* Brookfield, CT: Millbrook Press, 1992.

Greenhouse, Linda. "Court, Citing Religious Freedom, Voids a Ban on Animal Sacrifice." *New York Times,* June 12, 1993.

Hirst, Mike. *Freedom of Belief.* New York: Franklin Watts, 1997.

Klinker, Philip A. *The First Amendment.* Englewood Cliffs, NJ: Silver Burdett Press, 1991.

Rohter, Larry. "Santeria Faithful Hail Court Ruling." *New York Times,* June 13, 1993.

Sherrow, Victoria. *Freedom of Worship.* Brookfield CT: Millbrook Press, 1997.

World Religions, New York: Macmillan Library Reference USA, 1987.

The First Amendment says "Congress shall make no law . . . abridging the freedom of speech." Along with the First Amendment freedoms of religion, assembly, and the press, the freedom of speech is part of the larger freedom of expression. It is the right to think, believe, and learn what we want, share our thoughts with others, and listen to what others have to say.

Throughout history governments have restricted the freedom of speech. They feared that the free flow of ideas would threaten their power and lead to social disorder. In 1621 free speech restrictions in England by King James I led Parliament to issue a declaration of freedoms. During the French Revolution in 1789, the French Declaration of the Rights of Man included the freedom of expression. When Americans drafted a Bill of Rights for the new U.S. Constitution in 1789, this history influenced them to include the freedom of speech in the First Amendment. (Adopted in 1791, the Bill of Rights contains the first ten constitutional amendments.)

The Bill of Rights applies only to the federal government, so state governments did not have to recognize freedom of speech for a long time.

Then in 1868, after the American Civil War (1861–65) ended, the United States adopted the Fourteenth Amendment. Part of it says states may not "deprive any person of life, liberty, or property without due process of law." In *Gitlow v. New York* (1925), the U.S. Supreme Court decided that free speech is a "liberty" that is protected by the Fourteenth Amendment. Because of this, state governments today must allow freedom of speech.

The arguments for free speech

The U.S. Constitution protects free speech for many reasons. Free speech is essential for people to develop as individuals. It allows people to learn and explore what they want, which allows each person to be unique and special. It also spreads knowledge to more people, which helps Americans become better informed.

Free speech is also essential to the U.S. form of government. The United States's political leaders are elected by the people. Citizens could not make intelligent decisions on election day if they could not learn about the various candidates. Free speech also helps Americans stay informed about what their political leaders are doing, both good and bad.

Finally, free speech is essential for social change. For example, slavery was legal when the United States was formed. It took decades of discussion about the evils of slavery to spark the American Civil War, which ended slavery. If the government had been allowed to stop people from talking about the evils of slavery, it might have taken even longer to build a strong opposition.

Many types of speech

Supreme Court cases deal with three kinds of speech: pure, symbolic, and speech plus conduct. Pure speech is the most basic kind of First Amendment speech. It covers words that are written or spoken. Pure speech includes books, magazines, newspapers, radio, television, the Internet, motion pictures, public speeches, and much more. Pure speech is so important that the First Amendment prevents the government from regulating it based on its content, meaning the message it contains. For example, a state could not pass a law preventing people from writing books about legal ways to avoid taxes.

This is true even when speech is hateful or offensive. For example, in ***Brandenburg v. Ohio*** (1969), the Ku Klux Klan held a rally to protest against the federal government. During the rally, Klansmen shouted racist language about African Americans and said all Jews should be sent to Israel. Although the language was offensive, the Supreme Court said it was protected by the constitutional guarantee of freedom of speech. In the 1990s laws designed to prevent hate crimes often violated the First Amendment by prohibiting such hateful speech.

The second kind of speech is symbolic speech. Neither written nor spoken, symbolic speech involves action that is meant to convey a message. For example, in ***Tinker v. Des Moines Independent Community School District*** (1969), the Supreme Court decided that students who wore black armbands to school to protest the Vietnam War (1954-1975) were exercising their right to free speech.

The most controversial cases concerning symbolic speech have involved the American flag. In 1898 Pennsylvania started a trend by passing a law that made it a crime to damage the American flag. Other states followed with their own laws, including laws about other flags. In 1919 opposition to communism led California to pass a law banning displays of red-colored flags. In *Stromberg v. California* (1931), the Supreme Court overturned the law, saying it violated the right to engage in symbolic speech. It was not until *Texas v. Johnson* (1989), however, that the Court finally decided that flag burning is a form of symbolic speech protected by the First Amendment. The Court said that government "may not prohibit the expression of an idea simply because society finds the idea itself offensive or disagreeable."

The third kind of speech is called speech plus conduct. It combines the exercise of free speech with some course of conduct. This makes it hard to distinguish from symbolic speech. For instance, ***United States v. O'Brien*** (1968) involved Vietnam War opponents who burned their military draft cards—documents they were required to carry in preparation for being called into military service. The Supreme Court said that even though the protesters were exercising free speech, the government could outlaw the conduct of burning draft cards. The protesters still could oppose the military draft with other forms of speech.

No coverage for obscenity

Some speech is not protected by the First Amendment. Obscenity has little value and does not meaningfully contribute to the free flow of ideas. Obscenity, however, is hard to define. It generally means material of a sexual nature that is offensive. But different people are offended by different things. For example, some people would be offended by an artist's painting of nude people having sex, while others would consider the painting to have artistic value. To handle obscenity cases, the Supreme Court decides whether the material is sexually offensive and lacks literary, artistic, political, or scientific value. If so, the material is not protected by the First Amendment.

Fighting words also are not covered by the right to freedom of speech. ***Chaplinsky v. New Hampshire*** (1942) concerned a Jehovah's Witness who created a public disturbance by calling a city marshal a "damned racketeer" and a "damned Fascist." Chaplinsky was convicted under a state law making it a crime to call another person offensive names in public. The Supreme Court decided the conviction did not violate the freedom of speech guarantee. It said the First Amendment does not protect "fighting words," words that by themselves tend to cause injury or an immediate breach of the peace.

Not an absolute freedom

The First Amendment says Congress shall make "no law" interfering with free speech. Some people think "no law" means what it says, that government cannot pass any laws that interfere with free speech. Most people, however, do not think "no law" means "no law." Instead, they believe government can interfere with speech to serve an important governmental purpose.

The Supreme Court agrees with the latter view, that the freedom of speech is not absolute. The Court has not, however, been able to create a consistent test for determining whether a law violates freedom of speech. Instead, it has created many tests over the years to handle different situations. The best one can do to understand freedom of speech is to study some of these tests.

Clear and present danger test

In U.S. history, federal and state governments have passed sedition laws to prevent people from speaking against the government. Sedition laws were designed to foster respect for the government and to prevent people from starting a violent revolution. In ***Schenck v. United States*** (1919), the U.S. Supreme Court decided whether the federal Sedition Act of

1918 violated freedom of speech. Passed during World War I (1914–18), the Sedition Act made it a crime to say anything to cause disrespect for the U.S. government.

Schenck, the secretary of the Socialist Party in America, was convicted under the Sedition Act for distributing pamphlets urging people to resist the military draft. The Supreme Court ruled that Schenck's conviction did not violate freedom of speech. In the Court's decision, Justice Oliver Wendell Holmes, Jr., made a famous observation about freedom of speech. He said free speech is not absolute because a person is not allowed to shout "fire" in a crowded theater when there is no fire. In other words, the government may punish words that create a "clear and present danger" of causing evils the government has a right to prevent. Because Congress had a right to stop people from avoiding the military draft, punishing Schenck for encouraging such conduct did not violate the First Amendment.

It is important to realize that sedition laws usually are enacted during times of great national stress, such as war. Generally, the First Amendment says government may not prevent people from speaking against war.

A balancing act

Besides protecting itself, government has many other reasons to pass laws that restrict speech. Often it is trying to protect a societal interest, such as a defendant's right to a fair trial or the public's interest in fair elections. If the Supreme Court finds the interest compelling, meaning very important, it will balance the interest against freedom of speech to decide which is more important. Sometimes it asks if the government has restricted speech as little as necessary to serve the compelling interest. The balancing test makes it hard to predict which way the Court will rule in a particular case.

For instance, in *Ward v. Rock Against Racism* (1989), Rock Against Racism began holding concerts in New York's Central Park in 1979. After people complained about the volume, New York City's government decided to require bands to use a sound system and sound engineer approved by the city so it could control the noise. Rock Against Racism filed a lawsuit saying that stopping the bands from using their own equipment and engineers violated freedom of speech. They said it prevented bands from making the music sound the way they wanted. The

Supreme Court balanced the freedom of speech against the city's interest in controlling noise to rule in favor of New York City.

Commerce, jails, and schools

The government does not always have to show a compelling interest to restrict speech. The Supreme Court has decided that certain categories of speech deserve less protection than others. For a long time, commercial speech, such as advertising, did not receive any protection. Today the Court says commercial speech is protected by the First Amendment. Government, however, can regulate commercial speech as long as it does not stop it.

Speech in prison also receives less First Amendment protection. The Supreme Court says that government has an interest in maintaining order in jails. It also says criminals have given up the full right to free speech by breaking the law. This means the government can restrict speech in jails more than out in public.

The same thing happens in schools. The Supreme Court has ruled that students do not give up their freedom of speech by going to school. Schools, however, have an interest in maintaining order and discipline while teaching good values. This means schools can restrict speech more than other settings. For example, in ***Bethel School District No. 403 v. Fraser*** (1986), a high school student named Matthew Fraser gave an assembly speech nominating a fellow student for class vice president. He described the student using language that had a double meaning that referred to sexual intercourse.

Bethel High School suspended Fraser for using language that was obscene. The U.S. Supreme Court ruled that the suspension did not violate the right to freedom of speech, even though Fraser would have been free to speak as he did outside school or in another place. The Court said, "A high school assembly or classroom is no place for a sexually explicit monologue." The school was allowed to enforce the "fundamental values of public school education."

Time, place, and manner restrictions

Restrictions on speech in public are much less severe. In fact, the Supreme Court has ruled that government must allow people to exercise free speech in public places. Cities, for example, cannot prohibit speech in parks, on sidewalks, or in other areas where people traditionally gather to express themselves.

Government, however, is allowed to regulate speech for public convenience and safety. In *Cox v. New Hampshire* (1941), sixty-eight Jehovah's Witnesses were convicted for marching in a parade without getting a permit. They argued that the permit requirement violated their freedom of speech. The Supreme Court disagreed. It said that as long as government issues permits fairly to all persons, government may control the time, place, and manner of free speech for public convenience and safety. This rule, for example, allows the government to prevent someone from using a loudspeaker on neighborhood streets in the middle of the night.

Suggestions for further reading

Evans, J. Edward. *Freedom of Speech.* Minneapolis, MN: Lerner Publications, Inc., 1990.

Farish, Leah. *The First Amendment: Freedom of Speech, Religion, and the Press.* Hillside, NJ: Enslow Publishers, Inc., 1998.

King, David C. *The Right to Speak Out.* Brookfield, CT: Millbrook Press, 1997.

Klinker, Philip A. *The First Amendment.* Englewood Cliffs, NJ: Silver Burdett Press, 1991.

Pascoe, Elaine. *Freedom of Expression: The Right to Speak Out in America.* Brookfield, CT: Millbrook Press, 1992.

Steele, Philip, Philip Skele, and Penny Clarke. *Freedom of Speech?* New York: Franklin Watts, 1997.

Zeinert, Karen. *Free Speech: From Newspapers to Music Lyrics.* Hillside, NJ: Enslow Publishers, Inc., 1995.

Schenck v. United States
1919

Appellant: Charles T. Schenck

Appellee: United States

Appellant's Claim: That his speech was protected by the First Amendment.

Chief Lawyers for Appellant: Henry J. Gibbons, Henry John Nelson

Chief Lawyers for Appellee: John Lord O'Brian

Justices for the Court: Louis D. Brandeis, John Hessin Clarke, William Rufus Day, Oliver Wendell Holmes (writing for the Court), Charles Evans Hughes, Joseph McKenna, James Clark McReynolds, Willis Van Devanter, Edward Douglass White

Justices Dissenting: None

Date of Decision: March 3, 1919

Decision: Schenck's speech was not protected by the First Amendment and his conviction under the Espionage Act was upheld

Significance: This case marked the first time the Supreme Court ruled directly on the extent to which the U.S. government may limit speech. The opinion written by Justice Oliver Wendell Holmes produced two of that famous justice's most memorable and most often quoted statements on the law.

Associate Justice Oliver Wendell Holmes first used the term "clear and present danger."
Courtesy of the Library of Congress.

The Socialist party opposes the draft

On June 15, 1917, just after the United States entered World War I (1914–18), Congress passed the Espionage Act. This made it a federal crime to hinder the nation's war effort. The law was passed shortly after the Conscription Act that was passed on May 18, 1917. The Conscription Act enabled the government to draft men for military service.

At this time a political organization existed in America called the Socialist party. It pushed for government ownership of factories, railroads, iron mines, and such. At a meeting at the party's headquarters in Philadelphia, Pennsylvania, in 1917, its leaders decided to print 15,000 leaflets. The leaflets were to go to men who had been drafted. The pamphlets included words from the first part of the Thirteenth Amendment to the Constitution, which reads:

> **Neither slavery nor involuntary servitude, except as a punishment for crime whereof the party shall have been duly convicted, shall exist within the United States or any place subject to their jurisdiction.**

The leaflets went on to state that a draftee was like a criminal convict. They felt that drafting men, called conscription, was an unfair use of the government's authority. The leaflets further read, "Do not submit to intimidation," and urged readers to petition the government to repeal, or cancel, the Conscription Act. The message in the pamphlets also suggested that there was a conspiracy between politicians and the press. The party felt people were helping the conspiracy by not speaking out against the conscription law.

Charles T. Schenck

As general secretary of the Socialist party, Charles T. Schenck was in charge of the Philadelphia headquarters that mailed the leaflets. Officials arrested him. They charged him with conspiring to cause a rebellion in the armed forces, and getting in the way of the recruitment and enlistment of troops. Congress had made these acts crimes under various "sedition" laws. (Sedition is any illegal action that attempts to disrupt or overthrow the government.)

The government, however, produced no evidence that Schenck had influenced even one draftee. Instead, the prosecutors considered the publication of the pamphlets enough proof of his guilt.

The defense presented a simple argument: Schenck had exercised a right guaranteed by the First Amendment. This is the right to speak freely on a public issue. Nonetheless, the court found him guilty. Schenck then appealed to the federal courts and finally to the U.S. Supreme Court. All along he insisted on his right to freedom of speech.

Schenck's defense lawyer argued to the Supreme Court that there was not enough evidence to prove that Schenck mailed out the leaflets. Justice Oliver Wendell Holmes reviewed the testimony in the case. He pointed out that Schenck was the general secretary of the Socialist party, and was in charge of the headquarters that mailed the pamphlets. Justice Holmes noted that the general secretary's report of August 20, 1917 read, "Obtained new leaflets from printer and started work addressing envelopes." Justice Holmes also pointed out that Schenck was to receive $125 for mailing the leaflets. Justice Holmes concluded that "No reasonable man could doubt that the defendant Schenck was largely instrumental in sending the circulars about."

"Clear and Present Danger"

Justice Holmes wrote the opinion that all of the justices signed. Noting that prosecutors had not shown that the leaflets had caused any revolt, he pointed out that the pamphlets were mailed because they "intended to have some effect." He said the effect that was intended was to influence people subject to the draft from not participating in it.

Justice Holmes agreed with the defense that the leaflets deserved First Amendment protection, but only in peacetime—not in wartime. In one of his most memorable statements on the law he said:

> **We admit that in many places and in ordinary times the defendants in saying all that was said . . . would have been within their constitutional rights. But the character of every act depends upon the circumstances in which it is done. The most stringent [strongest] protection of free speech would not protect a man in falsely shouting fire in a theater and causing a panic.**

In another of the justice's memorable phrases he said:

> **The question in every case is whether the words used are used in such circumstances and are of such a nature as to create a clear and present danger that they will bring about the substantive [actual] evils that Congress has a right to prevent.**

Justice Holmes said the "clear and present danger," is a question of "proximity and degree." When a nation is at war, things that might be said in time of peace become obstacles to the nation's effort. Such things will not be endured so long as men fight, and no court could consider them protected by any constitutional right.

Finally, Justice Holmes observed, it made no difference that Schenck and his associates had failed to get in the way of military recruiting. "The statute," he said, "punishes conspiracies to obstruct [block] as well as actual obstruction." Justice Holmes said that the way a paper is circulated and the purpose for which it is done need not have successful results to make the act a crime.

With that, the Supreme Court upheld the judgment of the lower courts. Charles T. Schenck had been sentenced to spend ten years in prison for each of the three counts charged against him, which meant thirty years behind bars. (However, he served the three terms at the same time and actually spent a total of ten years in jail.)

The Schenck case, in establishing the "clear and present danger" test, marked a turning point in First Amendment free speech cases. Until then, Chief Justice Edward White and other justices had permit-

THE GREAT DISSENTER

Justice Oliver Wendell Holmes, who wrote the majority opinion for the *Schenck* case, frequently dissented, or disagreed, with his more conservative colleagues on the Court. Thus, he won the nickname "The Great Dissenter." Justice Holmes even dissented from his own opinions—or, at least, from the way his fellow justices sometimes applied them.

In *Abrams v. United States,* a Russian-born American named Jacob Abrams was found guilty of violating the Espionage Act. Abrams had scattered leaflets protesting the sending of U.S. troops into Russia after the Revolution of 1917. Although seven of his colleagues upheld the conviction on the grounds that Abrams presented a "clear and present danger"—Justice Holmes's own words—Holmes disagreed. He insisted that Abrams had a right to his opinion under the First Amendment. Since Abrams had acted during peacetime, his actions posed no danger. (Schenck had acted during wartime and that is why his speech was not protected under the First Amendment.)

In 1927, the Court upheld the conviction of Socialist Benjamin Gitlow, who produced a publication that supported overthrowing the government. Again, Justice Holmes dissented from those who had cited his own words, saying that there was "no present danger of an attempt to overthrow the Government by force" in Gitlow's papers.

ted the government to silence any speech that displayed a "dangerous tendency."

Suggestions for further reading

Bowen, Catherine Drinker. *Yankee from Olympus: Justice Holmes and His Family.* Boston: Little, Brown and Co., 1943.

Burton, David H. *Oliver Wendell Holmes, Jr.* Boston: Twayne Publishers, Div. of G. K. Hall & Co., 1980.

Commager, Henry Steele, and Milton Cantor. *Documents of American History.* Englewood Cliffs, NJ: Prentice Hall, 1988.

Friedman, Leon, and Fred L. Israel, eds. *The Justices of the United States Supreme Court 1789–1969: Their Lives and Major Opinions.* New York: Chelsea House, 1969.

Johnson, John W., ed. *Historic U.S. Court Cases, 1690–1990: An Encyclopedia.* New York: Garland Publishing, 1992.

Novick, Sheldon M. *Honorable Justice: The Life of Oliver Wendell Holmes.* Boston: Little, Brown and Co., 1989.

Schnayerson, Robert. *The Illustrated History of the Supreme Court of the United States.* New York: Harry N. Abrams, 1986.

Witt, Elder, ed. *The Supreme Court and Individual Rights.* Washington, DC: Congressional Quarterly, 1980.

Chaplinsky v. New Hampshire 1942

Appellant: Walter Chaplinsky

Appellee: State of New Hampshire

Appellant's Claim: That a state law making it a crime to call people offensive names in public violated the right to freedom of speech.

Chief Lawyer for Appellant: Hayden C. Covington

Chief Lawyer for Appellee: Frank R. Kenison

Justices for the Court: Hugo Lafayette Black, James Francis Byrnes, William O. Douglas, Felix Frankfurter, Robert H. Jackson, Frank Murphy (writing for the Court), Stanley Forman Reed, Owen Josephus Roberts, Harlan Fiske Stone

Justices Dissenting: None

Date of Decision: March 9, 1942

Decision: The law did not violate the freedom of speech because it prohibited the use only of words that tend to provoke violence or a breach of the peace.

Significance: The decision created categories of speech, including "fighting words," that are not protected by the guarantee of freedom of speech.

Associate Justice Frank Murphy.
Courtesy of the Library of Congress.

Chaplinsky v. New Hampshire

A ruckus about "rackets"

Walter Chaplinsky was a Jehovah's Witness who was distributing religious material in the streets of Rochester, New Hampshire, on a busy Saturday afternoon. Jehovah's Witnesses is a sect of Christianity that believes other organized religions are evil. Chaplinsky's activity drew a crowd. Some citizens complained to the city marshal, Bowering, that Chaplinsky was likening all religion to a "racket." (A racket is a dishonest or illegal organization that takes people's money.)

Bowering told the citizens that Chaplinsky was not breaking the law, but he also warned Chaplinsky that the crowd was getting restless. A short time later, Bowering was informed that a riot was in progress. On his way to check out the situation, Bowering ran into Chaplinsky, who was being taken to the police station by a police officer. Bowering told Chaplinsky that he had warned him earlier not to start a riot. Chaplinsky responded by calling Bowering a "damned racketeer" and a "damned Fascist." (A racketeer is somebody who runs a racket. A fascist is an oppressive dictator.)

New Hampshire charged Chaplinsky with violating a state law that made it a crime to call someone an "offensive" name in public. The jury convicted Chaplinsky, and the Supreme Court of New Hampshire affirmed, or approved, the conviction. Chaplinsky appealed to the U.S. Supreme Court. He argued that convicting him of a crime for calling Bowering names violated the constitutional right to freedom of speech.

FREEDOM OF SPEECH

Fighting words

With a unanimous decision, the Supreme Court affirmed Chaplinsky's conviction. Writing for the Court, Justice Frank Murphy rejected Chaplinsky's argument that his conviction violated the right to freedom of speech.

The First Amendment says "Congress shall make no law . . . abridging the freedom of speech." Justice Murphy said states must recognize freedom of speech under the Due Process Clause of the Fourteenth Amendment. Murphy said, however, "that the right of free speech is not absolute at all times and under all circumstances." He explained that there are categories of speech that are not protected by the First Amendment, including obscenity, profanity, libel, and "fighting words." (Obscenity is sexually offensive material. Profanity is cursing. Libel is injuring someone's reputation with lies.)

Justice Murphy described fighting words as words that "inflict injury or tend to incite an immediate breach of the peace." He said fighting words are not protected by the First Amendment because they have almost no social value. They do not contribute meaningfully to the free flow of ideas in society, which is what the First Amendment was designed to protect.

Justice Murphy decided that the names "damned racketeer" and "damned Fascist" would obviously provoke the average person to fight and cause a breach of the peace. That meant they were fighting words that were unprotected by the First Amendment. Chaplinsky's conviction for using those words did not violate the right to freedom of speech.

The Court's position on free speech has been modified since the *Chaplinsky* decision came down in 1942. Today profanity is protected by the First Amendment. For example, in ***Cohen v. California*** (1971), the Supreme Court reversed the conviction of a man who wore a jacket that said "Fuck the Draft" in a courtroom. Libel also receives some First Amendment protection. Fighting words are still unprotected, but only if they provoke an immediate hostile reaction rather than simply tending to cause a breach of the peace. Obscenity is still unprotected under the First Amendment.

Suggestions for further reading

Evans, J. Edward. *Freedom of Speech.* Minneapolis, MN: Lerner Publications, Inc., 1990.

HATE SPEECH

Speech that promotes hatred toward a particular race, religion, gender, or other group is called hate speech. Hate speech seemed to be on the rise in the United States at the end of the twentieth century. Many governments and universities have created laws and rules to prohibit hate speech. They believe hate speech discourages the targeted people from participating in society as equal citizens.

Laws prohibiting hate speech, however, may violate the First Amendment guarantee of freedom of speech. Many feel it is dangerous for the government to outlaw speech that some or even most people find to be offensive. It can be the first step to eliminating all free speech. Perhaps, they say, the United States should fight hate speech by encouraging tolerance and acceptance instead of outlawing categories of speech.

Farish, Leah. *The First Amendment: Freedom of Speech, Religion, and the Press.* Hillside, NJ: Enslow Publishers, Inc., 1998.

King, David C. *The Right to Speak Out.* Brookfield, CT: Millbrook Press, 1997.

Klinker, Philip A. *The First Amendment.* Englewood Cliffs, NJ: Silver Burdett Press, 1991.

Pascoe, Elaine. *Freedom of Expression: The Right to Speak Out in America.* Brookfield, CT: Millbrook Press, 1992.

Steele, Philip, Philip Skele, and Penny Clarke. *Freedom of Speech?* New York: Franklin Watts, 1997.

Zeinert, Karen. *Free Speech: From Newspapers to Music Lyrics.* Hillside, NJ: Enslow Publishers, Inc., 1995.

West Virginia State Board of Education v. Barnette 1943

Appellants: West Virginia State Board of Education, et al.

Appellees: Walter Barnette, et al.

Appellants' Claim: That a law requiring students to salute the American flag and say "The Pledge of Allegiance" was constitutional.

Chief Lawyer for Appellants: W. Holt Wooddell

Chief Lawyer for Appellees: Hayden C. Covington

Justices for the Court: Hugo Lafayette Black, William O. Douglas, Robert H. Jackson (writing for the Court), Frank Murphy, Wiley Blount Rutledge, Harlan Fiske Stone

Justices Dissenting: Felix Frankfurter, Stanley Forman Reed, Owen Josephus Roberts

Date of Decision: June 14, 1943

Decision: The law was unconstitutional because it violated the freedom of speech.

Significance: After *Barnette,* the right to freedom of speech prevents the government from forcing people to say things they do not believe.

THE FLAG SALUTE

Can schoolchildren be compelled to state the Pledge of Allegiance or salute the U.S. flag? Those who say yes believe that children do not have a constitutional right to refuse to do so. Advocates say that loyalty to the nation and the government is important and that saluting the flag is one way to teach children to have loyalty for the country.

But those opposed to enforced flag salutes say that children should not have to make a statement of loyalty if they do not wish. To make them do so, in turn, makes the action worthless. They also believe that children who are compelled to say the Pledge of Allegiance or salute the flag may one day resent the country that forced them to make these false statements or gestures.

"I pledge allegiance to the flag...."

Jehovah's Witnesses is a form of Christianity. Its members believe that obeying God is more important than obeying man's laws. One of the Bible's commands is that people should not worship anything except God. For this reason, Jehovah's Witnesses refuse to salute the American flag. They believe it is a form of worship that God forbids.

In ***Minersville School District v. Gobitis*** (1940), Jehovah's Witnesses in Minersville, Pennsylvania, challenged a state law requiring their children to salute the American flag in school. They said it violated the freedom of religion, which is protected by the First Amendment. The U.S. Supreme Court disagreed. It decided that schools can encourage national unity and respect for the government by requiring school children to say "The Pledge of Allegiance" each morning.

Play it again, Uncle Sam

The West Virginia Board of Education was encouraged by the Court's decision in *Minersville*. The Board decided to require all students and teachers in West Virginia to salute the flag and say "The Pledge of

Allegiance" each day. The Board modified the salute after some people complained that it looked too much like the way German Nazis saluted Adolph Hitler. The Board refused, however, to give Jehovah's Witnesses an exception to the new rule. In fact, any student who did not say "The Pledge of Allegiance" could be expelled from school and treated like a juvenile delinquent.

Many Jehovah's Witnesses, including Walter Barnette, filed a lawsuit in federal court in West Virginia. They asked the court to prevent West Virginia from forcing their children to salute the flag. As in *Minersville,* the Jehovah's Witnesses argued that the law violated the freedom of religion by forcing their children to do something forbidden by their religion. This time, however, they also argued that the law violated the freedom of speech by forcing their children to say things they did not believe. The federal court ruled in favor of the Jehovah's Witnesses, so the Board of Education appealed to the U.S. Supreme Court.

Overruling Minersville

This time the Jehovah's Witnesses won. With a 6–3 vote, the Supreme Court affirmed (approved) the decision of the federal court in West Virginia. Writing for the Supreme Court, Justice Robert H. Jackson said that the case was a battle between the power of the government and the rights of individual people.

Justice Jackson agreed with the Board of Education that West Virginia was allowed to encourage patriotism. Justice Jackson said that all states could do so by requiring students to study American history and learn about the government. Learning about the laws and freedoms in America would foster respect for the government.

The government, however, cannot violate individual freedoms. One of those freedoms is the freedom of speech. The First Amendment states, "Congress shall make no law . . . abridging [limiting] the freedom of speech." State governments, including the West Virginia Board of Education, must also obey the freedom of speech under the Due Process Clause of the Fourteenth Amendment. (The Due Process Clause of the Fourteenth Amendment prevents state and local governments from violating a person's right to life, liberty [or freedom], and property.)

Justice Jackson said that saluting the American flag is a form of speech known as symbolism. Symbolism is the expression of thoughts and ideas using an object, like the flag, instead of only words. Justice

THE FIRST PLEDGE OF ALLEGIANCE

The year 1892 was the 400th anniversary of Christopher Columbus's voyage to America. To celebrate the event, a children's magazine called *The Youth's Companion* published "The Youth's Companion Flag Pledge." It said, "I pledge allegiance to my Flag and to the Republic for which it stands–one Nation indivisible–with liberty and justice for all." On the very first Columbus Day in 1892, twelve million children throughout the country recited the salute. Since then the words have been changed, and the salute is now called "The Pledge of Allegiance."

Jackson said that requiring students to salute the flag forces them to say things they might not believe, which violates their freedom of speech.

After *Barnette,* the freedom of speech includes not only the right to say what you believe, but also the right not to be forced to say something you do not believe. As Justices Hugo Lafayette Black and William O. Douglas explained in a separate opinion, "Love of country must spring from willing hearts and minds."

Suggestions for further reading

Evans, J. Edward. *Freedom of Speech.* Minneapolis: Lerner Publications, Inc., 1990.

Farish, Leah.*The First Amendment: Freedom of Speech, Religion, and the Press.* Hillside, NJ: Enslow Publishers, Inc., 1998.

Kallen, Stuart A. *The Pledge of Allegiance.* Edina, MN: Abdo and Daughters, 1994.

King, David C. *The Right to Speak Out.* Brookfield, CT: Millbrook Press, 1997.

Klinker, Philip A. *The First Amendment.* Englewood Cliffs, NJ: Silver Burdett Press, 1991.

Pascoe, Elaine. *Freedom of Expression: The Right to Speak Out in America.* Brookfield, CT: Millbrook Press, 1992.

Steele, Philip, Philip Skele, and Penny Clarke. *Freedom of Speech?* New York: Franklin Watts, 1997.

Stevens, Leonard A. *Salute! The Case of the Bible vs. the Flag.* New York: Coward, McCann and Geoghegan, Inc., 1973.

Swanson, June. *I Pledge Allegiance.* Minneapolis: Carolrhoda Books, 1990.

Zeinert, Karen. *Free Speech: From Newspapers to Music Lyrics.* Hillside, NJ: Enslow Publishers, Inc., 1995.

Feiner v. New York
1951

Petitioner: Irving Feiner

Respondent: State of New York

Petitioner's Claim: That convicting him for disorderly conduct for speaking to a public crowd violated his freedom of speech.

Chief Lawyer for Petitioner: Sidney H. Greenberg

Chief Lawyer for Respondent: Dan J. Kelly

Justices for the Court: Harold Burton, Tom C. Clark, Felix Frankfurter, Robert H. Jackson, Stanley Forman Reed, Fred Moore Vinson

Justices Dissenting: Hugo Lafayette Black, William O. Douglas, Sherman Minton

Date of Decision: January 15, 1951

Decision: Feiner's conviction did not violate the First Amendment.

Significance: Freedom of speech does not allow people to incite riots.

On his soapbox

In 1948, city officials in Syracuse, New York, gave O. John Rogge a permit to speak at a public school building. A group that was working for equal rights for African Americans, called the Young Progressives, organized the speech. The planned subject of Rogge's talk was racial discrimination and civil rights.

FREEDOM OF SPEECH

On the day of the speech, Syracuse cancelled the permit. The Young Progressives then arranged for Rogge to speak at the Hotel Syracuse. Irving Feiner, a college student, announced the change of plans to the public on a street corner. Standing on a wooden box and using a loudspeaker attached to an automobile, Feiner attracted a crowd of about seventy-five people, both white and black.

Associate Justice Fred Moore Vinson.
Courtesy of the Supreme Court of the United States.

During his announcement, Feiner made comments about public officials. He called President Harry S. Truman and the mayor of Syracuse "bums." Feiner said the local government was run by "corrupt politicians" and that the American Legion was a "Nazi Gestapo." At least one witness recalled Feiner saying African Americans should "rise up in arms and fight for their rights."

The law arrives

After receiving a call about a public disturbance, two policemen arrived at the scene of Feiner's speech. The crowd was blocking foot traffic on the sidewalk and spilling into the street, so the police moved the crowd onto the sidewalk. The officers said Feiner's speech caused mumbling, grumbling, and shoving in the crowd. After Feiner made the comment about African Americans fighting for their rights, one man told the officers that if they did not stop Feiner, he would.

The police then decided the crowd was getting out of control. They approached Feiner and asked him to disperse the crowd. Feiner kept talking, urging everyone to attend Rogge's speech that evening at the Hotel Syracuse. The officers then told Feiner to get down, but Feiner continued to talk. As the crowd moved forward towards Feiner, the officers told Feiner he was under arrest and ordered him to get down. Feiner stepped down saying, "the law has arrived, and I suppose they will take over now."

In New York, the law of disorderly conduct made it a crime to cause a breach of the peace by using insulting language, annoying others, or disobeying a police order to move from a public street. Feiner was convicted of disorderly conduct and sentenced to thirty days in prison. Feiner appealed. He argued that his conviction violated the First Amendment freedom of speech. The First Amendment says, "Congress shall make no law . . . abridging [limiting] the freedom of speech." States, including New York, must obey the First Amendment under the Due Process Clause of the Fourteenth Amendment.

During his appeals, Feiner argued that the police arrested him because the city did not like his criticism of public officials or his support for equal rights for African Americans. Feiner said convicting him for such speech violated the First Amendment. The county court and the New York Court of Appeals rejected this argument and affirmed Feiner's conviction, so Feiner took his case to the U.S. Supreme Court.

No freedom to riot

With a 6–3 decision, the Supreme Court ruled in favor of New York and affirmed Feiner's conviction. Writing for the Court, Justice Fred Moore Vinson said the evidence clearly showed that the police did not arrest Feiner to stop his speech. Instead, after Feiner spoke for about thirty minutes, the police decided that the crowd, which was blocking foot and automobile traffic, was getting out of control. According to the Court, the police arrested Feiner to protect public safety, not to interfere with Feiner's freedom of speech.

Justice Vinson quoted from a previous case, ***Cantwell v. Connecticut*** (1940), to support the Court's decision. "When clear and present danger of riot, disorder, interference with traffic upon the public streets, or other immediate threat to public safety, peace, or order, appears, the power of the State to prevent or punish is obvious."

Justice Vinson emphasized that the police cannot arrest a speaker just because the crowd does not like what it hears and that the freedom of speech is designed to protect unpopular speech. But when the speaker encourages a riot that may cause a breach of the peace, the freedom of speech ends and public safety takes over. The Court believed Feiner encouraged a riot by urging African Americans to "rise up in arms and fight for their rights."

Official censorship

Three justices disagreed with the Court's decision. Justice William O. Douglas wrote a dissenting opinion. He said the evidence did not prove that Feiner was urging African Americans to start a riot. Instead, Feiner said the crowd should "rise up and fight for their rights by going arm in arm to the Hotel Syracuse, black and white alike, to hear John Rogge." Justice Douglas said the police should have protected Feiner while he made this speech.

Justice Hugo Lafayette Black also wrote a dissenting opinion. He said the evidence did not prove that the crowd was about to riot. Instead, one man complained to the police officers about Feiner's speech. Justice Black said the police should have protected Feiner's freedom of speech by stopping the man who threatened to stop Feiner. Justice Black feared that the Court's decision meant "minority speakers can be silenced in any city."

Suggestions for further reading

Evans, J. Edward. *Freedom of Speech.* Minneapolis: Lerner Publications, Inc., 1990.

Farish, Leah. *The First Amendment: Freedom of Speech, Religion, and the Press.* Hillside, NJ: Enslow Publishers, Inc., 1998.

King, David C. *The Right to Speak Out.* Brookfield, CT: Millbrook Press, 1997.

Klinker, Philip A. *The First Amendment.* Englewood Cliffs, NJ: Silver Burdett Press, 1991.

Mikula, Mark, and L. Mpho Mabunda, eds. *Great American Court Cases.* Vol. 1. Detroit: Gale Group, 1999.

Pascoe, Elaine. *Freedom of Expression: The Right to Speak Out in America.* Brookfield, CT: Millbrook Press, 1992.

TERMINIELLO V. CHICAGO

Cases in which speakers cause a public disturbance do not always have the same result. In *Terminiello v. Chicago* (1949), decided only three years before *Feiner*, the Supreme Court reversed the conviction of a man who actually caused a riot. The man was Father Terminiello, a priest from Birmingham, Alabama, who was prejudiced against Jews, African Americans, and almost anyone who was not a white Christian.

In 1946, a group called the Christian Veterans of America invited Father Terminiello to give a speech at the West End Women's Club in Chicago, Illinois. During his speech to a crowd of eight hundred people, Terminiello criticized Jews, African Americans, and President Franklin D. Roosevelt. An angry group of one thousand protestors outside began to riot. They threw rocks, bricks, bottles, and stink bombs, breaking 28 windows and leading to 17 arrests.

Father Terminiello was convicted for disturbing the peace. The U.S. Supreme Court, however, reversed Terminiello's conviction. The Court said it violates the First Amendment to convict someone for using speech that angers other people. The very reason for the freedom of speech is to protect the right to say things that others might not like to hear. Unfortunately, this same reasoning did not influence the Court's decision in *Feiner.*

Steele, Philip, Philip Skele, and Penny Clarke. *Freedom of Speech?* New York: Franklin Watts, 1997.

Zeinert, Karen. *Free Speech: From Newspapers to Music Lyrics.* Hillside, NJ: Enslow Publishers, Inc., 1995.

Roth v. United States 1957

Petitioner: Samuel Roth

Respondent: United States of America

Petitioner's Claim: That publishing and selling obscene material is protected by the First Amendment.

Chief Lawyers for Petitioner: David von G. Albrecht and O. John Rogge

Chief Lawyer for Respondent: Roger D. Fisher

Justices for the Court: William J. Brennan, Jr. (writing for the Court), Harold Burton, Tom C. Clark, Felix Frankfurter, Earl Warren, Charles Evans Whittaker

Justices Dissenting: Hugo Lafayette Black, William O. Douglas, John Marshall Harlan II

Date of Decision: June 24, 1957

Decision: Federal and state laws that prohibit the publication and sale of obscene material are constitutional.

Significance: The Supreme Court officially declared that obscenity is not protected by the freedom of speech. It also defined obscenity for future trials.

Samuel Roth ran a business in New York City. He published and sold books, magazines, and photographs that dealt with the subject of 0sex. Roth advertised his goods by mailing descriptive material to potential cus-

Associate Justice William J. Brennan, Jr.
Courtesy of the Supreme Court of the United States.

tomers. He was convicted in federal court for violating a federal law that made it a crime to mail obscene material.

In a separate case, David S. Alberts ran a mail order business in Los Angeles, California. Alberts also sold material that dealt with the subject of sex. Alberts was convicted in a California state court of violating a state law that made it a crime to sell obscene material.

Roth and Alberts both took their cases to the U.S. Supreme Court. They said their convictions violated the freedom of speech. The First Amendment says, "Congress shall make no law . . . abridging [limiting] the freedom of speech."

Roth was convicted under federal law, which is governed by the First Amendment. Although the First Amendment only mentions the federal government, state and local governments must obey it under the Due Process Clause of the Fourteenth Amendment. This allowed Alberts to argue that his conviction under California's obscenity law violated the freedom of speech. The U.S. Supreme Court decided to review both cases to determine whether the First Amendment protects obscenity.

Obscenity declared worthless

In a 6–3 decision, the Supreme Court affirmed the convictions of both Roth and Alberts. Writing for the Court, Justice William J. Brennan, Jr., said obscenity is not protected by the freedom of speech.

Justice Brennan made that conclusion after reviewing the history of the freedom of speech in America. He noted that in 1792, after the First Amendment was adopted, fourteen states made profanity or blasphemy a crime. (Profanity or blasphemy was speech that was anti-religious.) As early as 1712, Massachusetts made it a crime to publish "filthy, obscene, or profane" material about religion. Justice Brennan determined that history showed that the First Amendment was not designed to protect every kind of speech.

Brennan decided that the First Amendment only protects speech that contains valuable ideas about science, politics, art, religion, and other things that make up American society. The freedom of speech was not designed to protect worthless speech. Justice Brennan said obscenity is worthless because it does not make a valuable contribution to the flow of ideas in America. Therefore, obscenity is not protected by the freedom of speech.

The most important part of the Court's decision, however, was its definition of obscenity. Brennan said material dealing with sex is not automatically obscene. Sex in art, literature, and scientific works can be valuable to society. Brennan defined obscenity as material that deals with sex in a manner that is offensive to the average person. In an obscenity trial, the jury's duty would be to decide if the material would offend the average person in the jury's community.

What about art?

Justice William O. Douglas filed a dissenting opinion, meaning he disagreed with the Court's decision. Justice Douglas had two main concerns. First, the federal and California laws at issue made it illegal to sell or mail material that caused people to have sexual thoughts. Justice Douglas said the First Amendment was designed to allow people to speak or publish anything unless it caused harmful action. For Justice Douglas, punishing speech that causes bad thoughts but not bad action is a serious violation of the freedom of speech.

Second, Justice Douglas was afraid to allow juries to decide obscenity cases based on what would offend the average person. He said, "[t]he list of books that judges or juries can place in that category is endless." Justice Douglas feared that the Court's decision would allow communities to ban valuable works of art, literature, and science.

ROBERT MAPPLETHORPE

Robert Mapplethorpe was an American photographer. He was popular for his photographs of flowers, celebrities, and nude men. Mapplethorpe died in March 1989 while an exhibition of his photographs was touring the country. Called "The Perfect Moment," the exhibition contained shocking photographs of nude men. People in the art world said Mapplethorpe was a "brilliant artist." Opponents thought his photographs of nude men were offensive and disgusting.

In June 1990, the Contemporary Arts Center ("CAC") in Cincinnati, Ohio, displayed "The Perfect Moment" exhibition. Afterwards it became the first art gallery in America to face obscenity charges in court. In October 1990, a jury found the gallery not guilty of violating obscenity laws. Although the jury decided that Mapplethorpe's photographs were sexually offensive, it could not say they had no artistic value. The case showed the fine line between worthless obscenity and valuable art.

Obscenity changes

Over the years the Court listened to Justice Douglas's concerns and revised the definition of obscenity. In *Miller v. California* (1973), the Court said material is obscene if it: (1) appeals to abnormal sexual desire; (2) depicts sex offensively; and (3) lacks literary, artistic, political, or scientific value.

At this point Justice Brennan, who wrote the decision in *Roth,* decided that it was impossible for the justices to agree on a definition of obscenity. Without a definition, it is impossible for people to know what the obscenity laws prohibit and what they allow. For this reason, Justice Brennan concluded that obscenity laws are unconstitutional because they are too vague. The Supreme Court, however, still says obscenity is not protected by the freedom of speech, and it still uses the *Miller* test to determine what is obscene.

Suggestions for further reading

Evans, J. Edward. *Freedom of Speech.* Minneapolis: Lerner Publications, Inc., 1990.

Farish, Leah. *The First Amendment: Freedom of Speech, Religion, and the Press.* Hillside, NJ: Enslow Publishers, Inc., 1998.

King, David C. *The Right to Speak Out.* Brookfield, CT: Millbrook Press, 1997.

Klinker, Philip A. *The First Amendment.* Englewood Cliffs, NJ: Silver Burdett Press, 1991.

Morrisroe, Patricia. *Mapplethorpe: A Biography.* New York: Random House, Inc., 1995.

Pascoe, Elaine. *Freedom of Expression: The Right to Speak Out in America.* Brookfield, CT: Millbrook Press, 1992.

Steele, Philip, Philip Skele, and Penny Clarke. *Freedom of Speech?* New York: Franklin Watts, 1997.

Zeinert, Karen. *Free Speech: From Newspapers to Music Lyrics.* Hillside, NJ: Enslow Publishers, Inc., 1995.

New York Times Company v. Sullivan 1964

Appellant: The New York Times Company

Appellee: L. B. Sullivan

Appellant's Claim: That when the Supreme Court of Alabama upheld a libel judgment against *The New York Times,* it violated the newspaper's free speech and due process rights. Also, that an advertisement published in the *Times* was not libelous.

Chief Lawyers for Appellant: Herbert Brownell, Thomas F. Daly, and Herbert Wechsler

Chief Lawyers for Appellee: Sam Rice Baker, M. Roland Nachman, Jr., and Robert E. Steiner III

Justices for the Court: Hugo Lafayette Black, William J. Brennan, Jr. (writing for the Court), Tom C. Clark, William O. Douglas, Arthur Goldberg, John Marshall Harlan II, Potter Stewart, Earl Warren, and Byron R. White

Justices Dissenting: None

Date of Decision: March 9, 1964

Decision: The Alabama courts' decisions were reversed.

Significance: The U.S. Supreme Court greatly expanded Constitutional guarantees of freedom of speech and the press. It halted the rights of states to award damages in libel suits according to state laws.

ACTUAL MALICE STANDARDS

Until 1964, each state used its own standards to determine what was considered libelous. This changed after the decision in *New York Times Company v. Sullivan.* This landmark case established the criteria that would be used nationwide when determining libel cases involving public officials.

The Court stated that "actual malice" must be shown by the publishers of alleged libelous materia, when the falseness of the material is proven. This standard was later broadened by the Supreme Court to include not only public officials, but also "public figures." This includes well-known individuals outside of public office who receive media attention, such as athletes, writers, entertainers, and others who have celebrity status.

On March 23, 1960, an organization called the "Committee to Defend Martin Luther King and the Struggle for Freedom in the South" paid *The New York Times* to publish a full-page advertisement. The ad called for public support and money to defend Reverend Martin Luther King Jr. who was struggling to gain equal rights for African Americans. The ad ran in the March 29, 1960 edition of the *Times* with the title "Heed Their Rising Voices" in large, bold print.

The ad criticized several southern areas, including the city of Montgomery, Alabama, for breaking up civil rights demonstrations. In addition, the ad declared that "Southern violators of the Constitution" were determined to destroy King and his civil rights movement. No person was mentioned by name. The reference was to the entire South, not just to Montgomery or other specific cities.

Sullivan sues

Over 600,000 copies of the March 29, 1960 *Times* edition with the ad were printed. Only a couple hundred went to Alabama subscribers. Montgomery City Commissioner L. B. Sullivan learned of the ad through an editorial in a local newspaper. On April 19, 1960, an angry Sullivan sued the *Times* for libel (an attack against a person's reputation) in the Circuit Court of Montgomery County, Alabama. He claimed that the ad's reference to Montgomery and to "Southern violators of the Constitution" had the effect of defaming him, meaning attacking and abusing his reputation. He demanded $500,000 in compensation for damages.

On November 3, 1960, the Circuit Court found the *Times* guilty. The court awarded Sullivan the full $500,000 for damages. The Alabama Supreme Court upheld the Circuit Court judgment on August 30, 1962. In its opinion, or written decision, the Alabama Supreme Court gave an extremely broad definition of libel. The opinion stated that libel occurs when printed words: injure a person's reputation, profession, trade, or business; accuse a person of a punishable offense; or bring public contempt upon a person.

Supreme Court protects the press

The *Times*'s chief lawyers took the case to the U.S. Supreme Court. On January 6, 1964, the two sides appeared at a hearing before the Court in Washington, D.C. On March 9, 1964, the Supreme Court unanimously (in total agreement) reversed the Alabama courts' decisions. The Court held, meaning decided, that Alabama libel law violated the *Times*'s First Amendment rights to freedom of the press.

The Court recognized what Alabama's own newspapers had written. The newspapers had reported that Alabama's libel law was a powerful tool in the hands of anti-civil rights officials. The Court's decision canceled out Alabama's overly general libel law so that it could no longer be used to threaten freedom of the press.

Next, Justice William J. Brennan, Jr., stated that a new federal rule regarding libel law was needed. The new rule stopped a public official from recovering damages for a defamatory falsehood, or lie, about his official conduct unless he proved that the statement was made with actual malice (ill will).

Sullivan had not proven that the *Times* had acted with actual malice. What is actual malice? The Court defined it as knowingly printing false information or printing it "with reckless disregard of whether it was false or not."

MONTGOMERY DEMONSTRATIONS

Montgomery was the site of a lot of civil rights activity, largely because of the events set off by Rosa Parks. In 1955, Parks, then a forty-three-year-old seamstress working at a Montgomery department store, was on her way home from work. At that time, Montgomery city buses were segregated. Whites sat up front, blacks sat in the back. When Parks could not find a seat in the back, she sat in the middle of the bus. The driver told her to move to make room for new white passengers. Parks refused—and was arrested.

Parks had been a civil rights activist for some time, working with the local chapter of the National Association for the Advancement of Colored People (NAACP). Now she worked with local civil rights leaders who decided to use her case to end segregation on public transportation.

Parks's pastor, the twenty-seven-year-old Martin Luther King Jr., led a boycott of Montgomery city buses. (A boycott is a refusal to buy, use, or sell a thing or service.) Local officials bitterly resisted the boycott. Police arrested Parks a second time for refusing to pay her fine. They also arrested King. First on a drunk-driving charge, and then for conspiring (secretly planning) to organize an illegal boycott. The boycott of the city buses lasted for over a year. It ended with the November 1956 Supreme Court decision against the bus segregation. Montgomery continued to be a center of civil rights activity throughout the early 1960s.

Court broadens freedom of speech and press

In libel suits after *New York Times Company v. Sullivan,* the Court continued to expand the First Amendment's protection of freedom of speech and press. The Court decided that for any "public figure" to sue for libel and win, she or he would have to prove "actual malice." Public figures include anyone widely known in the community, such as athletes, writers, entertainers, and others with celebrity status. Also, the requirement for actual malice protects anyone accused of libel, not just newspapers like the *Times.*

The *Sullivan* case was a huge advance for freedom of speech. It prevented genuine criticism from being silenced by the threat of damaging and expensive libel lawsuits. *Sullivan* has not, however, become a license for the newspapers to print anything that they want to print. Defendants who act with ill will can receive severe penalties.

Suggestions for further reading

Bain, George. "A Question of Honor, Malice and Rights." *Maclean's* (October 1984): p. 64.

Friedman, Robert. "Freedom of the Press: How Far Can it Go?" *American Heritage* (October–November 1982): pp. 16–22.

Hopkins, W. Wat. *Actual Malice: Twenty-Five Years After Times v. Sullivan.* New York: Praeger, 1989.

Johnson, John W., ed. *Historic U.S. Court Cases, 1690–1990: An Encyclopedia.* New York: Garland Publishing, 1992.

Lewis, Anthony. *Make No Law: The Sullivan Case and the First Amendment.* New York: Random House, 1991.

Winfield, Richard N. *New York Times v. Sullivan: The Next Twenty Years.* New York: Practicing Law Institute, 1984.

Memoirs v. Massachusetts
1966

Appellants: A book named *John Cleland's Memoirs of a Woman of Pleasure,* et al.

Appellee: William I. Cowin, Assistant Attorney General of Massachusetts

Appellants' Claim: That the Supreme Judicial Court of Massachusetts erred when it decided that a book called *Memoirs of a Woman of Pleasure* (more popularly known as *Fanny Hill*) was obscene and not protected by the freedom of speech.

Chief Lawyer for Appellants: Charles Rembar

Chief Lawyer for Appellee: William I. Cowin, Assistant Attorney General of Massachusetts

Justices for the Court: Hugo Lafayette Black, William J. Brennan, Jr., William O. Douglas, Abe Fortas, Potter Stewart, Earl Warren

Justices Dissenting: Tom C. Clark, John Marshall Harlan II, Byron R. White

Date of Decision: March 21, 1966

Decision: Because the Supreme Judicial Court of Massachusetts admitted that *Fanny Hill* had some literary value, its decision that the book was obscene was in error. The Supreme Court sent the case back to Massachusetts for a retrial.

Significance: After *Memoirs,* the freedom of speech protected offensive books about sex unless they had absolutely no literary value.

Around 1750, John Cleland wrote a novel called *Memoirs of a Woman of Pleasure.* The book eventually became known as *Fanny Hill,* the name of the book's main character. In the novel, Fanny Hill is a young woman who becomes a prostitute, which is someone who has sexual intercourse for money. The novel contains over fifty descriptions of sex that are offensive to many people. By the end of the novel, Fanny Hill discovers that sex without love is meaningless, so she marries her first lover.

In 1957, the U.S. Supreme Court decided obscenity is not protected by the freedom of speech under the First Amendment. That meant state and federal governments could ban the publication of obscene books without violating the First Amendment. At the time, the Supreme Court defined obscenity as material that depicts sex in an offensive, worthless manner.

Literature or smut?

In the mid-1960s, G.P. Putnam's Sons published *Fanny Hill* in America. At that time, Massachusetts had a law that allowed the state to file a lawsuit against a book to have it declared obscene. In effect, the state could sue the book. If a court found the book obscene, the state could stop it from being published. Massachusetts Assistant Attorney General William I. Cowin filed such a lawsuit against *Fanny Hill.* G. P. Putnam's Sons intervened, which means joined the lawsuit, to defend its right to publish the book.

At the book's trial, the judge heard evidence to determine if *Fanny Hill* was obscene. Some witnesses testified that *Fanny Hill* was nothing but a worthless, offensive book about sex. Many professors from well known colleges and universities, however, testified in favor of the book. They called it a "work of art" having "literary merit" and "historical value." One witness said *Fanny Hill* is a piece of "social history of interest to anyone who is interested in fiction as a way of understanding society in the past." Another witness said the book "belongs to the history of English literature rather than the history of smut."

The trial judge rejected the testimony in favor of the book. Instead he ruled that *Fanny Hill* was obscene because it appealed to abnormal sexual desire, was sexually offensive, and was "utterly without redeeming social importance." G. P. Putnam's Sons appealed to the Supreme Judicial Court of Massachusetts. That court said the professors' testimony proved that *Fanny Hill* had some literary value. The court ruled in favor of Massachusetts, however, saying the book need not be completely worthless to be obscene. G. P. Putnam's Sons appealed to the U.S. Supreme Court.

Literature prevails

With a 6–3 decision, the Supreme Court ruled in favor of the book. The six justices who voted in favor of the book, however, could not agree on a reason for their decision. Many of them wrote separate opinions explaining their votes. Justice William J. Brennan, Jr., delivered the Court's decision and wrote an opinion for himself and for Justice Abe Fortas and Chief Justice Earl Warren.

According to Justice Brennan, the Supreme Judicial Court of Massachusetts was wrong when it said a book does not have to be completely worthless to be obscene. Brennan said that to be obscene and thus not protected by the First Amendment, a book must appeal to abnormal sexual desire, be offensive, and be completely worthless. Because the Massachusetts court admitted that *Fanny Hill* had some literary value, its decision that the book was obscene was wrong. The Supreme Court sent the whole case back to Massachusetts for another trial.

Filthy result?

Three justices wrote dissenting opinions, meaning they disagreed with the Court's decision. Justice Tom C. Clark voiced the strongest objection. He disagreed that a book had to be completely worthless to be obscene. Clark said the Court's decision would protect worthless material as long as it is well written. Clark feared this would prevent the states from fighting against criminal sexual behavior, such as rape, that many people think is caused by obscene material. As Justice Clark put it, the Court's decision "gives the smut artist free rein to carry on his dirty business."

Impact

Memoirs is one of many Supreme Court decisions to wrestle with the definition of obscenity. The Supreme Court's most recent definition is in *Miller v. California* (1973). There the Supreme Court said obscenity is material that (1) appeals to abnormal sexual desire, (2) is sexually offensive, and (3) taken as a whole, lacks literary, artistic, political, or scientific value.

SALMAN RUSHDIE

The story of Salman Rushdie explains why the United States protects the freedom of speech. Rushdie is an Indian novelist who published *The Satanic Verses* worldwide in 1988. The book is a novel about good and evil that refers to many aspects of Islam, the religion practiced by Muslims. In *The Satanic Verses,* a major character named Mahound resembles the Islamic prophet Mohammed.

Many Muslims considered *The Satanic Verses* to be an insult to their religion. Ayatollah Khomeni, the leader of Iran, was particularly insulted. He called *The Satanic Verses* blasphemy, an Iranian crime punishable by death, and issued a death sentence for Rushdie. Khomeni said every Muslim must use "everything he has, his life and wealth, to send [Rushdie] to hell."

Rushdie reacted by hiding in Great Britain, where he had lived since 1966. Meanwhile, the Iranian government called for every copy of *The Satanic Verses* in the world to be seized and burned. It was an extreme but real example of what can happen in a country that does not protect the freedom of speech.

At that point, Justice Brennan, who wrote the Court's decision in *Memoirs,* decided it was impossible for the justices to agree on a definition obscenity. Without a definition, it is impossible for people to know what obscenity laws prohibit and what they allow. For this reason, Brennan concluded that laws banning obscenity are unconstitutional. The Supreme Court, however, still says obscenity is not protected by the freedom of speech, and it still uses the *Miller* test to determine what is obscene.

Suggestions for further reading

Evans, J. Edward. *Freedom of Speech.* Minneapolis: Lerner Publications, Inc., 1990.

Farish, Leah. *The First Amendment: Freedom of Speech, Religion, and the Press.* Hillside, NJ: Enslow Publishers, Inc., 1998.

King, David C. *The Right to Speak Out.* Brookfield, CT: Millbrook Press, 1997.

Klinker, Philip A. *The First Amendment.* Englewood Cliffs, NJ: Silver Burdett Press, 1991.

Noble, William. *Bookbanning in America.* Middlebury: Paul S. Eriksson, 1990.

Pascoe, Elaine. *Freedom of Expression: The Right to Speak Out in America.* Brookfield, CT: Millbrook Press, 1992.

Steele, Philip, Philip Skele, and Penny Clarke. *Freedom of Speech?* New York: Franklin Watts, 1997.

The World Book Encyclopedia, 1997 ed., entry on "Rushdie, Salman." Chicago: World Book, 1997.

Zeinert, Karen. *Free Speech: From Newspapers to Music Lyrics.* Hillside, NJ: Enslow Publishers, Inc., 1995.

United States v. O'Brien 1968

Petitioner: United States of America

Respondent: David Paul O'Brien

Petitioner's Claim: That a federal law prohibiting the destruction of draft cards did not violate the freedom of speech.

Chief Lawyer for Petitioner: Erwin N. Griswold, U.S. Solicitor General

Chief Lawyer for Respondent: Marvin M. Karpatkin

Justices for the Court: Hugo Lafayette Black, William J. Brennan, Jr., Abe Fortas, John Marshall Harlan II, Potter Stewart, Earl Warren, Byron R. White

Justices Dissenting: William O. Douglas (Thurgood Marshall did not participate)

Date of Decision: May 27, 1968

Decision: The Supreme Court upheld the federal statute and O'Brien's conviction for violating it.

Significance: *O'Brien* limited protection for symbolic speech under the First Amendment.

The Vietnam War, which lasted from 1955 until 1974, was a battle between North and South Vietnam. North Vietnam wanted to unite the country under communism. South Vietnam resisted with help from the United States. By the end of 1965, there were 180,000 American troops fighting in Vietnam.

Many anti-war demonstrators showed their displeasure with the government during the Vietnam War by burning their draft cards. Reproduced by permission of the Corbis Corporation.

Although the war was ten years old in 1965, there was no sign that North Vietnam would be defeated. Many Americans became opposed to the war. Some thought a civil war in Vietnam was not America's concern. They were angry to see young Americans die while fighting for another country. Others were generally opposed to human beings killing each other. Protests against the war became common in America. In *United States v. O'Brien,* the U.S. Supreme Court had to decide whether one form of protest—burning draft cards—was protected by the freedom of speech.

Burning mad

The United States built an army to fight in Vietnam using the Selective Service System. It required all American males to register with a local draft board when they reached the age of eighteen. Each young man received a registration certificate and a classification certificate. The certificates were commonly called draft cards. They contained important information, including a reminder that registrants had to notify their local draft board of address changes. The local draft boards used the addresses to notify young men when they had been selected, or drafted, to fight in Vietnam.

On March 31, 1966, David Paul O'Brien and three other men burned their draft cards on the steps of the South Boston Courthouse. They did so to protest against the Vietnam War and the military draft. A crowd of citizens, including agents from the Federal Bureau of Investigation (FBI), watched the event. Immediately after the burning, angry members of the crowd attacked O'Brien and his companions.

An FBI agent rushed O'Brien to safety inside the courthouse. The agent then arrested O'Brien for violating a federal law that made it a crime to destroy draft cards. O'Brien admitted he had violated the federal law because of his beliefs.

The United States charged O'Brien with violating the federal law. At his trial, O'Brien told the jury he burned his draft card to convince others to adopt his anti-war beliefs. He said burning his draft card was "symbolic speech." (Symbolic speech conveys an idea or message with symbols or actions instead of words.) O'Brien argued that convicting him for using symbolic speech would violate his freedom of speech.

The district court rejected this argument and the jury found O'Brien guilty. On appeal, however, the U.S. Court of Appeals for the First Circuit reversed the conviction. It said the federal law violated the freedom of speech. The United States took the case to the U.S. Supreme Court.

Cooler heads prevail

With a 7–1 decision, the Supreme Court ruled in favor of the United States. Writing for the Court, Chief Justice Earl Warren applied the First Amendment, which says "Congress shall make no law . . . abridging [limiting] the freedom of speech." Justice Warren said the freedom of speech did not give O'Brien the right to burn his draft card.

Warren explained that only pure speech gets full protection under the First Amendment. By contrast, O'Brien's protest involved both "speech" and "conduct." The speech part was whatever O'Brien meant to say in protest against the Vietnam War. The conduct part was burning the draft card. Warren said the federal government can limit the "conduct" part of speech if it satisfies a two part test. First, it must have a substantial interest in limiting the speech. Second, it must interfere with the "speech" as little as necessary.

Under this test, the federal law making it a crime to destroy draft cards did not violate the First Amendment. The U.S. Constitution gives the federal government the power to raise an army to fight in wars. Using the Selective Service System to raise an army for the Vietnam War was an appropriate exercise of that power. This meant the government had a substantial interest in making sure that draft cards were handled properly and not misused. Otherwise it might have problems building an army for the Vietnam War.

The federal law also satisfied the second part of the test. It interfered with pure speech as little as necessary to serve the government's interest in building an army. Protestors still could speak against the Vietnam War and the military draft using words and other symbols other than burning draft cards. Because the federal law did not violate the freedom of speech, O'Brien's conviction was valid.

Aftermath

Soon after *O'Brien,* the United States began to withdraw troops from Vietnam. Protestors, however, continued to burn their draft cards. In all there were 31,831 reported violations ending in just 544 imprisonments. Then in 1973 the United States ended the draft and established an all vol-

EARL WARREN

Earl Warren, who wrote the decision in *O'Brien,* was the fourteenth chief justice of the U.S. Supreme Court. Warren was born in Los Angeles, California, in 1891. He grew up poor and lost his father to murder. Justice Warren put himself through college and law school at the University of California. He then devoted most of his working life to public service.

One of the Warren Court's most important decisions was ***Brown v. Board of Education*** (1954). In *Brown,* Justice Warren convinced the Supreme Court to vote unanimously to end segregation in public schools. Segregation was the practice of schooling black and white students in "separate but equal" facilities. Unfortunately, schools for black students usually were not as good as the ones for white students. In the Court's decision, Justice Warren wrote that separate is not truly equal in the United States of America.

unteer army. North Vietnam ultimately won the war in 1974 and united the country under communism in 1976. Meanwhile in America, *O'Brien* continues to limit First Amendment protection of symbolic speech that the government calls "conduct."

Suggestions for further reading

Evans, J. Edward. *Freedom of Speech.* Minneapolis: Lerner Publications, Inc., 1990.

Farish, Leah. *The First Amendment: Freedom of Speech, Religion, and the Press.* Hillside, NJ: Enslow Publishers, Inc., 1998.

King, David C. *The Right to Speak Out.* Brookfield, CT: Millbrook Press, 1997.

Klinker, Philip A. *The First Amendment.* Englewood Cliffs, NJ: Silver Burdett Press, 1991.

Pascoe, Elaine. *Freedom of Expression: The Right to Speak Out in America.* Brookfield, CT: Millbrook Press, 1992.

FREEDOM OF SPEECH

Steele, Philip, Philip Skele, and Penny Clarke. *Freedom of Speech?* New York: Franklin Watts, 1997.

The Supreme Court: Selections from the Four-Volume Encyclopedia of the American Constitution and Supplement. New York: Macmillan Library Reference USA, 1999.

Zeinert, Karen. *Free Speech: From Newspapers to Music Lyrics.* Hillside, NJ: Enslow Publishers, Inc., 1995.

Tinker v. Des Moines Independent Community School District 1969

Petitioners: John P. Tinker, Mary Beth Tinker, and Christopher Eckhardt

Respondents: Des Moines Independent Community School District, et al.

Petitioners' Claim: That suspending them from school for wearing black armbands to protest the Vietnam War violated the freedom of speech.

Chief Lawyer for Petitioners: Dan L. Johnston

Chief Lawyer for Respondents: Allan A. Herrick

Justices for the Court: William J. Brennan, Jr., William O. Douglas, Abe Fortas, Thurgood Marshall, Potter Stewart, Earl Warren, Byron R. White

Justices Dissenting: Hugo Lafayette Black, John Marshall Harlan II

Date of Decision: February 24, 1969

Decision: The Supreme Court struck down the school regulation that resulted in the suspensions.

Significance: Students do not give up their freedom of speech in school.

FREEDOM OF SPEECH

Whose war is it?

The Vietnam War, which lasted from 1955 until 1974, was a battle between North and South Vietnam. North Vietnam wanted to unite the country under communism. South Vietnam resisted with help from the United States. By the end of 1965, there were 180,000 American troops fighting in Vietnam.

Although the war was ten years old in 1965, there was no sign that North Vietnam would be defeated. Many Americans became opposed to the war. Some thought a civil war in Vietnam was not America's concern. They were angry to see young American die while fighting for another country. Others were generally opposed to human beings killing each other. Vietnam War protests became common in America.

Peaceful protest

In December 1965, a group of adults and school children gathered in Des Moines, Iowa. They met to discuss ways to voice their opposition to America's involvement in the Vietnam War. They eventually decided to wear black armbands with the peace symbol for the remainder of the holiday season. They also decided to fast, meaning live without eating, on December 16 and on New Year's Eve.

Mary Beth and John Tinker were suspended from school for wearing armbands protesting the Vietnam War. Reproduced by permission of the Corbis Corporation.

The students at the meeting included sixteen-year-old Christopher Eckhardt, fifteen-year-old John P. Tinker, and thirteen-year-old Mary Beth Tinker. Christopher and John attended high schools in Des Moines, and John's sister Mary attended junior high school. They decided to join their parents by wearing black armbands and fasting too.

The principals of the Des Moines public schools learned about these plans. They were worried the protest would cause trouble because a former student who had been killed in Vietnam still had friends at one of the high schools. Some students said they would wear different colored armbands to support the war. To avoid any conflict, on December 14 the principals adopted a policy that any student wearing a black armband would be asked to remove it and would be suspended if he refused.

Christopher, John, and Mary knew about the new policy but decided to follow their plan. John and Mary wore their black armbands to school on December 16, and Christopher wore his the next day. Although the armbands did not disrupt school, all three students were suspended and told not to return until they removed the armbands. The students did not return until after New Year's Day, when their protest ended.

Meanwhile, the students and their parents filed a lawsuit in federal district court. They asked the court to stop the schools from punishing them for wearing the black armbands. The district court dismissed the case, saying the schools were allowed to prevent disturbances. The students appealed, but the federal court of appeals affirmed (approved) the district court's decision. They then took their case to the U.S. Supreme Court. They argued that the schools had violated their right to free speech.

Free speech in school

With a 7–2 decision, the Supreme Court ruled in favor of the students. Writing for the Court, Justice Abe Fortas said wearing black armbands to protest the Vietnam War was a form of speech called "symbolic" speech. Symbolic speech conveys a message or idea with symbols or actions instead of words.

The First Amendment protects all kinds of speech, including symbolic speech. It says, "Congress shall make no law . . . abridging [limiting] the freedom of speech." State and local governments, including public schools in Des Moines, Iowa, must obey the freedom of speech under the Due Process Clause of the Fourteenth Amendment.

Justice Fortas said students have free speech rights under the First Amendment just like adults. "Students in school as well as out of school are 'persons' under our Constitution." Students do not give up the freedom of speech when they go to school. Justice Fortas said this means schools can interfere with free speech only when it is necessary to prevent actual disruptions.

The evidence showed that the students had not caused any disruptions. Instead, they had made a peaceful protest against the Vietnam War. The schools stopped them because other students might not like the protest; but, the freedom of speech protects the right to say things other people might not like to hear. After all, these same schools let students wear buttons to support political campaigns, and even allowed one student to wear an Iron Cross, the symbol of the German Nazis from World War II. Justice Fortas said the freedom of speech prevented the schools from allowing some political speech but punishing Christopher, John, and Mary for their protest.

Children should be seen and not heard

Justice Hugo Lafayette Black wrote a dissenting opinion, meaning he disagreed with the Court's decision. Justice Black said the First Amendment does not give people the freedom to say anything, anywhere, anytime. "Iowa's public schools . . . are operated to give students an opportunity to learn, not to talk politics by actual speech, or by 'symbolic' speech." Justice Black thought schools should be allowed to prevent speech that interferes with the job of learning.

Justice Black feared the Court's decision would give students the right to disobey school rules anytime they wanted to exercise free speech. He said "the Federal Constitution [does not compel] the teachers, parents, and elected school officials to surrender control of the American public school system to public school students."

Since *Tinker,* the Supreme Court has limited the freedom of speech for students in school. In ***Bethel School District No. 403 v. Fraser*** (1986), the Court said Bethel High School was allowed to suspend a student for giving a speech during a school assembly that referred to sexual intercourse. The Court said schools can limit free speech in order to teach good morals.

Suggestions for further reading

Evans, J. Edward. *Freedom of Speech.* Minneapolis: Lerner Publications, Inc., 1990.

Farish, Leah. *The First Amendment: Freedom of Speech, Religion, and the Press.* Hillside, NJ: Enslow Publishers, Inc., 1998.

BOMB THREAT

Does the freedom of speech allow a student to write a story about exploding a nuclear bomb in class? That question arose at Tallwood High School in Virginia Beach, Virginia, in May 1999.

Christopher Bullock, a sixteen-year-old junior, wrote the story for a required state writing test. The story's main character gave a speech to announce a gift for his school. Strapped to the character's chest, the gift turned out to be a nuclear bomb that the character exploded at the end of his speech. He said, "I have chosen this gift because school has given me nothing but stress, heartache, and pain. . . . I hope you all enjoy the light show for what little time you have left."

Tallwood High School suspended Bullock after learning about the story, and the police filed criminal charges. Bullock explained that the story was a fantasy and not a real threat. According to attorney Ann Beason, the freedom of speech protects the right to write a fantasy story about a bomb threat. The police eventually dropped the criminal charges, and Tallwood allowed Bullock to return to school.

King, David C. *The Right to Speak Out.* Brookfield, CT: Millbrook Press, 1997.

Klinker, Philip A. *The First Amendment.* Englewood Cliffs, NJ: Silver Burdett Press, 1991.

Mathews, Jay. "Student's Fantasy Violence Has Real Consequences." *Washington Post,* May 29, 1999.

Mathews, Jay. "Va. Student Cleared in Bomb Essay." *Washington Post,* June 11, 1999.

Pascoe, Elaine. *Freedom of Expression: The Right to Speak Out in America.* Brookfield, CT: Millbrook Press, 1992.

Steele, Philip, Philip Skele, and Penny Clarke. *Freedom of Speech?* New York: Franklin Watts, 1997.

Zeinert, Karen. *Free Speech: From Newspapers to Music Lyrics.* Hillside, NJ: Enslow Publishers, Inc., 1995.

Brandenburg v. Ohio 1969

Appellant: Clarence Brandenburg

Appellee: State of Ohio

Appellant's Claim: That convicting him for threatening the government at a Ku Klux Klan rally violated his freedom of speech.

Chief Lawyer for Appellant: Allen Brown

Chief Lawyer for Appellee: Leonard Kirschner

Justices for the Court: Hugo Lafayette Black, William J. Brennan, Jr., William O. Douglas, Abe Fortas, John M. Harlan II, Thurgood Marshall, Potter Stewart, Earl Warren, Byron R. White (unsigned decision)

Justices Dissenting: None

Date of Decision: June 9, 1969

Decision: The Supreme Court reversed Brandenburg's conviction as unconstitutional.

Significance: After *Brandenburg*, the First Amendment protects speech unless it encourages immediate violence or other unlawful action.

Threats against the government present a special problem for the freedom of speech. The First Amendment of the U.S. Constitution says, "Congress shall make no law . . . abridging [limiting] the freedom of speech." State and local governments must obey the freedom of speech under the Due Process Clause of the Fourteenth Amendment. The freedom of speech prevents the government from punishing someone for speaking his mind.

Governments naturally want to prevent revolutions or other violence against them. In the United States, however, the freedom of speech protects the right to criticize the government and to speak in favor of changing it. The question becomes whether this freedom allows people to speak in favor of violence against the government. That was the question in *Brandenburg v. Ohio*.

Revenge!

In 1919, Ohio passed a law called a criminal syndicalism statute. The law made it a crime to support sabotage, violence, or other unlawful ways to change the government. It also made it a crime to assemble a group of people to teach or support such conduct. The law originally was designed to fight communists, who supported violent revolution against American governments.

By the 1960s, communism was not a big threat in America. The civil rights movement, however, became strong. The civil rights movement was an effort by African Americans to achieve equal rights in America. The government helped the civil rights movement by passing laws to give equal rights to all people in America. Some white Americans who did not like the civil rights movement formed groups to oppose it. One of those groups was the Ku Klux Klan (KKK). Its members believed that white Protestant people were better than black people and members of other religions.

Clarence Brandenburg was the leader of a KKK group in Hamilton County, Ohio. One day he organized a KKK rally and asked a Cincinnati news reporter to cover the event. The reporter attended the rally with a cameraman, who filmed the event.

The rally included Brandenburg and eleven other members, all dressed in KKK uniforms and some carrying firearms. The Klansmen burned a cross. Some made hateful comments about African Americans and Jews. In a speech, Brandenburg said the KKK might have to seek revenge if the president, Congress, and the Supreme Court continued to suppress white Americans. Brandenburg also said he believed blacks should be returned to Africa and Jews to Israel.

The television reporter broadcast the rally on the local news. Afterward Ohio charged Brandenburg with violating the criminal syndical-

FREEDOM OF SPEECH

First Amendment rights must be protected equally for all people and groups, even groups that many citizens find objectionable. Courtesy of the Library of Congress.

ism statute by supporting violence against the government. Brandenburg was convicted and fined $1,000 and sentenced to one to ten years in prison. He appealed, saying the state of Ohio violated his freedom of speech by convicting him for speaking against the government. The court of appeals rejected this argument and affirmed (approved) Brandenburg's conviction. Brandenburg appealed again, but the Supreme Court of Ohio rejected the case. As his last resort, Brandenburg appealed to the U.S. Supreme Court.

Justice For All

With a unanimous decision, the Supreme Court ruled in favor of the man who had threatened it. The Court said Brandenburg's comments at the KKK rally were protected by the freedom of speech. His conviction, then, was unconstitutional.

The Court made its decision by distinguishing between two kinds of violent speech. One kind incites, or encourages, immediate violence against the government. For example, Brandenburg would have encouraged immediate violence if he had said, "let's go right now and burn down the building where they're passing laws to help the civil rights movement." The Supreme Court said speech that encourages immediate violence and is likely to succeed is not protected by the freedom of speech. It is too dangerous.

Brandenburg, however, did not encourage immediate violence. He said if the government continued to support the civil rights movement, the KKK might have to seek revenge in the future. The Supreme Court ruled that the First Amendment protects such speech. The spirit of the Court's decision was that such speech can be valuable because it gets society talking about what is good and bad about the government. It allows people to explore what is working, and what needs to be changed. Although the Supreme Court did not agree with Brandenburg's opinions, it said the freedom of speech protected his right to share those opinions with others.

Impact

Brandenburg made it harder for the government to convict people for speaking in favor of violence. This certainly was a victory for the freedom of speech. Some people, however, believe it also protects speech that has no value in society.

CROSS BURNING CASE

The Supreme Court also protected hateful, racist speech in *R.A.V. v. St. Paul* (1992). In that case, an African American couple with five children moved into a mostly white neighborhood in St. Paul, Minnesota. Several months later they awoke one night to find a burning cross in their front yard. Police arrested four white teenagers, one of whom lived across the street from the black family. Police charged one of the teenagers with violating a local law that made it a crime to display racial hate symbols in public. The U.S. Supreme Court, however, determined that the law violated the First Amendment freedom of speech. The Court said government cannot forbid categories of speech just because it does not like the speaker's message.

This became the focus of a sad case in the 1990s. In 1993, Lawrence Horn hired James Perry to kill Horn's eight-year-old, brain-damaged son. Perry killed the boy and the boy's mother and nurse by following the instructions in a book called *Hit Man*. Families of the victims sued Paladin Enterprises, the company that published the book. Paladin admitted that it published the book for murderers to use to learn how to kill people. Groups across the country, however, fought to protect Paladin's right to publish such books. The case raised serious questions about what kinds of speech the First Amendment protects.

Suggestions for further reading

Evans, J. Edward. *Freedom of Speech.* Minneapolis: Lerner Publications, Inc., 1990.

Farish, Leah. *The First Amendment: Freedom of Speech, Religion, and the Press.* Hillside, NJ: Enslow Publishers, Inc., 1998.

"Hate Speech." *Issues and Controversies on File.* June 4, 1999.

Hentoff, Nat. "Can a Book Be Liable for Murder?" *Washington Post,* May 8, 1999.

King, David C. *The Right to Speak Out.* Brookfield, CT: Millbrook Press, 1997.

Klinker, Philip A. *The First Amendment.* Englewood Cliffs, NJ: Silver Burdett Press, 1991.

Pascoe, Elaine. *Freedom of Expression: The Right to Speak Out in America.* Brookfield, CT: Millbrook Press, 1992.

Steele, Philip, Philip Skele, and Penny Clarke. *Freedom of Speech?* New York: Franklin Watts, 1997.

Cohen v. California
1971

Appellant: Paul Robert Cohen

Appellee: State of California

Appellant's Claim: That convicting him for wearing a jacket that said "F——— the Draft" in a county courthouse violated his freedom of speech.

Chief Lawyer for Appellant: Melville B. Nimmer

Chief Lawyer for Appellee: Michael T. Sauer

Justices for the Court: William J. Brennan, Jr., William O. Douglas, John Marshall Harlan II, Thurgood Marshall, Potter Stewart

Justices Dissenting: Hugo Lafayette Black, Harry A. Blackmun, Warren E. Burger, Byron R. White

Date of Decision: June 7, 1971

Decision: The Supreme Court overturned Cohen's conviction for disturbing the peace because it violated the First Amendment.

Significance: *Cohen* says the First Amendment protects profanity and other offensive language that is not obscene and does not provoke violence.

The Vietnam War, which lasted from 1955 until 1974 was a battle between North and South Vietnam. North Vietnam wanted to unite the country under communism. South Vietnam resisted with help from the United States. The

STUDENT PROTESTS, 1964–1967

The student protest movement began in 1964 in Berkeley, California. In what became known as the Free Speech Movement, students pressed issues against an academic bureaucracy out of touch with the problems of contemporary society. Students staged sit-ins, strikes, sang folk songs, and created slogans to identify the targets of their protests. By 1965, with escalating events in Vietnam coming to the forefront, students rallied in opposition to the war. "Make Love Not War" became a new slogan. The draft system of the Selective Service was the most visible target of the government war policy spurring draft card burnings, sit-ins, and picketing of local draft boards. From 1965 to1967 the nature of the student protests slowly changed from peaceful demonstrations to more aggressive tactics including calls for outright revolution. During this time period student activism and protests dramatically increased on college campuses nationwide.

United States used a military draft to build an army of Americans to fight in the war. By 1968, over 500,000 American troops were fighting in Vietnam.

Although the war was almost fifteen years old in 1968, there was no sign that North Vietnam would be defeated. Many Americans became opposed to the war. Some thought a civil war in Vietnam was not America's concern. They were angry to see young Americans die in a fight for another country. Others were generally opposed to human beings killing each other. Protests against the war became common in America. In *Cohen v. California,* the U.S. Supreme Court considered the case of a protestor in Los Angeles, California.

Disagreeing with the Draft

On April 26, 1968, police saw Paul Robert Cohen in the hall of a Los Angeles County courthouse wearing a jacket that said "F——— the Draft." There were men, women, and children in the hall. When Cohen entered one of the courtrooms, a police officer asked the judge to punish Cohen for contempt of court. (Contempt means being disrespectful of the court or the judge.) The judge refused, so the officer arrested Cohen for disturbing the peace after Cohen returned to the hallway. California law made it a crime to disturb the peace with "offensive conduct."

At his trial, Cohen testified that he wore the jacket to share with the public his deep feelings against the Vietnam War and the military draft. The evidence showed that Cohen did not provoke any violence or make any loud noises. Despite this evidence, Cohen was convicted for disturbing the peace and sentenced to thirty days in jail.

Cohen appealed to the California Court of Appeals, which affirmed (approved) Cohen's conviction. In its decision, the court defined "offensive conduct" as behavior that tends to provoke violence or disturb the peace. The court said that Cohen's behavior could have angered someone enough to make him or her attack Cohen or try to remove Cohen's jacket. Cohen appealed again, but the Supreme Court of California decided not to review the case. As a last resort, Cohen appealed to the U.S. Supreme Court.

Cohen argued to the Supreme Court that his conviction violated the freedom of speech. The First Amendment protects free speech by saying "Congress shall make no law . . . abridging [limiting] the freedom of speech." States, including California, must obey the freedom of speech under the Due Process Clause of the Fourteenth Amendment. The Due Process Clause prevents a state or local government from passing a law that violates a person's right to life, liberty (or freedom), and property.

Cohen argued that wearing his jacket in the courthouse did not create a disturbance. Indeed, there was no evidence that the jacket offended anyone. Cohen said that the lack of evidence meant that California was punishing him only for protesting against the draft with vulgar language. In other words, California was punishing his speech.

Free speech prevails

With a 5–4 decision, the Supreme Court ruled in favor of Cohen and reversed his conviction. Writing for the Court, Justice John Marshall Harlan II agreed that California convicted Cohen solely because of his speech. Justice Harlan said that the conviction could not stand unless Cohen's speech was outside the protection of the First Amendment.

JOHN MARSHALL HARLAN II

Justice John Marshall Harlan II served on the U.S. Supreme Court from 1955 to 1971. (His grandfather, John Marshall Harlan, served on the Supreme Court from 1877 to 1911.) Before joining the Supreme Court, Harlan II enjoyed a career as a trial lawyer in New York, a military and public servant, and a judge on the United States Court of Appeals for the Second Circuit.

As a Supreme Court Justice, Harlan worked hard to achieve fairness in every case. Justice Harlan strongly believed that the Court should respect the other branches of the federal government, as well as the individual state governments. At the same time, he often sided with the rights of individuals. Four years before the Supreme Court recognized a general right of privacy, Justice Harlan called marital privacy a "fundamental right." Justice Harlan also wrote opinions protecting the First Amendment freedoms of speech and assembly. Speaking about Justice Harlan, Judge Henry Friendly said Justice Harlan enjoyed "nearly uniform respect" from his fellow justices and judges.

For instance, the First Amendment does not protect obscenity—speech about sex that is offensive and worthless. Justice Harlan said that Cohen's jacket was not obscene because it made a political statement, not a sexual one. The First Amendment also does not protect fighting words—words used to start a fight or cause violence. Justice Harlan said that Cohen's speech was not directed at anyone to start a fight, rather Cohen simply was protesting against the military draft.

Justice Harlan said that the ultimate question was whether the government may punish people for using an offensive four-letter word. The answer was "no" because the First Amendment protects the right to use such language, especially in political speech. The United States adopted the First Amendment to allow people to criticize the government, which is exactly what Cohen had done. Justice Harlan said that if the government could prohibit certain words, it would have the power to prohibit the expression of emotions and ideas. The end result—government censorship of unpopular views—is forbidden by the freedom of speech.

Suggestions for further reading

Encyclopedia of the American Constitution. New York: Macmillan Publishing Company, 1986.

Evans, J. Edward. *Freedom of Speech.* Minneapolis: Lerner Publications, Inc., 1990.

Farish, Leah. *The First Amendment: Freedom of Speech, Religion, and the Press.* Hillside, NJ: Enslow Publishers, Inc., 1998.

King, David C. *The Right to Speak Out.* Brookfield, CT: Millbrook Press, 1997.

Klinker, Philip A. *The First Amendment.* Englewood Cliffs, NJ: Silver Burdett Press, 1991.

Pascoe, Elaine. *Freedom of Expression: The Right to Speak Out in America.* Brookfield, CT: Millbrook Press, 1992.

Steele, Philip, Philip Skele, and Penny Clarke. *Freedom of Speech?* New York: Franklin Watts, 1997.

Zeinert, Karen. *Free Speech: From Newspapers to Music Lyrics.* Hillside, NJ: Enslow Publishers, Inc., 1995.

Federal Communications Commission v. Pacifica Foundation 1978

Petitioner: Federal Communications Commission (FCC)

Respondents: Pacifica Foundation, et al.

Petitioner's Claim: That the federal government can control the time for broadcasting offensive radio programs.

Chief Lawyer for Petitioner: Joseph A. Marino

Chief Lawyer for Respondent: Harry A. Plotkin

Justices for the Court: Harry A. Blackmun, Warren E. Burger, Lewis F. Powell, Jr., William H. Rehnquist, John Paul Stevens

Justices Dissenting: William J. Brennan, Jr., Thurgood Marshall, Potter Stewart, Byron R. White

Date of Decision: July 3, 1978

Decision: The federal government can penalize a radio station for broadcasting an indecent program when children are likely to be listening.

Significance: *Pacifica* defined indecent broadcast material and recognized the FCC's power to control the time of such broadcasts.

FREEDOM OF SPEECH

The First Amendment protects the freedom of speech in America by saying, "Congress shall make no law . . . abridging [limiting] the freedom of speech." When Americans think of free speech, they usually imagine speeches delivered in public, or books, magazines, and newspapers sold in stores and newsstands.

George Carlin's show, "Dirty Words," was found to be offensive by the Supreme Court because it contained "obscene, indecent, or profane language."
Reproduced by permission of Archive Photos, Inc.

The freedom of speech, however, also applies to the broadcast media of television and radio. In Washington, D.C., the Federal Communications Commission ("FCC") regulates these media by making rules for radio and television stations to follow. The FCC was created by Congress to ensure that radio and television stations serve a beneficial public interest.

Although the FCC regulates the broadcast media, it is not to interfere with the freedom of speech. That means it cannot stop a radio station from broadcasting a program just because the government does not like the program. After a program airs, however, the FCC can fine the radio station if the program violates one of the FCC's rules. Under a law passed by Congress, one of those rules is that radio stations may not use "obscene, indecent, or profane language." In *Federal Communications Commission v. Pacifica Foundation,* (1978) a radio station challenged that rule, saying it violated the freedom of speech.

Dirty words

The case began in the early 1970s, when a comedian named George Carlin had a twelve minute act called "Dirty Words." One night he recorded the act before a live audience in California. In the act, Carlin listed seven words that he called "the curse words and the swear words, the cuss words and the words you can't say, that you're not supposed to say all the time." After listing the seven dirty words, Carlin spent the remainder of the act using them many, many times. Carlin's goal was to show that it was silly for people to be offended by words.

On October 30, 1973, a New York radio station called Pacifica Foundation broadcast "Dirty Words" at 2 o'clock in the afternoon. A few weeks later, a man who heard the broadcast while driving with his young son wrote a complaint to the FCC. The FCC sent the complaint to Pacifica, which explained that it did not mean to offend anyone with the broadcast. Instead, it had aired "Dirty Words" during a program that examined society's attitudes about language. Pacifica said "Carlin is not mouthing obscenities, he is merely using words to satirize how harmless and essentially silly our attitudes towards those words."

On February 21, 1975, the FCC decided Pacifica had violated the law against "indecent" broadcasts. The FCC said a broadcast is indecent when it exposes children to offensive language about sexual or excretory actions or body parts. Pacifica violated the law by airing such a program in the middle of the day, when children were likely to be listening. The FCC said it would fine Pacifica in the future if it ever violated the law again.

Pacifica appealed to the United States Court of Appeals for the Third Circuit. That court reversed and ruled in favor of Pacifica. One of the three judges on the panel said the FCC had violated Pacifica's freedom of speech. The FCC took the case to the U.S. Supreme Court.

Cleaning up the act

With a 5–4 decision, the Supreme Court reversed and ruled in favor of the FCC. Writing for the Court, Justice John Paul Stevens agreed that Carlin's act was speech under the First Amendment. He said, however, that it was "vulgar, offensive, and shocking." Justice Stevens said such language has almost no social value, so it is not entitled to full protection under the freedom of speech.

HOWARD STERN

After the Supreme Court's decision in *Pacifica,* the FCC worked hard to discourage indecent radio broadcasts. One of its targets was Howard Stern, a radio disc jockey in New York City whose morning program was broadcast in major cities throughout the country. Stern was called a "shock jock" because his programs contained shocking references to sexual intercourse, ethnic and religious groups, and other sensitive topics. Stern's program offended many people who did not want their children to listen to Stern's airwave antics.

During a Christmas show in 1988, Stern referred to a man playing a piano with his penis. The FCC called the broadcast "indecent" and fined Stern's employer, Infinity Broadcasting Corporation. Over the next seven years the FCC issued a total of $1.7 million in fines for various Stern broadcasts.

Infinity fought the fines, arguing that Stern had a constitutional right to express his opinions on the radio. On September 1, 1995, however, Infinity gave up the fight and agreed to pay the fines. Although Infinity did not admit to any wrongdoing, the FCC said the settlement was a victory for regulations against indecent broadcasts.

As rationale for the decision, Justice Stevens said radio and television had become so powerful in America, invading the privacy of everyone's home. Children had easy access to such programs, even without their parents' permission. That meant is was reasonable for the FCC to limit the broadcast of indecent material to times when children were not likely to be listening. This did not violate the freedom of speech because broadcasters could air such programs at other times, such as between midnight and six in the morning.

Dirty decision?

Four justices dissented, meaning they disagreed with the Court's decision. Justice William J. Brennan, Jr., a strong supporter of the freedom of speech, wrote a dissenting opinion. Justice Brennan said that while obscenity is not protected by the First Amendment, indecent language is. He said the Court's decision would force adults to listen to nothing but children's programming during the day. He also feared the decision would allow the FCC to ban all broadcasts that contain "four-letter words." Such a restriction, he wrote, would include plays by Shakespeare, a good deal of political speech, and even portions of the Bible.

Suggestions for further reading

Evans, J. Edward. *Freedom of Speech.* Minneapolis: Lerner Publications, Inc., 1990.

Farhi, Paul. "Stern Indecency Case Settled." *Washington Post,* September 2, 1995.

Farish, Leah. *The First Amendment: Freedom of Speech, Religion, and the Press.* Hillside, NJ: Enslow Publishers, Inc., 1998.

King, David C. *The Right to Speak Out.* Brookfield, CT: Millbrook Press, 1997.

Klinker, Philip A. *The First Amendment.* Englewood Cliffs, NJ: Silver Burdett Press, 1991.

Pascoe, Elaine. *Freedom of Expression: The Right to Speak Out in America.* Brookfield, CT: Millbrook Press, 1992.

Steele, Philip, Philip Skele, and Penny Clarke. *Freedom of Speech?* New York: Franklin Watts, 1997.

World Book Encyclopedia, 1997 ed., s.v. "Federal Communications Commission."

Zeinert, Karen.*Free Speech: From Newspapers to Music Lyrics.* Hillside, NJ: Enslow Publishers, Inc., 1995.

Island Trees Union Free School District Board of Education v. Pico 1982

Petitioners: Island Trees Union Free School District Board of Education, et al.

Respondents: Steven A. Pico, et al.

Petitioners' Claim: That removing vulgar and racist books from public school libraries does not violate the First Amendment.

Chief Lawyer for Petitioners: George W. Lipp, Jr.

Chief Lawyer for Respondents: Alan H. Levine

Justices for the Court: Harry A. Blackmun, William J. Brennan, Jr., Thurgood Marshall, John Paul Stevens, Byron R. White

Justices Dissenting: Warren E. Burger, Sandra Day O'Connor, Lewis F. Powell, Jr., William H. Rehnquist

Date of Decision: June 25, 1982

Decision: Removing books from public school libraries because of their political or social ideas violates the freedom of speech.

Significance: *Island Trees* limits the ability of public schools to remove offensive books from their libraries.

BANNED BOOKS

The 1994 book, *Banned in the U.S.A.,* offers a list of the fifty books most often banned or challenged in the 1990s. Some of the books included in the top five of this list are *Of Mice and Men, by John Steinbeck (1937), challenged mainly on the basis of the profanity contained in it;* The Catcher in the Rye, by J. D. Salinger (1951); *The Adventures of Huckleberry Finn, by Mark Twain (1885), for its racial epithets; and* The Chocolate War, by Robert Cormier (1974), because it portrays school and church in a negative light.

A significant number of books on the list have won Newbery, National Book, Pulitzer, or even Nobel prizes: *A Wrinkle in Time, by Madeleine L'Engle,* I Know Why the Caged Bird Sings, by Maya Angelou, and *One Hundred Years of Solitude,* by Gabriel Garcia Marquez.

Richard Ahrens, Frank Martin, and Patrick Hughes were members of the Board of Education of the Island Trees Union Free School District No. 26 in New York. In September 1975, they attended a conference sponsored by Parents of New York United ("PONYU"). PONYU was a group of conservative parents that was concerned about education in New York's public schools. At the conference, Ahrens, Martin, and Hughes got lists of books that PONYU considered to be inappropriate for public school students.

When they returned from the conference, the board members learned that their high school library had nine of the books on the lists, and the junior high school library had one. The books included *Slaughterhouse Five,* by Kurt Vonnegut, Jr., and *Best Short Stories of Negro Writers,* edited by Langston Hughes. Some of the books contained graphic descriptions of sexual intercourse. One criticized President George Washington for owning slaves. Some of the books said hateful things about Jesus Christ and Jews.

The board ordered the school principals to remove the nine books from the libraries so the board could study them. In a press release, the board said the books were "anti-American, anti-Christian, anti-Semitic, and just plain filthy." (Anti-Semitic means hateful of Jews.) The board said its duty was to protect students from moral dangers in books just like it protected them from physical and medical dangers.

A short time later, the board formed a committee of parents and school personnel to study the books. The committee's job was to determine if the books had any educational value. The committee recommended that the board return five of the nine books to the libraries, and make one more available to students with parental permission. The board, however, rejected this recommendation, returned only one book to the high school library, and made one other available with parental permission only.

Fighting censorship

Richard A. Pico and three other students filed a lawsuit against the Island Trees Board of Education in federal district court. The students said the board removed the books not because they lacked educational value, but because they offended the board's social, political, and moral tastes. The students argued that removing books for those reasons violated the First Amendment freedom of speech. The First Amendment says, "Congress shall make no law . . . abridging [limiting] the freedom of speech." State and local governments, including public school boards, must obey the freedom of speech under the Due Process Clause of the Fourteenth Amendment.

The district court granted summary judgment for the board, which means it ruled in favor of the board without holding a trial. The court said it would be unwise for it to interfere with a decision made by the Island Trees Board of Education. It also said removing "vulgar" books from public school libraries does not violate the freedom of speech.

On appeal, the United States Court of Appeals for the Second Circuit reversed the district court's decision. It said Pico and the other students deserved a trial to force the Board of Education to give a good reason for removing the books from the libraries. The Island Trees Board of Education took the case up to the U.S. Supreme Court.

Read all about it

In a close decision, the Supreme Court voted 5–4 in favor of Pico and the students. Writing for the Court, Justice William J. Brennan, Jr., said the

AMERICA'S FIRST BOOK BURNING

Burning books has been a popular form of censorship. America's first book burning happened in Boston, Massachusetts, in 1650. That year William Pynchon, founder of Springfield, Massachusetts, wrote a religious pamphlet called *The Meritorious Price of Our Redemption.* In it he challenged part of the Puritan religion as taught by the ministers of the Massachusetts Bay Colony in Boston.

When the book arrived in Boston from London, where it was published, it caused a scandal. Puritan authorities confiscated as many copies as they could find. The General Court, which served as both the legislature and court in Massachusetts, condemned the book and ordered it to be burned. The burning occurred on October 20, 1650 in the Boston marketplace, with only four copies escaping the fire.

The General Court ordered Pynchon to appear before it to take back his offensive remarks. Pynchon only retracted some statements and so was sent back to England. There he wrote more religious texts, including two expanded versions of his controversial book. Pynchon died in England on October 29, 1662.

students deserved a trial to determine if the board's reason for removing the books violated the freedom of speech.

Justice Brennan said public schools are allowed to prepare students to be good citizens by teaching them good morals. Schools, however, cannot violate the First Amendment while doing so. Quoting ***Tinker v. Des Moines Independent Community School,*** Justice Brennan said students do not "shed their constitutional rights to freedom of speech and expression at the schoolhouse gate."

Justice Brennan said the freedom of speech was designed to allow Americans to discuss, debate, and share information and ideas. Authors could not share information in books if people were not allowed to read them. That means the freedom of speech also includes the right to receive information and ideas. "[S]tudents must always remain free to inquire, to study and to evaluate, to gain new maturity and understanding."

Justice Brennan decided that when a school removes books from the library because it doesn't like the political or social ideas in them, it violates the right to receive information. Removing books because they are vulgar or lack educational value, however, is proper for teaching students to be good citizens with good morals. Pico and the other students, then, deserved a trial to determine the real reason the Island Trees Board of Education removed the books from the libraries.

Who rules school?

Four justices dissented, meaning they disagreed with the Court's decision. Chief Justice Warren E. Burger wrote a dissenting opinion. He said the question in the case was whether local schools should be run "by elected school boards, or by federal judges and teenage pupils." Justice Burger strongly urged that school boards have the final say about what books to include in public school libraries. He disagreed that the freedom of speech includes a right to receive information. Warren said school boards are allowed to remove vulgar books that may prevent the development of good morals.

Suggestions for further reading

Evans, J. Edward. *Freedom of Speech.* Minneapolis: Lerner Publications, Inc., 1990.

Farish, Leah. *The First Amendment: Freedom of Speech, Religion, and the Press.* Hillside, NJ: Enslow Publishers, Inc., 1998.

Hentoff, Nat. *The Day They Came to Arrest the Book: A Novel.* New York: Dell Publishing Company, 1982.

King, David C. *The Right to Speak Out.* Brookfield, CT: Millbrook Press, 1997.

Klinker, Philip A. *The First Amendment.* Englewood Cliffs, NJ: Silver Burdett Press, 1991.

Noble, William. *Bookbanning in America.* Middlebury: Paul S. Ericksson, 1990.

Pascoe, Elaine. *Freedom of Expression: The Right to Speak Out in America.* Brookfield, CT: Millbrook Press, 1992.

Springfield Library website, www.springfieldlibrary.org/Pynchon/pynchon.html.

Steele, Philip. *Censorship.* New York: Discovery Books, 1992.

Steele, Philip, Philip Skele, and Penny Clarke. *Freedom of Speech?* New York: Franklin Watts, 1997.

aylor, C.L. *Censorship.* New York: Franklin Watts, 1986.

Zeinert, Karen. *Free Speech: From Newspapers to Music Lyrics.* Hillside, NJ: Enslow Publishers, Inc., 1995.

Bethel School District No. 403 v. Fraser 1986

Petitioners: Bethel School District, et al.

Respondents: Matthew N. Fraser, et al.

Petitioners' Claim: That punishing Fraser for using offensive language in high school assembly speech did not violate the freedom of speech.

Chief Lawyer for Petitioners: William A. Coats

Chief Lawyer for Respondents: Jeffrey T. Haley

Justices for the Court: Harry A. Blackmun, William J. Brennan, Jr., Warren E. Burger, Sandra Day O'Connor, Lewis F. Powell, Jr., William H. Rehnquist, Byron R. White

Justices Dissenting: Thurgood Marshall, John Paul Stevens

Date of Decision: July 7, 1986

Decision: Bethel High School did not violate the freedom of speech by punishing Fraser.

Significance: *Bethel* says students in school have less freedom of speech than adults in public. Schools can encourage good values by punishing offensive speech that people may use outside school.

The First Amendment of the U.S. Constitution protects the freedom of speech in America. It says, "Congress shall make no law . . . abridging [limiting] the freedom of speech." State and local governments must obey the freedom of speech under the Due Process Clause of the Fourteenth Amendment. The Due Process Clause prevents state and local governments from violating a person's right to life, liberty (or freedom), and property.

In ***Tinker v. Des Moines Independent Community School*** (1969), the Supreme Court said that students do not lose their freedom of speech when they go to school. Students, like adults, are people under the Constitution, so they are also protected by the First Amendment. In *Tinker,* the Court said that schools can limit free speech only when it interferes with learning.

School assembly

Matthew N. Fraser was an outstanding student at Bethel High School in Pierce County, Washington. In April 1983, Fraser prepared to give a speech at a school assembly. The assembly was part of a school program to teach about government. In his speech, Fraser would nominate a fellow classmate, Jeff Kuhlman, as student vice-president. Fraser prepared a speech that referred to Kuhlman using many metaphors about male sexuality.

Before the assembly, Fraser shared his speech with three teachers. One teacher told Fraser that the speech was inappropriate and that Fraser "probably should not deliver it." Another said the speech would cause problems "in that it would raise eyebrows." Evidence indicated that another person said the speech would have severe consequences. None of the teachers, however, told Fraser that the speech violated the student handbook.

Fraser delivered his speech at the assembly on April 26, 1983. Six hundred students were in the audience, some as young as fourteen. During Fraser's speech, some students hooted and yelled, and a few mimicked the sexual activities they thought Fraser was describing. Other students appeared to be embarrassed by Fraser's speech. There was no evidence, however, that the speech offended anyone.

Bethel High's student handbook had a rule that prevented students from interfering with education by using obscene or profane language. The day after the assembly, the assistant principal called Fraser into her office and told him that she believed he had violated the rule. The principal had letters from five teachers describing Fraser's speech. One teacher said she had to skip a part of her lesson to discuss the speech with her class.

Fraser admitted that he used sexual references in his speech. As a punishment, Bethel High School suspended Fraser for three days and removed his name from a list of candidates for graduation speaker. Fraser challenged his punishment. A hearing officer, however, approved the punishment after deciding that Fraser's speech was "indecent, lewd, and offensive." Fraser served two days of his suspension and was allowed to return to school on the third day.

Fraser sues

Fraser sued Bethel High School in federal district court. He argued that the school violated the First Amendment by punishing him for his assembly speech. The district court agreed and awarded Fraser over $13,000 for damages and attorneys' fees. The court also said that the Bethel School District could not prevent Fraser from being the graduation speaker. After being elected by his classmates, Fraser gave a graduation speech on June 8, 1983.

Meanwhile, Bethel School District appealed the case. The U.S. Court of Appeals for the Ninth Circuit affirmed (approved) the district court's decision. It said that under *Tinker,* schools cannot punish a student for speech unless he disrupts education. Even if Fraser's speech was offensive, it did not disrupt learning at Bethel High. Bethel School District disagreed and took the case to the U.S. Supreme Court.

Fraser loses

With a 7–2 decision, the Supreme Court reversed and ruled in favor of Bethel School District. Chief Justice Warren E. Burger wrote the Court's opinion.

Justice Burger agreed that under *Tinker,* the First Amendment protects students even when they are in school. Justice Burger said, however, that one of the purposes of school is to teach students how to be good citizens. Part of being a good citizen is learning how to behave in public. Therefore, the freedom of speech in school must be balanced against the school's need to teach socially appropriate behavior.

Justice Burger also agreed that the freedom of speech allows adults to use offensive language, even in public. He said, however, that students in school have less protection under the First Amendment than adults in

OLFF V. EAST SIDE UNION HIGH SCHOOL DISTRICT

In 1969, Robert Olff was a fifteen-year-old student in good standing at James Lick High School in San Jose, California. The school had the following rule for boy's hair: "Hair shall be trim and clean. A boy's hair shall not fall below the eyes in front and shall not cover the ears, and it shall not extend below the collar in the back."

On September 10, 1969, when Olff went to school to register for the year, a teacher sent him to see the vice- principal. The vice- principal said that Olff's hair violated the school rule. Olff was not allowed to attend school until he cut his hair.

Olff sued the school in federal district court. He argued that the school's rule violated his freedom of expression. Teachers for the school said that long hair on boys created "a less serious atmosphere, more [wasted] time, more discipline problems, more class distractions, and less education." Although the district court ruled in Olff's favor, the court of appeals reversed. It said that the hair rule did not violate the freedom of expression or the right of privacy. Instead, it was a valid rule designed to foster education at James Lick High School. The U.S. Supreme Court refused to review the case.

public. Fraser's speech about male sexuality may have offended teenage girls. It also may have caused problems for younger students who were just learning about sexuality. Justice Burger decided that Bethel High was allowed to punish Fraser to make the point that vulgar language is wrong under the values taught by public education.

No warning

Two justices dissented, meaning they disagreed with the Court's decision. Justice Thurgood Marshall did not think that Fraser's speech had disrupted learning at Bethel High. Justice John Paul Stevens agreed with Justice Marshall. Justice Stevens also thought that Fraser's punishment was unfair because neither the student handbook nor the three teachers had warned Fraser that he could be suspended for giving his speech. Justice Stevens said that the Fourteenth Amendment of the U.S. Constitution prevents public schools from punishing students without fair warning.

Suggestions for further reading

Evans, J. Edward. *Freedom of Speech.* Minneapolis: Lerner Publications, Inc., 1990.

Farish, Leah. *The First Amendment: Freedom of Speech, Religion, and the Press.* Hillside, NJ: Enslow Publishers, Inc., 1998.

King, David C. *The Right to Speak Out.* Brookfield, CT: Millbrook Press, 1997.

Klinker, Philip A. *The First Amendment.* Englewood Cliffs, NJ: Silver Burdett Press, 1991.

Pascoe, Elaine. *Freedom of Expression: The Right to Speak Out in America.* Brookfield, CT: Millbrook Press, 1992.

Steele, Philip, Philip Skele, and Penny Clarke. *Freedom of Speech?* New York: Franklin Watts, 1997.

Zeinert, Karen. *Free Speech: From Newspapers to Music Lyrics.* Hillside, NJ: Enslow Publishers, Inc., 1995.

Frisby v. Schultz
1988

Appellants: Russell Frisby, Supervisor of the Town of Brookfield, Wisconsin, et al.

Appellees: Sandra C. Schultz and Robert C. Braun

Appellants' Claim: That a law banning picketing in front of residential homes did not violate the freedom of speech.

Chief Lawyer for Appellants: Harold H. Furhman

Chief Lawyer for Appellees: Steven Frederick McDowell

Justices for the Court: Harry A. Blackmun, Anthony M. Kennedy, Sandra Day O'Connor, William H. Rehnquist, Antonin Scalia, Byron R. White

Justices Dissenting: William J. Brennan, Jr., Thurgood Marshall, John Paul Stevens

Date of Decision: June 27, 1988

Decision: The law banning picketing was constitutional under the First Amendment.

Significance: Freedom of speech does not give picketers the right to harass people in their homes.

Abortion is ending a woman's pregnancy before the fetus or child is born. (Abortion supporters call the unborn a fetus. Abortion protestors call the unborn a child.) In the landmark decision of ***Roe v. Wade*** (1973), the U.S. Supreme Court decided that women have a constitutional right to have abortions. Since then, abortion supporters have fought hard to

WHEN IS PICKETING CONSTITUTIONALLY PROTECTED?

Picketing is normally a peaceful carrying of signs and banners clearly advertising a grievance or the purpose of a demonstration. It is a recognized means of communication.

Beginning in the 1930s, some states sought to hinder the development of labor unions by passing laws prohibiting picketing. The states argued picketing is conduct, not speech, and therefore not protected by the First Amendment. In 1941 the Supreme Court concluded that peaceful picketing is a constitutionally protected means of transmitting ideas.

The guarantee of free expression has often been weighed against a state's desire to preserve public peace through picketing restrictions. Normally, picketing that becomes an instrument of force, vandalism, intimidation, or coercion is not protected by the First Amendment. Similarly, First Amendment protection does not apply to picketing that is part of other conduct that violates state law.

protect this right. Abortion protestors, who believe abortion is murder, have fought equally hard for the rights of the unborn.

Picket fencing

Brookfield, Wisconsin, is a residential suburb of Milwaukee and was home to an abortion doctor. Abortion protestors, including Sandra C. Schultz and Robert C. Braun, decided to picket on a public street outside the doctor's home to protest against abortion. Schultz and Brown picketed with many other protestors six times during April and May 1985. The groups ranged from eleven to over forty people who picketed for between one and two hours.

The picketing was orderly and peaceful. No one violated any laws against blocking the streets, making loud noises, or disorderly conduct.

The Town Board, however, believed the picketers were harassing the doctor. To stop the picketers, the Town Board enacted a new law on May 15, 1985. The law made it illegal "for any person to engage in picketing before or about the residence or dwelling of any individual in the Town of Brookfield." The law said its goal was to protect privacy in residential homes.

After the board enacted the new law, Schultz and Braun stopped picketing and filed a lawsuit in federal district court. They said the law violated the freedom of speech. The First Amendment protects free speech by saying "Congress shall make no law . . . abridging [limiting] the freedom of speech." State and local governments, including the Town Board of Brookfield, must obey the freedom of speech under the Due Process Clause of the Fourteenth Amendment. Schultz and Braun asked the trial court to prevent Brookfield from enforcing the anti-picketing law. The trial court ruled in favor of Schultz and Braun, so Brookfield appealed all the way to the U.S. Supreme Court.

Privacy prevails

With a 6–3 decision, the Supreme Court reversed and ruled in favor of Brookfield. Writing for the Court, Justice Sandra Day O'Connor analyzed the freedom of speech and its limitations. Justice O'Connor said picketing is protected by the freedom of speech because it helps Americans consider and discuss important public issues.

The nature of the freedom depends on whether the speaker is in a public or non-public place. Justice O'Connor said picketers on public streets in a residential neighborhood deserve the greatest amount of protection under the First Amendment. Public streets have become a traditional place for the exercise of free speech in America.

By banning picketing "before or about" residential homes, Brookfield was trying to regulate the place where people could exercise free speech. Justice O'Connor said the government can restrict speech like this only if it satisfies a three part test. First, the law must give speakers other ways to express their ideas. Brookfield's anti-picketing law satisfied this test. It only prevented the picketers from gathering in front of a single home to harass the people inside. It did not prevent them from spreading their message by marching through neighborhoods, going door-to-door with anti-abortion literature, or calling people on the telephone.

AMERICA'S MOST WANTED

The battle between abortion doctors and protestors reached the internet in 1999. Two groups, the American Coalition of Life Activists and Advocates for Life Ministries, sponsored a website to protest against abortion. The website featured Old West style "Wanted" posters for abortion doctors. After three of the doctors were killed by abortion protestors, their names were crossed out on the website. When protestors injured a doctor, the doctor's name on the website turned gray.

Planned Parenthood and a group of doctors filed a lawsuit in federal court against the anti-abortion groups and twelve individuals. They said the website contained death threats that violated federal laws. On February 3, 1999, a federal jury in Portland, Oregon, agreed and awarded the plaintiffs $107 million in damages.

Abortion protestors said the verdict trampled on the freedom of speech. A lawyer for the plaintiffs, however, said the verdict protected freedom for abortion doctors. "They want the freedom to hug their child in front of a window." The verdict likely will be in appeals for many years.

The second part of the test was that the law must be designed to serve an important government interest. Brookfield's anti-picketing law did that because it was designed to protect privacy in people's homes. Quoting from a prior case, Justice O'Connor said the American home is "the last citadel of the tired, the weary, and the sick." She said the First Amendment does not require Americans to welcome unwanted speech into their homes.

The third part of the test was that the law must be written narrowly so that it does not prevent more speech than necessary to protect privacy. Justice O'Connor said Brookfield's anti-picketing law satisfied this part of the test as well. Again, the law only prevented people from gathering in front of a single home to harass the people inside. Because Brookfield's law satisfied each of the three conditions, Brookfield could stop the protestors from picketing in front of the abortion doctor's home.

Sorry, Charlie

Three justices dissented, meaning they disagreed with the Court's decision. Justice John Paul Stevens wrote a dissenting opinion. Justice Stevens thought the law banned all picketing, whether hostile or friendly. In fact, he said the law would prevent fifth graders from carrying a sign saying "GET WELL CHARLIE — OUR TEAM NEEDS YOU" in front of their sick teammate's home. Stevens said that violated the freedom of speech. Without a doubt, the case showed the difficulty of balancing the privacy rights of abortion doctors and the free speech rights of abortion protestors.

Suggestions for further reading

Evans, J. Edward. *Freedom of Speech.* Minneapolis: Lerner Publications, Inc., 1990.

Farish, Leah. *The First Amendment: Freedom of Speech, Religion, and the Press.* Hillside, NJ: Enslow Publishers, Inc., 1998.

King, David C. *The Right to Speak Out.* Brookfield, CT: Millbrook Press, 1997.

Klinker, Philip A. *The First Amendment.* Englewood Cliffs, NJ: Silver Burdett Press, 1991.

Pascoe, Elaine. *Freedom of Expression: The Right to Speak Out in America.* Brookfield, CT: Millbrook Press, 1992.

Steele, Philip, Philip Skele, and Penny Clarke. *Freedom of Speech?* New York: Franklin Watts, 1997.

Verhovek, Sam Howe. "Creators of Anti-Abortion Web Site Told to Pay Millions." *New York Times,* February 3, 1999.

Zeinert, Karen. *Free Speech: From Newspapers to Music Lyrics.* Hillside, NJ: Enslow Publishers, Inc., 1995.

Simon & Schuster v. Members of the New York State Crime Victims Board 1991

Petitioner: Simon & Schuster, Inc.

Respondents: Members of New York State Crime Victims Board, et al.

Petitioner's Claim: That New York's Son of Sam law, which required criminals to forfeit money made from stories about their crimes, violated the First Amendment freedom of speech.

Chief Lawyer for Petitioner: Ronald S. Rauchberg

Chief Lawyer for Respondents: Howard L. Zwickel, Assistant Attorney General of New York

Justices for the Court: Harry A. Blackmun, Anthony M. Kennedy, Sandra Day O'Connor, William H. Rehnquist, Antonin Scalia, David H. Souter, John Paul Stevens, Byron R. White

Justices Dissenting: None (Clarence Thomas did not participate)

Date of Decision: December 10, 1991

Decision: New York's Son of Sam law violated the First Amendment by limiting speech too much.

Significance: The Court emphasized that, except in rare cases, laws that limit speech based on its content violate the First Amendment.

Son of Sam

From 1976 through the summer of 1977, David Berkowitz committed a series of murders in New York City. In a letter to the police before he was caught, Berkowitz called himself the Son of Sam. After Berkowitz was caught, he planned to sell his story for publication. New York did not think Berkowitz should be allowed to profit from his story while his victims and their families went without payment for their injuries.

To stop Berkowitz, New York passed a statute called the Son of Sam law. The law required anyone who published a criminal's story to give payment for the story to the Crime Victims Board instead of to the criminal. The board would hold the money to pay any victims who sued the criminal and won. If no victim filed a lawsuit for five years, the board would return the money to the criminal.

Wiseguy

Henry Hill was part of an organized crime family in New York. In a twenty-six-year career that ended with his arrest in 1980, Hill committed

Murderer David Berkowitz (Son of Sam) was the reason for the controversial New York law. Reproduced by permission of AP/Wide World Photos.

robberies, extortion, and drug deals. After his arrest, Hill entered the federal witness protection program. The program allowed Hill to avoid prosecution for his crimes by testifying against his former partners.

In August 1981, author Nicholas Pileggi agreed to write a book about Hill's life. Hill and Pileggi then signed a contract for Simon & Schuster to publish the book. The book, called *Wiseguy,* was published in January 1986. In it, Hill admitted to what the Supreme Court called "an astonishing variety of crimes."

The New York State Crime Victims Board learned about *Wiseguy* soon after it was published. By then Simon & Schuster had paid Hill $98,250 and planned to pay him another $27,958. The board decided that Simon & Schuster had violated the Son of Sam law by paying Hill instead of giving the money to the board. It ordered Hill to turn over all the money he had received, and ordered Simon & Schuster to give Hill's future payments directly to the board.

In August 1987, Simon & Schuster sued the board in federal district court. It argued that the Son of Sam law violated the First Amendment freedoms of speech and the press. The First Amendment says, "Congress shall make no law . . . abridging [limiting] the freedom of speech, or of the press." States, including New York, must obey these freedoms under the Due Process Clause of the Fourteenth Amendment. The district court ruled in favor of the board and the court of appeals affirmed, so Simon & Schuster took the case to the U.S. Supreme Court.

Wise Justices

With a unanimous decision, the Supreme Court reversed and ruled in favor of Simon & Schuster. The Court said New York's Son of Sam law violated the First Amendment.

Writing for the Court, Justice Sandra Day O'Connor said restrictions that limit based on its substance ("content based restrictions") are the most serious violations of the First Amendment. For instance, New York's Son of Sam law only forced criminals writing about their crimes to forfeit their money. Criminals or other people writing about other subjects could keep their money. Content based restrictions are serious because they give the government the power to eliminate ideas it does not like.

Justice O'Connor said content based restrictions violate the First Amendment unless they satisfy two conditions. First, they must be need-

SON OF SINATRA

Frank Sinatra was a popular singer of American songs who became wealthy with his talent. In December 1963, Barry Keenan and two other men kidnapped Sinatra's 19-year-old son. Keenan's crew held Frank Jr. until Sinatra paid a $240,000 ransom. They released Frank Jr. unharmed after collecting the cash, but were caught days later when a family member turned them in.

Keenan spent four years in prison for his crime. In 1997, writer Peter Gilstrap interviewed Keenan and published a story about the kidnapping. Columbia Pictures then agreed to pay Keenan and others $1.5 million for the right to make the story into a movie.

California has a Son of Sam law that prevents felons from making money on stories about their crimes. Frank Sinatra Jr. filed a lawsuit to prevent Columbia Pictures from paying Keenan any money. Frank Jr.'s lawyer described Keenan's deal with Columbia as a "second ransom." Keenan, however, said he paid his debt to society by spending four years in jail. Keenan said the freedom of speech protects his right to sell his story. Frank Jr.'s attorney disagreed, saying "You shouldn't be able to put a gun to someone's ear and kidnap them, then cash in."

ed to serve a compelling, or highly important, state interest. The Son of Sam law satisfied this condition because it was needed to prevent criminals from profiting from their crimes while victims went without payment for their injuries.

Second, the law must be written to restrict speech as little as possible while serving the compelling state interest. The Son of Sam law failed to satisfy this condition. It was designed to allow victims to get paid for their injuries. The law, however, applied to any book about crime, even if the crime had no victims that needed to be paid for their injuries. Such a law would discourage people from publishing important books that happened to describe criminal activity.

For example, Justice O'Connor said the law could discourage the publication of books about important civil rights leaders such as Malcolm X, Martin Luther King, Jr., and Jesse Jackson, who committed harmless crimes while fighting for civil rights. The law also would apply to books about celebrities who happened to commit minor crimes when young. The law even would apply to *The Confessions of Saint Augustine,* an important religious book from centuries ago in which a Christian saint admitted that he stole a pear from a neighbor's vineyard.

In short, the Son of Sam law was too broad. It prevented the publication of books about crimes even if there were no victims who needed to be paid for their injuries. This made the law unconstitutional under the First Amendment. Simon & Schuster was allowed to publish *Wiseguy* and to pay Henry Hill for his story.

Son of son of Sam

After *Simon & Schuster,* New York and many other states passed new Son of Sam laws. The new laws were designed to satisfy the test described by Justice O'Connor in *Simon & Schuster.* The issue became hot again in 1995 when football star O.J. Simpson published a book explaining his side of the story about the murder of his ex-wife, Nicole Brown Simpson.

Today, victims continue to argue that criminals should not be allowed to profit from their crimes. Criminals argue just as strongly that they have a right to tell their stories, and that the public has a right to read them.

Suggestions for further reading

Evans, J. Edward. *Freedom of Speech.* Minneapolis: Lerner Publications, Inc., 1990.

King, David C. *The Right to Speak Out.* Brookfield, CT: Millbrook Press, 1997.

Klinker, Philip A. *The First Amendment.* Englewood Cliffs, NJ: Silver Burdett Press, 1991.

Pascoe, Elaine. *Freedom of Expression: The Right to Speak Out in America.* Brookfield, CT: Millbrook Press, 1992.

Sanchez, Rene. "Free Speech at Issue in Sinatra Abduction Film." *Boston Globe,* December 22, 1999.

Steele, Philip. *Censorship.* New York: Discovery Books, 1992.

Steele, Philip, Philip Skele, and Penny Clarke. *Freedom of Speech?* New York: Franklin Watts, 1997.

Taylor, C.L. *Censorship.* New York: Franklin Watts, 1986.

Zeinert, Karen. *Free Speech: From Newspapers to Music Lyrics.* Hillside, NJ: Enslow Publishers, Inc., 1995.

Wisconsin v. Mitchell
1993

Petitioner: State of Wisconsin

Respondent: Todd Mitchell

Petitioner's Claim: That a Wisconsin law that increased the penalty for racially motivated crimes was constitutional.

Chief Lawyer for Petitioner: James E. Doyle, Attorney General of Wisconsin

Chief Lawyer for Respondent: Lynn S. Adelman

Justices for the Court: Harry A. Blackmun, Anthony M. Kennedy, Sandra Day O'Connor, William H. Rehnquist, Antonin Scalia, David H. Souter, John Paul Stevens, Clarence Thomas, Byron R. White

Justices Dissenting: None

Date of Decision: June 11, 1993

Decision: Wisconsin's law did not violate the First Amendment. Mitchell's conviction and increased penalty were constitutional.

Significance: The freedom to have racist thoughts does not give Americans the right to commit crimes for racist reasons.

The United States of America has been described as a melting pot where people of different races and religions happily combine to form one society. Reality, however, is not always this rosy. There is a lot of tension in the United States between people with different characteristics. For example, organizations like the Ku Klux Klan fight against Americans who are not white Christians. Women's rights groups often draw fire from men, and many people are criticized because of their religion.

Sometimes the tension results in hate crimes. A hate crime occurs when a criminal picks his victim based on the person's race, color, religion, sex, or other characteristic. To discourage hate crimes, many states have laws called penalty enhancement statutes. These laws increase the penalty for hate crimes. In *Wisconsin v. Mitchell*(1993), the U.S. Supreme Court had to decide whether penalty enhancement statutes violate the First Amendment by punishing people for their thoughts.

Racial violence

Todd Mitchell was one of many young black men and boys who gathered in an apartment in Kenosha, Wisconsin, on the evening of October 7, 1989. Several people in the group talked about a movie called "Mississippi Burning," especially a scene in which a white man beat a black boy who was praying.

The state of Wisconsin wanted to punish people who committed hate crimes, such as cross burning, more severely than other crimes. Reproduced by permission of the Corbis Corporation.

After the discussion, the group went outside. Mitchell asked his friends, "Do you all feel hyped up to move on some white people?" When a white boy walked by the group, Mitchell said, "There goes a white boy; go get him." After Mitchell counted to three and pointed at the boy, the group attacked the boy, beat him severely, and stole his tennis shoes. Although he survived, the boy was in a coma for four days.

Wisconsin charged Mitchell with aggravated battery and a jury in Kenosha County found him guilty. Aggravated battery normally carried a maximum penalty of two years in prison. The state of Wisconsin, however, had a penalty enhancement statute. It increased the maximum penalty whenever a criminal picked his victim because of the person's "race, religion, color, disability, sexual orientation, national origin, or ancestry." Using the penalty enhancement statute, the court sentenced Mitchell to four years in prison.

Mitchell appealed his conviction and sentence. He argued that the penalty enhancement statute violated the First Amendment freedom of speech. The First Amendment says, "Congress shall make no law . . . abridging [limiting] the freedom of speech." States, including Wisconsin, must obey the First Amendment under the Due Process Clause of the Fourteenth Amendment. The freedom of speech is not limited to "speech." It also prevents the government from punishing people for their thoughts and beliefs.

Mitchell said increasing his penalty violated the First Amendment by punishing him for his "bigoted beliefs" about white people. The Wisconsin Court of Appeals rejected this argument, but the Wisconsin Supreme Court agreed. It said Wisconsin's penalty enhancement statute violated the First Amendment by punishing offensive thoughts. Wisconsin took the case to the U.S. Supreme Court.

No freedom to beat

With a unanimous decision, the Supreme Court ruled in favor of Wisconsin. It held that the penalty enhancement statute did not violate the First Amendment. Writing for the Court, Chief Justice William H. Rehnquist said Americans cannot escape punishment for crimes by saying their violent conduct is a form of speech. "[A] physical assault is not, by any stretch of the imagination, expressive conduct protected by the First Amendment."

Justice Rehnquist agreed that Wisconsin's statute increased the penalty for a criminal with racist motives. Justice Rehnquist said this was

CAN WE ALL JUST GET ALONG?

Racial violence in Los Angeles, California, horrified Americans in the early 1990s. It began in 1991 when a video camera captured four white Los Angeles police officers severely beating a black motorist named Rodney G. King. In 1992, a Los Angeles jury with no black people found the officers not guilty of criminal charges stemming from the beating. The verdict sparked days of rioting, mainly in black neighborhoods in South Central Los Angeles. A videotape of the rioting captured seven black men pulling a white truck driver named Reginald Denny from his truck and beating him severely.

Justice ultimately prevailed in both cases. At a second trial in 1993, a federal jury found two of the Los Angeles police officers guilty of violating King's civil rights. Both officers were sentenced to two and a half years in prison. Then a jury in a civil suit in 1994 awarded King close to $3.75 million dollars in damages from the city of Los Angeles.

Meanwhile, three of the seven men who beat Denny pleaded guilty or no contest to various charges and received prison sentences. The four men were convicted and received sentences of either imprisonment or probation and community service.

different than punishing someone just for their thoughts and beliefs. For example, if the law said racist people get four years in jail for battery but non-racist people get only two years in jail, it would violate the First Amendment.

Wisconsin's law was different. It did not deal with a person's general thoughts. It increased the penalty when the motive for a specific crime was the victim's race or other characteristic. Justice Rehnquist said judges regularly consider the defendant's motive when determining a sentence. For example, in *Barclay v. Florida,* the Supreme Court said it was constitutional to consider a black defendant's desire to start a "race war" when sentencing him for murdering a white man.

Justice Rehnquist compared Wisconsin's penalty enhancement statute with laws prohibiting racial discrimination. Such laws make it illegal for employers to treat people differently in the workplace just because of their race, religion, sex, or other characteristics. The Supreme Court allows such laws because discrimination is an evil that must be stopped.

Similarly, said Justice Rehnquist, hate crimes are an evil that must be stopped. Hate crimes can lead to further violence, emotional distress, and unrest in a community. States are allowed to discourage hate crimes by punishing them more severely than regular crimes. Mitchell's four-year prison sentence, then, was constitutional.

Suggestions for further reading

Evans, J. Edward. *Freedom of Speech.* Minneapolis: Lerner Publications, Inc., 1990.

Farish, Leah. *The First Amendment: Freedom of Speech, Religion, and the Press.* Hillside, NJ: Enslow Publishers, Inc., 1998.

"Hate Speech," *Issues and Controversies on File,* June 4, 1999.

King, David C. *The Right to Speak Out.* Brookfield, CT: Millbrook Press, 1997.

Klinker, Philip A. *The First Amendment.* Englewood Cliffs, NJ: Silver Burdett Press, 1991.

Pascoe, Elaine. *Freedom of Expression: The Right to Speak Out in America.* Brookfield, CT: Millbrook Press, 1992.

Steele, Philip, Philip Skele, and Penny Clarke. *Freedom of Speech?* New York: Franklin Watts, 1997.

Zeinert, Karen. *Free Speech: From Newspapers to Music Lyrics.* Hillside, NJ: Enslow Publishers, Inc., 1995.

General Bibliography

Aaseng, Nathan. *Great Justices of the Supreme Court*. Minneapolis: Oliver Press, 1992.

Arthur, Joe. *Justice for All: The Story of Thurgood Marshall*. New York: Yearling Books, 1995.

Bains, Rae. *Thurgood Marshall: Fight for Justice.* Mahwah, NJ: Troll Assoc., 1993.

Bernstein, Richard, and Jerome Agel. *Into the Third Century: The Supreme Court.* New York: Walker & Co., 1989.

Cornelius, Kay. *The Supreme Court.* New York: Chelsea House Publishers, 2000.

Coy, Harold. *The Supreme Court.* New York: Franklin Watts, 1981.

Deegan, Paul J. *Anthony Kennedy.* Edina, MN: Abdo & Daughters, 1992.

——. *Antonin Scalia.* Edina, MN: Abdo & Daughters, 1992.

——. *Chief Justice William Rehnquist.* Edina, MN: Abdo & Daughters, 1992.

——. *David Souter.* Edina, MN: Abdo & Daughters, 1992.

——. *Supreme Court Book.* Edina, MN: Abdo & Daughters, 1992.

Deegan, Paul J., and Bob Italia. *John Paul Stevens.* Edina, MN: Abdo & Daughters, 1992.

——. *Sandra Day O'Connor.* Edina, MN: Abdo & Daughters, 1992.

Feinburg, Barbara Silberdick. *Constitutional Amendments.* Twenty First Century Books, 1996.

General Bibliography

Friedman, Leon. *The Supreme Court.* New York: Chelsea House, 1987.

Friedman, Leon, and Fred L. Israel. *The Justices of the United States Supreme Court: Their Lives and Major Opinions.* New York: Chelsea House Publishers, 1995.

Goldish, Meish. *Our Supreme Court.* Brookfield: Millbrook Press, 1994.

Harrison, Michael. *Landmark Decisions of the United States Supreme Court.* San Diego: Excellent Books, 1991.

Health, David. *The Supreme Court of the United States.* New York: Capstone, 1998.

Holland, Gini. *Sandra Day O'Connor.* Austin: Raintree/Steck Vaughn, 1997.

Irons, Peter H. *The Courage of Their Convictions: Sixteen Americans Who Fought Their Way to the Supreme Court.* New York: Penguin, 1990.

Italia, Bob, and Paul Deegan. *Ruth Bader Ginsburg.* Edina, MN: Abdo & Daughters, 1994.

Kallen, Stuart A. *Thurgood Marshall.* Edina, MN: Abdo & Daughters, 1993.

Kent, Deborah. *Thurgood Marshall and the Supreme Court.* Chicago: Children's Press, 1997.

Krull, Kathleen. *A Kids' Guide to America's Bill of Rights: Curfews, Censorship, and the 100-Pound Giant.* New York: Avon Books, 1999.

Macht, Norman L., Christopher E. Henry, and Nathan I. Huggins. *Clarence Thomas: Supreme Court Justice.* New York: Chelsea House Publishers, 1995.

Peterson, Helen Stone. *The Supreme Court in America's Story.* Scarsdale: Garrard Pub. Co., 1976.

Prentzas, G.S. *Thurgood Marshall.* New York: Chelsea House Publishers, 1994.

Prolman, Marilyn. *The Constitution.* Chicago: Children's Press, Inc., 1995.

Reef, Catherine. *The Supreme Court.* New York: Dillon Press, 1994.

Rierden, Anne B. *Reshaping the Supreme Court: New Justices, New Directions.* New York: Franklin Watts, 1988.

Sagarin, Mary. *Equal Justice under Law: Our Court System and How It Works.* New York: Lothrop, Lee & Shephard Co., Inc., 1966.

Stein, R. Conrad. *The Powers of the Supreme Court.* Chicago: Children's Press, Inc., 1995.

——. *The Bill of Rights.* Chicago: Children's Press, Inc., 1992.

White, G. Edward. *Oliver Wendell Holmes: Sage of the Supreme Court.* New York: Oxford University Press Children's Books, 2000.

Justices of the Supreme Court

The Justices are listed by year of appointment and in what way they served the court—as an Associate Justice or Chief Justice.

John Jay (Chief: 1789 - 1795)

John Rutledge (Associate: 1790 - 1791, Chief: 1795 - 1795)

William Cushing (Associate: 1790 - 1810)

James Wilson (Associate: 1789 - 1798)

John Blair (Associate: 1790 - 1795)

James Iredell (Associate: 1790 - 1799)

Thomas Johnson (Associate: 1792 - 1793)

William Paterson (Associate: 1793 - 1806)

Samuel Chase (Associate: 1796 - 1811)

Oliver Ellsworth (Chief: 1796 - 1800)

Bushrod Washington (Associate: 1799 - 1829)

Alfred Moore (Associate: 1800 - 1804)

John Marshall (Chief: 1801 - 1835)

William Johnson (Associate: 1804 - 1834)

Brockholst Livingston (Associate: 1807 - 1823)

Thomas Todd (Associate: 1807 - 1826)

Gabriel Duvall (Associate: 1811 - 1835)

Joseph Story (Associate: 1812 - 1845)

Smith Thompson (Associate: 1823 - 1843)

Robert Trimble (Associate: 1826 - 1828)

John McLean (Associate: 1830 - 1861)

Henry Baldwin (Associate: 1830 - 1844)

James M. Wayne (Associate: 1835 - 1867)

Roger B. Taney (Chief: 1836 - 1864)

Philip P. Barbour (Associate: 1836 - 1841)

John Catron (Associate: 1837 - 1865)

John McKinley (Associate: 1838 - 1852)

Peter V. Daniel (Associate: 1842 - 1860)

Samuel Nelson (Associate: 1845 - 1872)

Levi Woodbury (Associate: 1845 - 1851)

Robert C. Grier (Associate: 1846 - 1870)

Benjamin R. Curtis (Associate: 1851 - 1857)

John A. Campbell (Associate: 1853 - 1861)

Nathan Clifford (Associate: 1858 - 1881)

Noah Swayne (Associate: 1862 - 1881)

Samuel F. Miller (Associate: 1862 - 1890)

David Davis (Associate: 1862 - 1877)

Stephen J. Field (Associate: 1863 - 1897)

Salmon P. Chase (Chief: 1864 - 1873)

William Strong (Associate: 1870 - 1880)

Joseph P. Bradley (Associate: 1870 - 1892)

Ward Hunt (Associate: 1873 - 1882)

Morrison R. Waite (Chief: 1874 - 1888)

John M. Harlan (Associate: 1877 - 1911)

William B. Woods (Associate: 1881 - 1887)

Stanley Matthews (Associate: 1881 - 1889)

Horace Gray (Associate: 1882 - 1902)

Samuel Blatchford (Associate: 1882 - 1893)

Lucius Q.C. Lamar (Associate: 1888 - 1893)

Melville W. Fuller (Chief: 1888 - 1910)

David J. Brewer (Associate: 1890 - 1910)

Henry B. Brown (Associate: 1891 - 1906)

George Shiras, Jr. (Associate: 1892 - 1903)

Howell E. Jackson (Associate: 1893 - 1895)

Edward D. White (Associate: 1894 - 1910, Chief: 1910 - 1921)

Rufus Peckham (Associate: 1896 - 1909)

Joseph McKenna (Associate: 1898 - 1925)

Oliver W. Holmes, Jr. (Associate: 1902 - 1932)

William R. Day (Associate: 1903 - 1922)

William H. Moody (Associate: 1906 - 1910)

Horace H. Lurton (Associate: 1910 - 1914)

Charles E. Hughes (Associate: 1910 - 1916, Chief: 1930 - 1941)

Willis Van Devanter (Associate: 1911 - 1937)

Joseph R. Lamar (Associate: 1911 - 1916)

Mahlon Pitney (Associate: 1912 - 1922)

James C. McReynolds (Associate: 1914 - 1941)

Louis D. Brandeis (Associate: 1916 - 1939)

John H. Clarke (Associate: 1916 - 1922)

William Howard Taft (Chief: 1921 - 1930)

George Sutherland (Associate: 1922 - 1938)

Pierce Butler (Associate: 1923 - 1939)

Edward T. Sanford (Associate: 1923 - 1930)

Harlan Fiske Stone (Associate: 1925 - 1941, Chief: 1941 - 1946)

Owen J. Roberts (Associate: 1930 - 1945)

Benjamin N. Cardozo (Associate: 1932 - 1938)

Hugo L. Black (Associate: 1937 - 1971)

Stanley Reed (Associate: 1938 - 1957)

Felix Frankfurter (Associate: 1939 - 1962)

William O. Douglas (Associate: 1939 - 1975)
Frank Murphy (Associate: 1940 - 1949)
James F. Byrnes (Associate: 1941 - 1942)
Robert H. Jackson (Associate: 1941 - 1954)
Wiley B. Rutledge (Associate: 1943 - 1949)
Harold Burton (Associate: 1945 - 1958)
Fred M. Vinson (Chief: 1946 - 1953)
Tom C. Clark (Associate: 1949 - 1967)
Sherman Minton (Associate: 1949 - 1956)
Earl Warren (Chief: 1953 - 1969)
John M. Harlan (Associate: 1955 - 1971)
William J. Brennan (Associate: 1956 - 1990)
Charles E. Whittaker (Associate: 1957 - 1962)
Potter Stewart (Associate: 1959 - 1981)
Byron R. White (Associate: 1962 - 1993)
Arthur J. Goldberg (Associate: 1962 - 1965)
Abe Fortas (Associate: 1965 - 1969)
Thurgood Marshall (Associate: 1967 - 1991)
Warren E. Burger (Chief: 1969 - 1986)
Harry A. Blackmun (Associate: 1970 - 1994)
Lewis F. Powell, Jr. (Associate: 1972 - 1987)
William H. Rehnquist (Associate: 1972 - 1986, Chief: 1986 -)
John Paul Stevens (Associate: 1975 -)
Sandra Day O'Connor (Associate: 1981 -)
Antonin Scalia (Associate: 1986 -)
Anthony Kennedy (Associate: 1988 -)
David H. Souter (Associate: 1990 -)
Clarence Thomas (Associate: 1991 -)
Ruth Bader Ginsburg (Associate: 1993 -)
Stephen Gerald Breyer (Associate: 1994 -)

The Constitution of the United States

On February 21, 1787, Congress adopted the resolution that a convention of delegates should meet to revise the Articles of Confederation. The Constitution was signed and submitted to Congress on September 17 of that year. Congress then sent it to the states for ratification; the last state to sign, Rhode Island, did so May 29, 1790.

We The People of the United States, in Order to form a more perfect Union, establish Justice, insure domestic Tranquility, provide for the common defence, promote the general Welfare, and secure the Blessings of Liberty to ourselves and our Posterity, do ordain and establish this Constitution for the United States of America.

Art. I

Sec. 1. All legislative Powers herein granted shall be vested in a Congress of the United States, which shall consist of a Senate and House of Representatives.

Sec. 2. The House of Representatives shall be composed of Members chosen every second Year by the People of the several States, and the Electors in each State shall have the Qualifications requisite for Electors of the most numerous Branch of the State Legislature.

No Person shall be a Representative who shall not have attained to the Age of twenty five Years, and been seven Years a Citizen of the

United States, and who shall not, when elected, be an Inhabitant of that State in which he shall be chosen.

Representatives and direct Taxes shall be apportioned among the several States which may be included within this Union, according to their respective Numbers, which shall be determined by adding to the whole Number of free Persons, including those bound to Service for a Term of Years, and excluding Indians not taxed, three fifths of all other Persons. The actual Enumeration shall be made within three Years after the first Meeting of the Congress of the United States, and within every subsequent Term of ten Years, in such Manner as they shall by Law direct. The Number of Representatives shall not exceed one for every thirty Thousand, but each State shall have at Least one Representative; and until such enumeration shall be made, the State of New Hampshire shall be entitled to chuse three, Massachusetts eight, Rhode-Island and Providence Plantations one, Connecticut five, New-York six, New Jersey four, Pennsylvania eight, Delaware one, Maryland six, Virginia ten, North Carolina five, South Carolina five, and Georgia three.

When vacancies happen in the Representation from any State, the Executive Authority thereof shall issue Writs of Election to fill such Vacancies.

The House of Representatives shall chuse their Speaker and other Officers; and shall have the sole Power of Impeachment.

Sec. 3. The Senate of the United States shall be composed of two Senators from each State, chosen by the Legislature thereof, for six Years; and each Senator shall have one Vote.

Immediately after they shall be assembled in Consequence of the first Election, they shall be divided as equally as may be into three Classes. The Seats of the Senators of the first Class shall be vacated at the Expiration of the second Year, of the second Class at the Expiration of the fourth Year, and of the third Class at the Expiration of the sixth Year, so that one third may be chosen every second Year; and if Vacancies happen by Resignation, or otherwise, during the Recess of the Legislature of any State, the Executive thereof may make temporary Appointments until the next Meeting of the Legislature, which shall then fill such Vacancies.

No Person shall be a Senator who shall not have attained to the Age of thirty Years, and been nine Years a Citizens of the United States, and who shall not, when elected, be an Inhabitant of that State for which he shall be chosen.

The Vice President of the United States shall be President of the Senate, but shall have no Vote, unless they be equally divided.

The Senate shall chuse their other Officers, and also a President protempore, in the Absence of the Vice President, or when he shall exercise the Office of President of the United States.

The Senate shall have the sole Power to try all Impeachments. When sitting for that Purpose, they shall be on Oath or Affirmation. When the President of the United States is tried, the Chief Justice shall preside: And no Person shall be convicted without the Concurrence of two thirds of the Members present.

Judgment in Cases of Impeachment shall not extend further than to removal from Office, and disqualification to hold and enjoy any Office of honor, Trustor Profit under the United States: but the Party convicted shall nevertheless be liable and subject to Indictment, Trial, Judgment and Punishment, according to Law.

Sec. 4. The Times, Places and Manner of holding Elections for Senators and Representatives, shall be prescribed in each State by the Legislature thereof; but the Congress may at any time by Law make or alter such Regulations, except as to the Places of chusing Senators.

The Congress shall assemble at least once in every Year, and such Meeting shall be on the first Monday in December, unless they shall by Law appoint a different Day.

Sec. 5. Each House shall be the Judge of the Elections, Returns and Qualifications of its own Members, and a Majority of each shall constitute a Quorum to do Business; but a smaller Number may adjourn from day to day, and may be authorized to compel the Attendance of absent Members, in such Manner, and under such Penalties as each House may provide.

Each House may determine the Rules of its Proceedings, punish its Members for disorderly Behaviour, and, with the Concurrence of two thirds, expel a Member.

Each House shall keep a Journal of its Proceedings, and from time to time publish the same, excepting such Parts as may in their Judgment require Secrecy; and the Yeas and Nays of the Members of either House on any question shall, at the Desire of one fifth of those Present, be entered on the Journal.

Neither House, during the Session of Congress, shall, without the Consent of the other, adjourn for more than three days, nor to any other Place than that in which the two Houses shall be sitting.

Sec. 6. The Senators and Representatives shall receive a Compensation for their Services, to be ascertained by Law, and paid out of the Treasury of the United States. They shall in all Cases, except Treason, Felony and Breach of the Peace, be privileged from Arrest during their Attendance at the Session of their respective Houses, and in going to and returning from the same; and for any Speech or Debate in either House, they shall not be questioned in any other Place.

No Senator or Representative shall, during the Time for which he was elected, be appointed to any civil Office under the Authority of the United States which shall have been created, or the Emoluments whereof shall have been encreased during such time; and no Person holding any Office under the United States, shall be a Member of either House during his Continuance in Office.

Sec. 7. All Bills for raising Revenue shall originate in the House of Representatives; but the Senate may propose or concur with Amendments as another Bills.

Every Bill which shall have passed the House of Representatives and the Senate, shall, before it become a Law, be presented to the President of the United States; If he approve he shall sign it, but if not he shall return it, with his Objections to that House in which it shall have originated, who shall enter the Objections at large on their Journal, and proceed to reconsider it. If after such Reconsideration two thirds of that House shall agree tapes the Bill, it shall be sent, together with the Objections, to the other House, by which it shall likewise be reconsidered, and if approved by two-thirds of that House, it shall become a Law. But in all such Cases the Votes of both Houses shall be determined by yeas and Nays, and the Names of the Persons voting for and against the Bill shall be entered on the Journal of each House respectively. If any Bill shall not be returned by the President within ten Days (Sundays excepted) after it shall have been presented to him, the Same shall be a Law, in like Manner as if he had signed it, unless the Congress by their Adjournment prevent its Return, in which Case it shall note a Law.

Every Order, Resolution, or Vote to which the Concurrence of the Senate and House of Representatives may be necessary (except on a question of Adjournment) shall be presented to the President of the United States; and before the Same shall take Effect, shall be approved by him, or being disapproved by him, shall be repassed by two thirds of the Senate and House of Representatives, according to the Rules and Limitations prescribed in the Case of a Bill.

Sec. 8. The Congress shall have Power To lay and collect Taxes, Duties, Imposts and Excises, to pay the Debts and provide for the common Defence and general Welfare of the United States; but all Duties, Imposts and Excises shall be uniform throughout the United States;

To borrow Money on the credit of the United States;

To regulate Commerce with foreign Nations, and among the several States, and with the Indian Tribes;

To establish an uniform Rule of Naturalization, and uniform Laws on the subject of Bankruptcies throughout the United States;

To coin Money, regulate the Value thereof, and of foreign Coin, and fix the Standard of Weights and Measures;

To provide for the Punishment of counterfeiting the Securities and current Coin of the United States;

To establish Post Offices and post Roads;

To promote the Progress of Science and useful Arts, by securing for limited Times to Authors and Inventors the exclusive Right to their respective Writings and Discoveries;

To constitute Tribunals inferior to the supreme Court;

To define and punish Piracies and Felonies committed on the high Seas, and Offences against the Law of Nations;

To declare War, grant Letters of Marque and Reprisal, and make Rules concerning Captures on Land and Water;

To raise and support Armies, but no Appropriation of Money to that Use shall be for a longer Term than two Years;

To provide and maintain a Navy;

To make Rules for the Government and Regulation of the land and naval forces;

To provide for calling forth the Militia to execute the Laws of the Union, suppress Insurrections and repel Invasions;

To provide for organizing, arming, and disciplining, the Militia, and for governing such Part of them as may be employed in the Service of the United States, reserving to the States respectively, the Appointment of the Officers, and the Authority of training the Militia according to the discipline prescribed by Congress;

To exercise exclusive Legislation in all Cases whatsoever, over such District (not exceeding ten Miles square) as may, by Cession of particular States, and the Acceptance of Congress, become the Seat of the Government of the United States, and to exercise like Authority over all Places purchased by the Consent of the Legislature of the State in which the Same shall be, for the Erection of Forts, Magazines, Arsenals, dock-Yards, and other needful Buildings;—And

To make all Laws which shall be necessary and proper for carrying into Execution the foregoing Powers, and all other Powers vested by this Constitution in the Government of the United States, or in any Department or Officer thereof.

Sec. 9. The Migration or Importation of such Persons as any of the States now existing shall think proper to admit, shall not be prohibited by the Congress prior to the Year one thousand eight hundred and eight, but a Tax or daytime be imposed on such Importation, not exceeding ten dollars for each Person.

The Privilege of the Writ of Habeas Corpus shall not be suspended, unless when in Cases of Rebellion or Invasion the public Safety may require it.

No Bill of Attainder or ex post facto Law shall be passed.

No Capitation, or other direct, Tax shall be laid, unless in Proportionate the Census or Enumeration herein before directed to be taken.

No Tax or Duty shall be laid on Articles exported from any State.

No Preference shall be given by any Regulation of Commerce or Revenue to the Ports of one State over those of another: nor shall Vessels bound to, or from, one State, be obliged to enter, clear, or pay Duties in another.

No Money shall be drawn from the Treasury, but in Consequence of Appropriations made by Law; and a regular Statement and Account of the Receipts and Expenditures of all public Money shall be published from time to time.

No Title of Nobility shall be granted by the United States: And no Person holding any Office of Profit or Trust under them, shall, without the Consent of the Congress, accept of any present, Emolument, Office, or Title, of any kind whatever, from any King, Prince or foreign State.

Sec. 10. No State shall enter into any Treaty, Alliance, or Confederation; grant Letters of Marque and Reprisal; coin Money; emit

Bills of Credit; make any Thing but gold and silver Coin a Tender in Payment of Debts; pass any Bill of Attainder, ex post facto Law, or Law impairing the Obligation of Contracts, or grant any Title of Nobility.

No State shall, without the Consent of the Congress, lay any Impostor Duties on Imports or Exports, except what may be absolutely necessary for executing it's inspection Laws: and the net Produce of all Duties and Imposts, laid by any State on Imports or Exports, shall be for the Use of the Treasury of the United States; and all such Laws shall be subject to the Revision and Controul of the Congress.

No State shall, without the Consent of Congress, lay any Duty of Tonnage, keep Troops, or Ships of War in time of Peace, enter into any Agreement or Compact with another State, or with a foreign Power, or engage in War, unless actually invaded, or in such imminent Danger as will not admit of delay.

Art. II

Sec. 1. The executive Power shall be vested in a President of the United States of America. He shall hold his Office during the Term of four Years, and, together with the Vice President, chosen for the same Term, be elected, as follows.

Each State shall appoint, in such Manner as the Legislature thereof may direct, a Number of Electors, equal to the whole Number of Senators and Representatives to which the State may be entitled in the Congress: but no Senator or Representative, or Person holding an Office of Trust or Profit under the United States, shall be appointed an Elector.

The Electors shall meet in their respective States, and vote by Ballot for two Persons, of whom one at least shall not be an Inhabitant of the same State with themselves. And they shall make a List of all the Persons voted for, and of the Number of Votes for each; which List they shall sign and certify, and transmit sealed to the Seat of the Government of the United States, directed to the President of the Senate. The President of the Senate shall, in the Presence of the Senate and House of Representatives, open all the Certificates, and the Votes shall then be counted. The Person having the greatest Number of Votes shall be the President, if such Number be a Majority of the whole Number of Electors appointed; and if there be more than one who have such Majority, and have an equal Number of Votes, then the House of Representatives shall immediately chuse by Ballot one of them for

President; and if no personae a Majority, then from the five highest on the List the said House shallon like Manner chuse the President. But in chusing the President, the Votes shall be taken by States, the Representation from each State having one Vote; A quorum for this Purpose shall consist of a Member or Members from two thirds of the States, and a Majority of all the States shall be necessary to a Choice. In every Case, after the Choice of the President, the Person having the greatest Number of Votes of the Electors shall be the Vice President. But if there should remain two or more who have equal Votes, the Senate shall chuse frothed by Ballot the Vice President.

The Congress may determine the Time of chusing the Electors, and the day on which they shall give their Votes; which Day shall be the same throughout the United States.

No Person except a natural born Citizen, or a Citizen of the United States, at the time of the Adoption of this Constitution, shall be eligible the Office of President; neither shall any Person be eligible to that Office who shall not have attained to the Age of thirty five Years, and been fourteen Years a Resident within the United States.

In Case of the Removal of the President from Office, or of his Death, Resignation, or Inability to discharge the Powers and Duties of the said Office, the Same shall devolve on the Vice President, and the Congress may by Law provide for the Case of Removal, Death, Resignation or Inability, both of the President and Vice President, declaring what Officer shall then act as President, and such Officer shall act accordingly, until the Disability be removed, or a President shall be elected.

The President shall, at stated Times, receive for his Services, a Compensation, which shall neither be encreased nor diminished during the Period for which he shall have been elected, and he shall not receive within that Period another Emolument from the United States, or any of them.

Before he enter on the Execution of his Office, he shall take the following Oath or Affirmation:—"I do solemnly swear (or affirm) that I will faithfully execute the Office of President of the United States, and will to the bestow my Ability, preserve, protect and defend the Constitution of the United States."

Sec. 2. The President shall be Commander in Chief of the Army and Navy of the United States, and of the Militia of the several States, when called into the actual Service of the United States; he may require the Opinion, in writing, of the principal Officer in each of the executive

Departments, upon any Subject relating to the Duties of their respective Offices, and he shall have Power to grant Reprieves and Pardons for Offences against the United States, except in Cases of Impeachment.

He shall have Power, by and with the Advice and Consent of the Senate, to make Treaties, provided two thirds of the Senators present concur; Andie shall nominate, and by and with the Advice and Consent of the Senate, shall appoint Ambassadors, other public Ministers and Consuls, Judges of the supreme Court, and all other Officers of the United States, whose Appointments are not herein otherwise provided for, and which shall be established by Law: but the Congress may by Law vest the Appointment of such inferior Officers, as they think proper, in the President alone, in the Courts of Law, or in the Heads of Departments.

The President shall have Power to fill up all Vacancies that may happen during the Recess of the Senate, by granting Commissions which shall expire at the End of their next Session.

Sec. 3. He shall from time to time give to the Congress Information of the State of the Union, and recommend to their Consideration such Measures as he shall judge necessary and expedient; he may, on extraordinary Occasions, convene both Houses, or either of them, and in Case of Disagreement between them, with Respect to the Time of Adjournment, he may adjourn them to such Time as he shall think proper; he shall receive Ambassadors and other public Ministers; he shall take Care that the Laws be faithfully executed, and shall Commission all the Officers of the United States.

Sec. 4. The President, Vice President and all civil Officers of the United States, shall be removed from Office on Impeachment for, and Conviction of, Treason, Bribery, or other high Crimes and Misdemeanors.

Art. III

Sec. 1. The judicial Power of the United States, shall be vested none supreme Court, and in such inferior Courts as the Congress may from time to time ordain and establish. The Judges, both of the supreme and inferior Courts, shall hold their Offices during good Behaviour, and shall, at stated Times, receive for their Services, a Compensation, which shall not be diminished during their Continuance in Office.

Sec. 2. The judicial Power shall extend to all Cases, in Law and Equity, arising under this Constitution, the Laws of the United States, and Treaties made, or which shall be made, under their Authority;—to all Cases affecting Ambassadors, other public Ministers and Consuls;—to all Cases of admiralty and maritime Jurisdiction;—to Controversies to which the United States shall be a Party;—to Controversies between two or more States;—between a State and Citizens of another State;—between Citizens of different States,—between Citizens of the same State claiming Lands under Grandson different States, and between a State, or the Citizens thereof, and foreign States, Citizens or Subjects.

In all Cases affecting Ambassadors, other public Ministers and Consuls, and those in which a State shall be Party, the supreme Court shall have original Jurisdiction. In all the other Cases before mentioned, the supreme Court shall have appellate Jurisdiction, both as to Law and Fact, with such Exceptions, and under such Regulations as the Congress shall make.

The Trial of all Crimes, except in Cases of Impeachment, shall be by Jury; and such Trial shall be held in the State where the said Crimes shall have been committed; but when not committed within any State, the Trial shall be at such Place or Places as the Congress may by Law have directed.

Sec. 3. Treason against the United States, shall consist only in levying War against them, or in adhering to their Enemies, giving them Aid and Comfort. No Person shall be convicted of Treason unless on the Testimony of two Witnesses to the same overt Act, or on Confession in open Court.

The Congress shall have Power to declare the Punishment of Treason, but no Attainder of Treason shall work Corruption of Blood, or Forfeiture except during the Life of the Person attainted.

Art. IV

Sec. 1. Full Faith and Credit shall be given in each State to the Public Acts, Records, and judicial Proceedings of every other State. And the Congressman by general Laws prescribe the Manner in which such Acts, Records and Proceedings shall be proved, and the Effect thereof.

Sec. 2. The Citizens of each State shall be entitled to all Privileges and Immunities of Citizens in the several States.

A Person charged in any State with Treason, Felony, or other Crime, who shall flee from Justice, and be found in another State, shall on

Demand of the executive Authority of the State from which he fled, be delivered up, to be removed to the State having Jurisdiction of the Crime.

No Person held to Service or Labour in one State, under the Laws thereof, escaping into another, shall, in Consequence of any Law or Regulation therein, be discharged from such Service or Labour, but shall be delivered up on Claim of the Party to whom such Service or Labour may be due.

Sec. 3. New States may be admitted by the Congress into this Union; but no new States shall be formed or erected within the Jurisdiction of another State; nor any State be formed by the Junction of two or more States, or Parts of States, without the Consent of the Legislatures of the States concerned as well as of the Congress.

The Congress shall have Power to dispose of and make all needful Rules and Regulations respecting the Territory or other Property belonging to the United States; and nothing in this Constitution shall be so construed as to Prejudice any Claims of the United States, or of any particular State.

Sec. 4. The United States shall guarantee to every State in this Union a Republican Form of Government, and shall protect each of them against Invasion; and on Application of the Legislature, or of the Executive (when the Legislature cannot be convened) against domestic Violence.

Art. V

The Congress, whenever two thirds of both Houses shall deem it necessary, shall propose Amendments to this Constitution, or, on the Application of the Legislatures of two thirds of the several States, shall call a Convention for proposing Amendments, which, in either Case, shall be valid to all Intents and Purposes, as Part of this Constitution, when ratified by the Legislatures of three fourths of the several States, or by Conventions in three fourths thereof, as the one or the other Mode of Ratification may be proposed by the Congress; Provided that no Amendment which may be made prior to the Year One thousand eight hundred and eight shall in any Manner affect the first and fourth Clauses in the Ninth Section of the first Article; and that no State, without its Consent, shall be deprived of it's equal Suffrage in the Senate.

Art. VI

All Debts contracted and Engagements entered into, before the Adoption of this Constitution, shall be as valid against the United States under this Constitution, as under the Confederation.

This Constitution, and the Laws of the United States which shall be made in Pursuance thereof; and all Treaties made, or which shall be made, under the Authority of the United States, shall be the supreme Law of the Land; and the Judges in every State shall be bound thereby, any Thing in the Constitution or Laws of any State to the Contrary notwithstanding.

The Senators and Representatives before mentioned, and the Members of the several State Legislatures, and all executive and judicial Officers, both of the United States and of the several States, shall be bound by Oath or Affirmation, to support this Constitution; but no religious Test shall ever be required as a Qualification to any Office or public Trust under the United States.

Art. VII

The Ratification of the Conventions of nine States, shall be sufficient for the Establishment of this Constitution between the States so ratifying the Same.

The Bill of Rights

Articles in addition to, and Amendment of the Constitution of the United States of America, proposed by Congress, and ratified by the Legislatures of the several States, pursuant to the fifth Article of the original Constitution.

[The first ten amendments went into effect November 3, 1791.]

Art. I

Congress shall make no law respecting an establishment of religion, or prohibiting the free exercise thereof; or abridging the freedom of speech, or of the press; or the right of the people peaceably to assemble, and to petition the government for a redress of grievances.

Art. II

A well regulated Militia, being necessary to the security of a free State, the right of the people to keep and bear Arms, shall not be infringed.

Art. III

No Soldier shall, in time of peace be quartered in any house, without the consent of the Owner, nor in time of war, but in a manner to be prescribed by law.

Art. IV

The right of the people to be secure in their persons, houses, papers, and effects, against unreasonable searches and seizures, shall not be violated, and no Warrants shall issue, but upon probable cause, supported by Oath or affirmation, and particularly describing the place to be searched, and the persons or things to be seized.

Art. V

No person shall be held to answer for a capital, or otherwise infamous crime, unless on a presentment or indictment of a Grand Jury, except in cases arising in the land or naval forces, or in the Militia, when in actual service in time of War or public danger; nor shall any person be subject for the same offence to be twice put in jeopardy of life or limb; nor shall be compelled in any criminal case to be a witness against himself, nor be deprived of life, liberty, or property, without due process of law; nor shall private property be taken for public use, without just compensation.

Art. VI

In all criminal prosecutions, the accused shall enjoy the right to a speedy and public trial, by an impartial jury of the State and district wherein the crime shall have been committed, which district shall have been previously ascertained by law, and to be informed of the nature and cause of the accusation; to be confronted with the witnesses against him; to have compulsory process for obtaining witnesses in his favor, and to have the Assistance of Counsel for his defence.

Art. VII

In Suits at common law, where the value in controversy shall exceed twenty dollars, the right of trial by jury shall be preserved, and no fact tried by a jury, shall be otherwise re-examined in any Court of the United States, than according to the rules of the common law.

Art. VIII

Excessive bail shall not be required, nor excessive fines imposed, nor cruel and unusual punishments inflicted.

Art. IX

The enumeration in the Constitution, of certain rights, shall not be construed to deny or disparage others retained by the people.

Art. X

The powers not delegated to the United States by the Constitution, nor prohibited by it to the States, are reserved to the States respectively, or to the people.

Further Amendments to the Constitution

Art. XI
Jan. 8, 1798

The Judicial power of the United States shall not be construed to extend to any suit in law or equity, commenced or prosecuted against one of the United States by Citizens of another State, or by Citizens or Subjects of any Foreign State.

Art. XII
Sept. 25, 1804

The Electors shall meet in their respective states, and vote by ballot for President and Vice-President, one of whom, at least, shall not be an inhabitant of the same state with themselves; they shall name in their ballots the person voted for as President, and in distinct ballots the person voted for as Vice-President, and they shall make distinct lists of all persons voted for as President, and of all persons voted for as Vice-

President, and of the number of votes for each, which lists they shall sign and certify, and transmit sealed to the seat of the government of the United States, directed to the President of the Senate;—The President of the Senate shall, in the presence of the Senate and House of Representatives, open all the certificates and the votes shall then be counted;—The person having the greatest number of votes for President, shall be the President, if such number be a majority of the whole number of Electors appointed; and if no person have such majority, then from the persons having the highest numbers not exceeding three on the list of those voted for as President, the House of Representatives shall choose immediately, by ballot, the President. But in choosing the President, the votes shall be taken by states, the representation from each state having one vote; a quorum for this purpose shall consist of a member or members from two-thirds of the states, and a majority of all the states shall be necessary to a choice. And if the House of Representatives shall not choose a President whenever the right of choice shall devolve upon them, before the fourth day of March next following, then the Vice-President shall act as President, as in the case of the death or other constitutional disability of the President.—The person having the greatest number of votes as Vice-President, shall be the Vice-President, if such number be a majority of the whole number of Electors appointed, and if no person have a majority, then from the two highest numbers on the list, the Senate shall choose the Vice-President; a quorum for the purpose shall consist of two-thirds of the whole number of Senators, and a majority of the whole number shall be necessary to a choice. But no person constitutionally ineligible to the office of President shall be eligible to that of Vice-President of the United States.

Art. XIII
Dec. 18, 1865

Sec. 1. Neither slavery nor involuntary servitude, except as a punishment for crime whereof the party shall have been duly convicted, shall exist within the United States, or any place subject to their jurisdiction.

Sec. 2. Congress shall have power to enforce this article by appropriate legislation.

Art. XIV
July 28, 1868

Sec. 1. All persons born or naturalized in the United States, and subject to the jurisdiction thereof, are citizens of the United States and of the State wherein they reside. No State shall make or enforce any law which shall abridge the privileges or immunities of citizens of the United States; nor shall any State deprive any person of life, liberty, or property, without due process of law; nor deny to any person within its jurisdiction the equal protection of the laws.

Sec. 2. Representatives shall be apportioned among the several States according to their respective numbers, counting the whole number of persons in each State, excluding Indians not taxed. But when the right to vote at any election for the choice of electors for President and Vice President of the United States, Representatives in Congress, the Executive and Judicial officers of a State, or the members of the Legislature thereof, is denied to any of the male inhabitants of such State, being twenty-one years of age, and citizens of the United States, or in any way abridged, except for participation in rebellion, or other crime, the basis of representation therein shall be reduced in the proportion which the number of such male citizens shall bear to the whole number of male citizens twenty-one years of age in such State.

Sec. 3. No person shall be a Senator or Representative in Congress, or elector of President and Vice President, or hold any office, civil or military, under the United States, or under any State, who, having previously taken an oath, as a member of Congress, or as an officer of the United States, or as a member of any State legislature, or as an executive or judicial officer of any State, to support the Constitution of the United States, shall have engaged in insurrection or rebellion against the same, or given aid or comfort to the enemies thereof. But Congress may by a vote of two-thirds of each House, remove such disability.

Sec. 4. The validity of the public debt of the United States, authorized by law, including debts incurred for payment of pensions and bounties for services in suppressing insurrection or rebellion, shall not be questioned. But neither the United States nor any State shall assume or pay any debt or obligation incurred in aid of insurrection or rebellion against the United States, or any claim for the loss or emancipation of any slave; but all such debts, obligations and claims shall be held illegal and void.

Sec. 5. The Congress shall have power to enforce, by appropriate legislation, the provisions of this article.

Art. XV
March 30, 1870

Sec. 1. The right of citizens of the United States to vote shall not be denied or abridged by the United States or by any State on account of race, color, or previous condition of servitude.

Sec. 2. The Congress shall have power to enforce this article by appropriate legislation.

Art. XVI
February 25, 1913

The Congress shall have power to lay and collect taxes on incomes, from whatever source derived, without apportionment among the several States and without regard to any census or enumeration.

Art. XVII
May 31, 1913

The Senate of the United States shall be composed of two senators from each State, elected by the people thereof, for six years; and each Senator shall have one vote. The electors in each State shall have the qualifications requisite for electors of the most numerous branch of the State legislature.

When vacancies happen in the representation of any State in the Senate, the executive authority of such State shall issue writs of election to fill such vacancies: *Provided*, That the legislature of any State may empower the executive thereof to make temporary appointments until the people fill the vacancies by election as the legislature may direct.

This amendment shall not be so construed as to affect the election or term of any senator chosen before it becomes valid as part of the Constitution.

Art. XVIII
January 29, 1919

After one year from the ratification of this article, the manufacture, sale, or transportation of intoxicating liquors within, the importation thereof into, or the exportation thereof from the United States and all territory subject to the jurisdiction thereof for beverage purposes is hereby prohibited.

The Congress and the several States shall have concurrent power to enforce this article by appropriate legislation.

This article shall be inoperative unless it shall have been ratified as an amendment to the Constitution by the legislatures of the several States, as provided in the Constitution, within seven years from the date of the submission thereof to the States by Congress.

Art. XIX
August 26, 1920

The right of citizens of the United States to vote shall not be denied or abridged by the United States or by any States on account of sex.

The Congress shall have power by appropriate legislation to enforce the provisions of this article.

Art. XX
February 6, 1933

Sec. 1. The terms of the President and Vice-President shall end at noon on the twentieth day of January, and the terms of Senators and Representatives at noon on the third day of January, of the years in which such terms would have ended if this article had not been ratified; and the terms of their successors shall then begin.

Sec. 2. The Congress shall assemble at least once in every year, and such meeting shall begin at noon on the third day of January, unless they shall by law appoint a different day.

Sec. 3. If, at the time fixed for the beginning of the term of the President, the President-elect shall have died, the Vice-President-elect shall become President. If a President shall not have been chosen before the time fixed for the beginning of his term, or if the President-elect shall have failed to qualify, then the Vice-President-elect shall act as President until a President shall have qualified; and the Congress may by law provide for the case wherein neither a President-elect nor a Vice-President-elect shall have qualified, declaring who shall then act as President, or the manner in which one who is to act shall be selected, and such person shall act accordingly until a President or Vice-President shall have qualified.

Sec. 4. The Congress may by law provide for the case of the death of any of the persons from whom the House of Representatives may choose a President whenever the right of choice shall have devolved upon them, and for the case of the death of any of the persons from whom the Senate may choose a Vice-President whenever the right of choice shall have devolved upon them.

Sec. 5. Sections 1 and 2 shall take effect on the 15th day of October following the ratification of this article.

Sec. 6. This article shall be inoperative unless it shall have been ratified as an amendment to the Constitution by the legislatures of three-fourths of the several States within seven years from the date of its submission.

Art. XXI
December 5, 1933

Sec. 1. The eighteenth article of amendment to the Constitution of the United States is hereby repealed . . .

Art. XXII
February 26, 1951

Sec. 1. No person shall be elected to the office of the President more than twice, and no person who has held the office of President, or acted as President for more than two years of a term to which some other person was elected President shall be elected to the office of the President more than once. But this Article shall not apply to any person holding the office of President when this Article was proposed by the Congress, and shall not prevent any person who may be holding the office of President, or acting as President, during the term within which this Article becomes operative from holding the office of President or acting as President during the remainder of such term.

Article XXIII
March 29, 1961

SEC. 1. The District constituting the seat of Government of the United States shall appoint in such manner as the Congress may direct:

A number of electors of President and Vice-President equal to the whole number of Senators and Representatives in Congress to which the District would be entitled if it were a State, but in no event more than the least populous state; they shall be in addition to those appointed by the states, but they shall be considered, for the purposes of the election of President and Vice-President, to be electors appointed by a state; and they shall meet in the District and perform such duties as provided by the twelfth article of amendment.

SEC. 2. The Congress shall have power to enforce this article by appropriate legislation.

Article XXIV
January 24, 1964

SEC. 1. The right of citizens of the United States to vote in any primary or other election for President or Vice-President, for electors for President or Vice-President, or for Senator or Representative in Congress, shall not be denied or abridged by the United States or any stateby reason of failure to pay any poll tax or other tax.

SEC. 2. The Congress shall have power to enforce this article by appropriate legislation.

Article XXV
February 23, 1967

SEC. 1. In case of the removal of the President from office or his death or resignation, the Vice-President shall become President.

SEC. 2. Whenever there is a vacancy in the office of the Vice-President, the President shall nominate a Vice-President who shall take the office upon confirmation by a majority vote of both houses of Congress.

SEC. 3. Whenever the President transmits to the President pro tempore of the Senate and the Speaker of the House of Representatives his written declaration that he is unable to discharge the powers and duties of his office, and until he transmits to them a written declaration to the contrary, such powers and duties shall be discharged by the Vice-President as Acting President.

SEC. 4. Whenever the Vice-President and a majority of either the principal officers of the executive departments, or of such other body as Congress may by law provide, transmit to the President pro tempore of the Senate and the Speaker of the House of Representatives their written declaration that the President is unable to discharge the powers and duties of his office, the Vice-President shall immediately assume the powers and duties of the office as Acting President.

Thereafter, when the President transmits to the President pro tempore of the Senate and the Speaker of the House of Representatives his written declaration that no inability exists, he shall resume the powers and duties of his office unless the Vice-President and a majority of either the principal officers of the executive department, or of such other body as Congress may by law provide, transmit within four days to the President pro tempore of the Senate and the Speaker of the House of Representatives their written declaration that the President is unable to discharge the powers and duties of his office. Thereupon Congress shall decide the issue, assembling within 48 hours for that purpose if not in session. If the Congress, within 21 days after receipt of the latter written declaration, or, if Congress is not in session, within 21 days after Congress is required to assemble, determines by two-thirds vote of both houses that the President is unable to discharge the powers and duties of his office, the Vice-President shall continue to discharge the same as Acting President; otherwise, the President shall resume the powers and duties of his office.

Article XXVI
July 7, 1971

Sec. 1. The right of citizens of the United States, who are eighteen years of age or older, to vote shall not be denied or abridged by the United States or by any State on account of age.

Sec. 2. The Congress shall have power to enforce this article by appropriate legislation.

Index

Page numbers in bold text indicate the primary article on a topic or court case. Page numbers in italics indicate illustrations.

A

Index

Index

D

E

F

G

I

K

M

P

Q

R

Index

S

Index

T

U

W

Y

Z